INSIDE TOPS

The Complete Guide to Networking Macs, PCs, and Printers

Supports Version 2.1

New Riders Publishing
Thousand Oaks, California

Inside TOPS
The Complete Guide to Networking Macs, PCs, and Printers

Published by:

New Riders Publishing
PO Box 4846
Thousand Oaks, CA 91360
U.S.A.

Copyright © 1989 by New Riders Publishing

First Edition 1989

Printed in the United States of America

Library of Congress Cataloging-in-Publication Data

Inside TOPS.

   1. Local area networks (Computer networks)
2. IBM microcomputers. 3. Macintosh (Computer)
I. New Riders Publishing.
TK5105.7.I56 1989   004.6   89-14492
ISBN 0-934035-72-5

■ About the authors

JESSE BERST has authored or co-authored more than a dozen computer books, including the bestsellers *Inside Xerox Ventura Publisher* and *Publishing Power with Ventura*. An honors graduate of the University of Puget Sound, he is currently Director of the Electronic Publishing Division of New Riders Publishing, where he uses a TOPS network daily.

Berst contributed to Chapters One, Two, Three, Four, Five, and Six.

INNOVISIONS is a Northwest microcomputer consulting firm, specializing in PC and Macintosh networking and Macintosh-based graphic design. Contributors included: Eric Chu, Macintosh specialist and InnoVisions leader; Kevin Kerr, technical writer and PC specialist, B.A. in English and History, University of Washington (UW); Jeremy Robkin, graphic designer, B.A. in Creative Writing, UW; Julie McGalliard, technical writer, B.A. in English, Western Washington University; and Eric Holton, technical writer, B.S. in Math Sciences, UW.

InnoVisions contributed Chapters Seven, Nine, Ten, and Eleven and portions of Chapters Five and Six.

STEVE MURTHA is Director of Marketing at Prometheus Products in Tigard, Oregon. He is the author of several computer books, including the best-selling *CP/M Primer*. He also programmed Desktop Manager, a file management utility for Xerox Ventura Publisher.

Murtha contributed Chapters Seven and Eight.

■ Production

Lead Editor: D. Keith Thompson

Copy Editor: Scott C. Dunn

Cover design: Jill Casty Design

Page design: Barbara Roll, Martha Lubow

Illustrations and layout: D. Keith Thompson, Barbara Roll

■ Acknowledgements

The authors and New Riders Publishing wish to thank the following companies for their support of this book, for their advice and suggestions, and for supplying evaluation hardware and software:

Belkin Components — BelTalk and QuikNet interface boxes.

CE Software — QuickMail.

DayStar Digital — FS100 LocalTalk File Server Board.

Farallon Computing, Inc. — PhoneNET interface boxes, Timbuktu software, Traffic Watch software, CheckNET Utility software.

Infosphere, Inc. — Liaison 2.0 software.

Irwin Magnetics — 5080 and 2080 tape drives.

Microsoft Corporation — Microsoft Word and Microsoft Mail software.

Nuvotech, Inc. — TurboNet interface boxes.

TOPS — TOPS software, TOPS Repeater, TOPS Tele-Connector, TOPS FlashCard, Inbox software.

■ Contents

Introduction

Part One

▌Installing TOPS

Part Two

■ Learning TOPS

Chapter Six

Exchanging Files with TOPS

Chapter Seven

Translating Files with TOPS

Chapter Eight

Printing with TOPS

Chapter Nine

Sending Electronic Mail on a TOPS Network

Appendix A

Glossary

Appendix B

Manufacturers Reference

Appendix C

TOPS Planning Checklists

■ Introduction

For most of this decade, connectivity has been touted by computer manufacturers. That's because the idea has so much to offer. By wiring computers together into a *local area network* (LAN), you can decrease costs, increase productivity and enjoy effortless interoffice communication. At least, that's what the ads say.

■ Why a network?

The appeal of networks is easy to understand. If you put a group of people in an office together, it's obvious they are going to need to trade information back and forth. It's equally obvious they can save money if they share expensive equipment like laser printers. If you're reading this book, you're probably aware of the things a network can do. To review just a few:

- Share information by trading files over the network cables.

- Share storage by making large hard disks accessible to anyone on the network.

- Share printers (and other high-priced peripherals) between several workstations.

- Share messages by setting up an electronic mail system.

Revenge of the nodes

Until recently, those promises of cost savings were more hype than reality. The cost per *node* — per network connection — turned out to be higher than expected. For one thing, many networking schemes needed a high-powered computer at the center, above and beyond the individual workstations. In addition, the cable turned out to be surprisingly expensive. And so did the task of rewiring existing offices to accomodate it.

On top of all that, most networks accepted only one type of computer. That forced everyone in the office to conform — even if their jobs could be done cheaper and easier on a different brand. Worst of all was the hassle and confusion. Most offices, even small ones, found they couldn't keep their networks up and running without a full-time LAN manager.

■ Why TOPS?

Until recently, then, networking was largely reserved for big corporations that could afford the equipment and the manpower. That changed, however, with the 1986 appearance of TOPS. TOPS solves most of the previous limitations:

- It doesn't require an expensive central file server (although you can use it that way if you prefer).

- It can exchange files between PCs, Macs, and other computers that are otherwise incompatible.

- It is easy to install and use.

- It uses inexpensive cabling.

- It optionally translates data formats so incompatible applications can communicate.

- It lets PCs print over a network to AppleTalk-compatible PostScript laser printers — a task previously reserved for Macintoshes.

TOPS is not the answer to all problems. It is not adequate for huge networks with hundreds of workstations. It is, however, the network of choice for small installations (including workgroups within a large company), especially for linking different kinds of computers. Hundreds of thousands of people use it on a daily basis.

■ Why this book?

We produced this book for several reasons. The first was to create a single, central information resource. Until this book, users were forced to search through dozens of manuals from different manufacturers to get the complete picture.

A second reason was to share information that was unavailable anywhere else. We've included real-life information you can't get from a reference manual. What works. What doesn't. Shortcuts. Tips. Warnings. Practical examples. And by the way, if there's a better, faster way to do things that doesn't involve TOPS, we tell you about it. And show you how.

A third motivation was to develop practical tools. For instance, Chapter Two includes a hands-on planning checklist. And almost all of the chapters include reference tables that list key commands and functions. As you progress with TOPS, you'll turn to these tools over and over again.

■ Who can use this book

We planned this book for beginners and advanced users alike. Novices will find step-by-step instructions and lots of illustrations, plus a glossary at the back of the book. But we didn't ignore the power users. They will find special *Speed Start* sections in many chapters, so they can skip the explanations and get right to work. In addition, we included advanced chapters on customizing and expanding the network.

■ How to use this book

The best way to use this book depends on your level of expertise and what you need to do. For instance, there's no need to bother with the installation chapters if TOPS is already up and running in your office. Still, we hope everyone, beginner and advanced alike, will skim Chapter One, "Getting Started with TOPS." Chapter One not only clarifies networking, but also gives important information you'll need in later chapters. In addition, it introduces you to our terminology. Unfortunately, almost every company involved in networking uses the same words to mean different things. Chapter One lays out the definitions we used throughout this book.

Once you've glanced through Chapter One, you can turn directly to the chapters that address your particular needs. Table I-1 may help you find what you need.

Table I-1. How to use this book

Task	Chapters
Installing TOPS	Chapter One — Getting Started with TOPS
	Chapter Two — Planning a TOPS Network
	Chapter Three — Connecting the Hardware
	Chapter Four — Installing TOPS Software
	Glossary
Learning TOPS	Chapter Five — Loading and Starting TOPS
	Chapter Six — Exchanging Files with TOPS
	Chapter Seven — Translating Files with TOPS
	Chapter Eight — Printing with TOPS
	Chapter Nine — Sending Electronic Mail with TOPS
Managing TOPS	Chapter Ten — Building Bigger and Better TOPS Networks
	Chapter Eleven — Customizing TOPS on the PC

There's no requirement to read all the chapters, or to read them in order. However, if you are installing TOPS for the first time, you'll have more success if you proceed through Chapters Two, Three, and Four one after the other. Each chapter assumes that you have successfully accomplished the tasks set out previously.

Beginners should read at the computer if possible. The fastest way to learn is to try things out as you go along. Advanced users, on the other hand, can skim for new ideas and techniques. They can also go straight to the Speed Start sections, and turn to the full explanations only if they run into problems.

Conventions

This book uses several terms in a general manner:

- Macintosh or *Mac* — any model of the Apple Macintosh

- PC — any personal computer compatible with the IBM PC/XT or the IBM AT

- DOS — any version of the Microsoft operating system for IBM PCs and compatibles. When IBM sells DOS, it calls it PC-DOS. Other companies usually call it MS-DOS. DOS should not be confused with IBM's new operating system, called OS/2.

Continuing on

During most of the 1980s, the focus was on individual computing. Now the attention has shifted to *workgroup* computing. Companies are exploring ways to empower their employees by linking their machines together.

Through the use of TOPS and the help of this book, you can get the benefits of networked computing simply, quickly, and inexpensively. The first step is to gain an overview of TOPS and to understand how it fits into the big picture. Chapter One will get you started.

Part One

Installing TOPS

To reap the benefits of TOPS, you need to install it properly. In the next four chapters, you will learn how to install TOPS hardware and software to create a network that meets your organization's needs.

Chapter One

Getting Started with TOPS

When people have problems with TOPS, it's usually because they are fuzzy on its underlying concepts. In this chapter, you will learn the fundamentals that make TOPS easy to understand and operate.

The CIA and the KGB would approve of this chapter. Clandestine organizations operate on a *need-to-know* basis. We did the same thing. We cut out the extraneous facts and concentrated on what you need to know to get up and running in a hurry. You won't find a lot of rambling about the history of networking. Or cute stories about Mr. Joe Average and his ever-so-typical TOPS installation. But you will find nuts-and-bolts networking basics you will need in later chapters:

- to plan your network (Chapter Two)
- to make the hardware connections (Chapter Three)
- to install the software (Chapter Four)
- to run the network efficiently (remaining chapters)

Who should read this chapter?

You should. Yes, you. Computer novices should read this chapter because it gets them started as painlessly as possible. Computer wizards should skim it to make sure they're familiar with the terms we use in the rest of the book.

Networking has its own language. Unfortunately, companies use the same terms to mean different things. To overcome this dilemma, we've come up with a consistent terminology, as defined in this chapter. Beginner or expert, you need to know what *we* mean when we use these phrases.

Please don't dive in until you can find 30 uninterrupted minutes to lay a good foundation. Then you can learn TOPS in detail, chapter by chapter, and begin putting it to use. So tell the butler to hold your calls for the next half hour. In that time, you should be able to master the basics of (1) networks in general and (2) TOPS in particular. Along the way, you'll get an informal tour of TOPS and its many capabilities.

■ Networking made simple

TOPS is a type of computer network. It makes sense, therefore, to learn a few networking basics before you tackle TOPS itself. This section defines key terms as they apply to TOPS and to the decisions you must make in later chapters.

Networks defined

A network is a scheme for connecting computers. Computers linked by cables talk back and forth with the help of network software.

It's important to make the distinction between a network and a *multi-user computer*. Mainframes and minicomputers often have many terminals attached to one central machine. Although they have many terminals, these multi-user computers possess only one *brain* — one *central processing unit* (CPU) (Figure 1-1).

By contrast, each computer in a network has its own CPU. The network is merely the highway that carries messages back and forth among these standalone devices (Figure 1-2).

Servers and clients

As long as we're defining networks, we might as well introduce two words you're going to see over and over again: server and client.

A *server* is a disk that stores files and makes them available to the network. A *dedicated server* is used for nothing else. Its sole task is to store and retrieve files for the network. (Some networks require a dedicated server to operate.) With a *distributed server*, by contrast, a workstation can act as a server

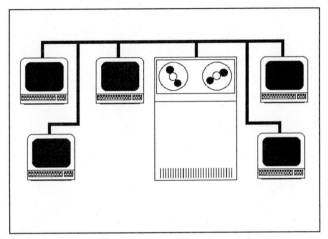

Figure 1-1. Multi-user computers have many terminals hooked up to a single CPU.

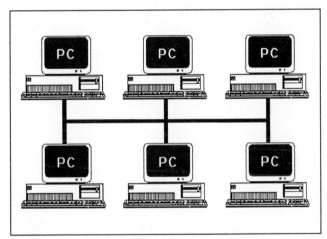

Figure 1-2. In a network, standalone computers communicate via a cable.

while also performing other computing chores. As you will see, TOPS can use either server strategy.

A *client* is any computer that can work with files from the server. Think of a server as a warehouse for storing files. A client, then, is anyone who has a key — anyone who's allowed to enter the warehouse to take things in or out (Figure 1-3).

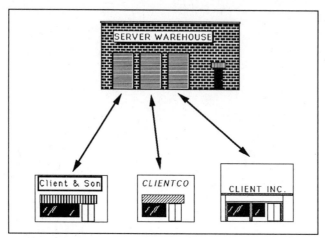

Figure 1-3. A server makes files available to the rest of the network. Clients can access those files.

Network benefits

Why connect computers? The three most important reasons are to:

- share information

- share resources

- centralize files

Networks make it possible to share expensive *peripherals*. Peripherals are devices that attach to computers — things like laserprinters, scanners, modems, plotters, and so on. By linking through a network, a single laserprinter can, for example, serve an entire five-person word-processing department (Figure 1-4).

Figure 1-5 illustrates the scale of the savings possible when you can share resources.

Equally important is the ability to share files. No longer must you copy files to a disk and carry them down the hall. The files you need are just a few keystrokes away, no matter where they are stored physically, because they can be sent over the cables from one workstation to another.

And networks can also centralize file storage, so everyone can access the same data. For instance, all of the clerks in the

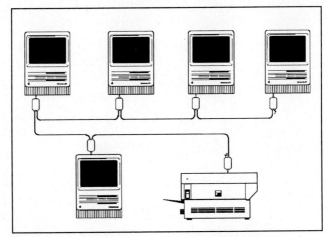

Figure 1-4. A network lets you share expensive resources such as plotters, modems, hard disks, or (as illustrated here) laserprinters.

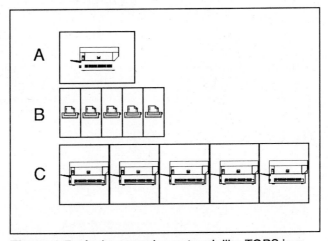

Figure 1-5. An inexpensive network like TOPS is a cost-effective way to share resources. Compare the cost of sharing one laserprinter among five users (A) versus the cost of buying each user a dot-matrix printer (B) or a laserprinter (D).

order entry department can use the same inventory database. There is no need to duplicate files, and no worry that changes made on one workstation will fail to be recorded on the others.

Network hardware

There's not a whole lot to learn about network hardware. It consists of only four main elements: devices, network circuitry, cables, and connectors.

Devices

In this book, a device is anything that hooks up to the network. It might be a computer (also called a *workstation*) or a peripheral, such as a printer. You'll also see us refer to devices as *nodes*. The word node sounds like something you'd go to a surgeon to remove, but in networking terms it is any point of connection.

Network circuitry

Before a computer can hook up to the network, it must have the necessary circuitry inside. This hardware provides a *port* — a connection to the cable that runs to the other devices. If necessary, it also translates the signal so it can be sent over the wire to the other machines. Macintosh computers and Sun workstations have networking circuitry built right in. PC compatibles, on the other hand, need an add-in board (Figure 1-6).

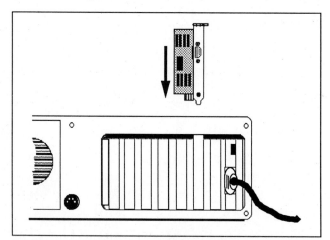

Figure 1-6. IBM PC-compatible computers must have a network add-in board. This board provides a connection to the cable, plus circuitry that makes the signals from the computer compatible with the network.

Cables

Cables are wires that connect the devices on the network. In Chapter Two, "Planning a TOPS Network," you'll need to know about cabling options so you can choose the right one. TOPS-compatible cables come in three varieties: *twisted-pair, coaxial*, and *fiber-optic*. Whether you realize it or not, you are already familiar with the first two.

Most TOPS installations use twisted-pair cable. As the name implies, it contains wires wrapped around one another. (The twisting reduces interference between the signals). Although it can't carry as much information as the other two types, twisted-pair cable is cheaper, easier to install, and perfectly adequate for smaller TOPS installations.

You're likely to encounter two varieties of twisted-pair wiring. We'll refer to the first as *LocalTalk* cable. This type was introduced by Apple. Many older TOPS networks still use this type. Far more popular, however, is modular *phone wire*. As it turns out, the same phone wire that connects your telephone to the wall jack is ideal for carrying network signals over short distances (Figure 1-7).

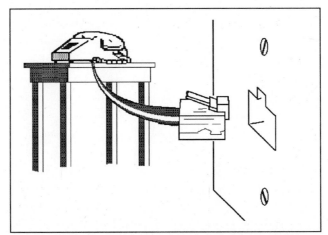

Figure 1-7. You can use ordinary modular phone wire to set up a TOPS network. You can usually spot phone wire by its thin appearance and by the *RJ11* plug at the end.

Coaxial cable is popular for larger networks. Its superior shielding lets it carry more information for longer distances.

You may have seen it used to bring cable TV into your home. You will use coaxial cable if you decide to install an Ethernet-compatible version of TOPS. (Newcomers: Ethernet is defined later in this chapter.)

Fiber-optic is the least common cable type. Glass or acrylic fibers transmit the data. Fiber-optic cable can carry more information than other types. However, it requires extra equipment to translate electrical signals into optical signals and back again. Its current use is restricted to specialized environments that can justify its higher costs. These include very large networks, and military/defense installations where security is an issue. (Fiber-optic cable makes it harder to eavesdrop electronically.)

Connectors and interface boxes

Connectors form the final part of the hardware puzzle. In this book, we use the term *connector* to mean a small jack or plug that attaches a cable to any device (Figure 1-8). *Interface boxes* are small devices that include special network circuitry and connect the computers to the rest of the network wiring.

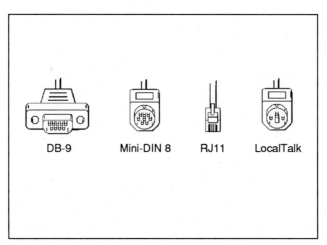

DB-9   Mini-DIN 8   RJ11   LocalTalk

Figure 1-8. A few of the connectors you may encounter while building your TOPS network.

Network software

No matter how many computers, cables, and connectors you own, you can't have a network without special software.

Why do you need extra software? One reason is to make sure your messages get to the right place — the right *address* in networking jargon. A second reason is to avoid collisions between different messages. Think of the cable as a party line for computers. If everybody talks at once, nobody can understand. To make sure collisions don't occur, network software follows special rules called *protocols*.

The network software makes sure everyone follows the protocols. It also arbitrates conflicts. Imagine that two users want to grab the same file at the same time. The software decides who gets it first and who has to wait.

Network software also provides security features. You may want your warehouse employees to have access to the inventory database. But you probably don't want them fooling around with your payroll files. Network software controls who has access to what and when.

Finally, network software may do some translation. TOPS, for instance, does the necessary interpreting to let different kinds of computers talk to each other.

Two types of network software

As you plan and install your TOPS network, you will encounter two types of network software. One is known as *network driver* software. It does the actual talking over the network. The second is the *network operating software* (NOS), which provides the interface to the user and the computer's native operating system.

We're telling you this because you'll want to know the distinctions when you install TOPS software. Here's one way to remember the differences: The driver is responsible for getting messages to their destinations. It takes care of obeying the rules of the road (the protocols) and avoiding collisions. The NOS (network operating software), on the other hand, is the portion that you will come into contact with when you operate the network.

It works something like a mansion in Victorian England. The lord of the manor (that's you) tells the butler to get a cup of tea. The butler tells the cook, who tells the scullery maid. In the case of a network, the user (that's you again) talks to the application software, which talks to the NOS, which talks to the driver.

An example: You tell an electronic mail program to send a message. The mail program passes it through to the NOS, which passes it to the network driver, which sends it out over the network. Figure 1-9 provides a simplified illustration of what's going on.

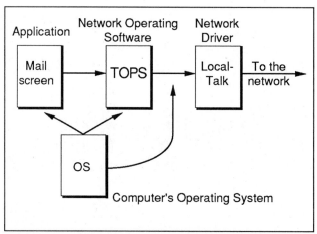

Figure 1-9. The network operating system provides the interface. The network driver takes care of getting messages to their destination.

Network topologies

You've already made a lot of progress. You've learned about network hardware and software. Before we move on to TOPS itself, we should finish up with a quick discussion of two other important topics: network topologies and network varieties.

Topology is a long word for a simple concept. It is nothing more than the way you string the machines together — the arrangement or the layout. In Chapter Two, you'll plan the layout for your system, so you need to understand the major options. For the moment, we'll content ourselves with defining two topologies popular for TOPS installations and two that have problems.

Daisy chain layout
If you are setting up a simple TOPS network, we recommend

this arrangement. To achieve a daisy chain layout, you simply string cables between machines (Figure 1-10).

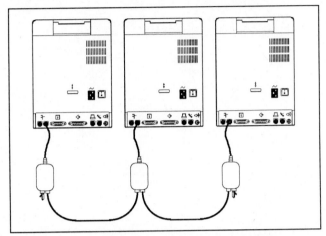

Figure 1-10. A daisy chain layout is the easiest, simplest way to arrange a small TOPS network.

The daisy chain topology has several advantages. Any workstation can send a message directly to any other. What's more, the network isn't dependent on any single device. You don't have to worry that the failure of a single device will shut down the entire network. And expansion is easy — just string some wire from the last machine to the new one.

Star layout

A star layout has a central hub (Figure 1-11). That hub can be active — where it performs some of the network functions — or passive — where it does nothing except provide a physical connection between machines.

In an *active* star, information goes from the workstation to the central node, which then sends it on to its destination. The central node manages and controls all the traffic on the network. Consequently, it becomes the bottleneck. If anything happens to it, the rest of the network can't communicate. Earlier in the chapter, we explained the concept of a dedicated server — a computer for the sole purpose of storing and distributing files. Obviously, you'd usually put a dedicated server at the center of a star network.

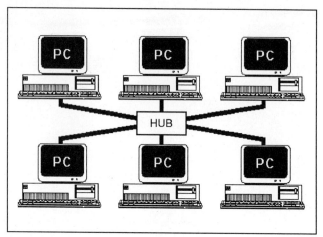

Figure 1-11. In a star configuration, connections pass through a central hub.

TOPS doesn't *require* a dedicated server, but it does allow you to use one if you prefer. You can arrange a TOPS network in an active star topology through devices such as Farallon Computing's StarController.

Trunk layout
To this point we've described two topologies that are appropriate for a TOPS network. Now we'll mention two that have problems. The first is the trunk layout. Think of a tree and you'll be able to visualize a trunk layout. Like a tree, it has a central trunk — in this case a cable. From there, other cables branch out (Figure 1-12).

At first glance, a trunk layout resembles a daisy chain. The difference is that extra length of wire that runs from the connector back to the central cable. For those of you with a technical background, the problems arise from excessive *ringing* and from the need to terminate each interface box. For those who are beginners, just remember that a trunk installation can cause difficulties.

Ring layout
In a ring configuration, all the machines are hooked up in a circle (Figure 1-13). All you need to know about this layout is that you shouldn't use it with TOPS.

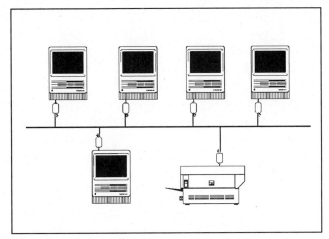

Figure 1-12. In trunk layouts, all the connections return to a central cable.

Figure 1-13. Do NOT use a ring configuration with TOPS.

Network varieties

We don't want to get into too many details in this section. You don't need to know much about the rest of the networking world to successfully install and use a TOPS system. Suffice it to say that there are dozens of different varieties. They are distinguished by their speed, cable type, capacity, topology, and compatibility.

For instance, some computers are compatible with only one

type of computer or one type of operating system. As you probably know already, TOPS is compatible with several operating systems, including those for PCs, Macintoshes, and Sun machines.

Network server strategies

Networks can also be classified by their server strategies. This does not have anything to do with who should serve first in doubles tennis. Rather, it concerns which computers and disks can act as servers.

Many networking schemes demand a *centralized server*. This machine serves all the other computers. The centralized method has several limitations. For instance, the failure of the server can bring down the whole network. In addition, only peripherals connected to the server are available to network users. In other words, if you want to share three laser printers, all three of them must be attached to the central server. Likewise, only the information on the central server is available to the rest of the network. If Bob wants to send a file to Kathy, he must first put it on the server. Only then can she retrieve it.

But you can overcome these shortcomings with a *decentralized server* strategy (also called a *distributed server*).

Under this system, any computer can be a server at any time. Consequently, any station can get information from any disk. You can also make any peripheral available to the network. Moreover, the failure of one machine doesn't affect the rest of the network.

Doesn't the distributed server sound like a better way to do things? It's the TOPS way. Notice that you can have a dedicated or centralized server if you want. But you don't have to. As you'll see, this advantage can save you time, trouble, and money.

■ TOPS made simple

So far we've spent our time understanding networks in general. These basics give you the foundation to explore TOPS itself. TOPS is an elegant solution to the problem of communicating between different computers. Yet its commands and procedures can mystify newcomers who don't understand what's going on under the hood. You don't need to be a computer expert to use TOPS. But you do need a grasp of three key areas:

1. TOPS hardware

2. TOPS software

3. TOPS functions

TOPS defined

TOPS is an inexpensive networking scheme that can link Macintoshes, PCs, Unix-based computers, and others. Two key features set TOPS apart from other networks: It is decentralized and it allows for mixed operating systems.

Decentralized, distributed servers

Some networks require a dedicated server. You won't have that problem with TOPS. (You may have other problems, like how to pay for all these computers and laserprinters you're hooking up, but at least you won't have that one.) Almost any disk on any computer can act as a server, and you can have more that one active at a time. If your network later expands, you can add a dedicated server to improve performance.

Mixed operating systems

Many networks work only with one type of operating system — Unix, for example, or MS-DOS. That's because different operating systems speak different languages. There's no way for them to talk directly.

TOPS, by contrast, can mix and match between different operating systems. In essence, TOPS translates between the native language of, for instance, a Macintosh and that of a PC. Thanks to the intervention of TOPS, incompatible machines can talk to each other over the network (Figure 1-14).

TOPS varieties

TOPS comes in two different flavors. The first is compatible with *LocalTalk*, a network cabling scheme originally

Figure 1-14. TOPS network software translates between operating systems so incompatible machines can communicate.

developed by Apple Computer. LocalTalk circuitry is built into Macintosh computers. It's slower than Ethernet (see below), but also cheaper and easier, since it can use inexpensive twisted-pair cabling.

You can also build a TOPS network compatible with *Ethernet,* a networking system originally developed by Xerox Corp. You still have the same functions, but your network communicates over Ethernet cabling. Ethernet compatibility requires more expensive hardware and higher-priced coaxial cable.

TOPS hardware

Figure 1-15 shows the key components of a typical TOPS network. To install and run TOPS, you should recognize and understand them all.

- *Nodes or devices.* Anything connected to the network, whether a computer, a printer, or any other equipment.

- *Interface box.* The physical link between the devices and the cable. On a TOPS network, every device requires an interface box.

- *Connector.* Some vendors use connector interchangeably with interface box. In this book, we use connector only for the plugs and jacks that attach cables. Different devices

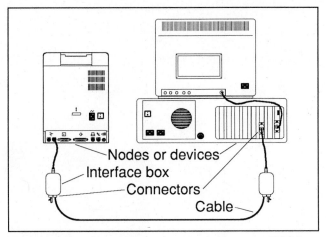

Figure 1-15. The hardware components of a TOPS network.

require different connectors, so it's important to know in advance which kind you need.

- *Cables.* They contain the wires that carry the signals from one machine to another.

- *Network circuitry.* Resides inside the computer. Sometimes it is built-in. In other cases, it comes as an add-in card.

Repeaters and gateways

Larger TOPS networks may include two additional hardware components. A *repeater* lets you extend the length of the network. When the cable gets too long — about 1000 feet usually — and the signal starts to fade, you insert a repeater to amplify the signal and send it further along (Figure 1-16).

A *gateway* is like a border crossing. It allows commerce between two otherwise hostile nations — in this case, information exchange between two otherwise incompatible networks. A gateway contains both hardware and software. The hardware lets different cable types interconnect. The software translates the signals from one network so they can be understood by the other.

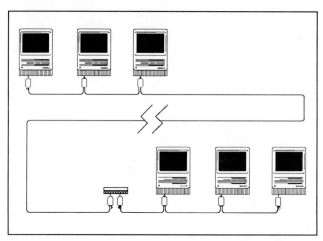

Figure 1-16. A repeater lets you create longer networks by amplifying the signal so it can go greater distances.

TOPS software

The hardware provides the physical connections and circuitry. It's the software that does most of the work.

TOPS software is *memory resident,* so it can work together with your other software. Once you load it, it remains in memory even if you load other programs. It can also work in *background mode.* Because TOPS functions behind the scenes, you can continue to work with other programs.

TOPS drivers

Let's get a little more technical. As you recall from our earlier discussion, network software consists of (1) the network driver and (2) the network operating software (NOS). Since TOPS comes in two varieties — Apple/LocalTalk-compatible and Ethernet-compatible — it stands to reason it has two matching drivers.

Like any networking system, LocalTalk has its own protocols, called *AppleTalk.* The AppleTalk driver available from Apple Computer is called *AppleShare.* The AppleTalk driver from TOPS is known as *FlashTalk.*

It's easy to confuse these terms, so let's review: LocalTalk is a local area network (LAN) cabling system. AppleTalk is a set of rules for that cabling system. AppleShare and FlashTalk are programs that know how to obey those rules.

If you are planning an Ethernet-compatible system, you will use a different network driver called (not surprisingly) Ether-Talk. This driver adapts LocalTalk protocols so they can run on the Ethernet cabling system.

TOPS network operating software

In addition to the driver software, you'll also use TOPS network operating software (NOS). The variety depends on your computer. On a PC-compatible, you run TOPS/DOS. On a Macintosh, you use TOPS/Macintosh. On a Sun workstation, you use TOPS/Sun. Remember — the NOS does not replace your normal operating system. It works together with it to provide additional network functions.

You can think of the NOS as residing between the native operating system and the applications software. When a program makes a request — to get the file called LETTER.TXT, for instance — TOPS intercepts it. If the request relates to a *local* disk drive (one that is physically attached to the computer), TOPS passes the request through to the operating system, which fetches the file as it would normally. However, if the file is on a *remote* drive, TOPS takes care of sending the request to the proper destination (Figure 1-17).

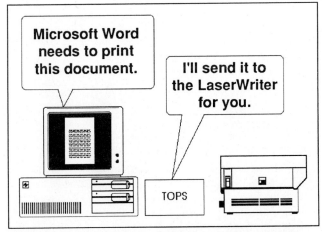

Figure 1-17. The TOPS network operating system intercepts messages from the applications program to make sure they get to their correct destination.

The functions are much the same from machine to machine. The interface — the way you interact with the program — differs greatly. For instance, Figures 1-18 and 1-19 show how differently the Mac and PC versions of TOPS look when accomplishing an identical file-handling function.

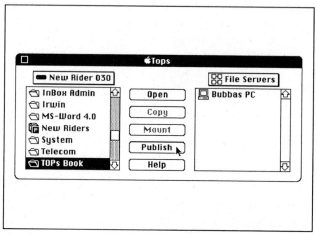

Figure 1-18. Your screen will look something like this when selecting folders to publish on a Macintosh.

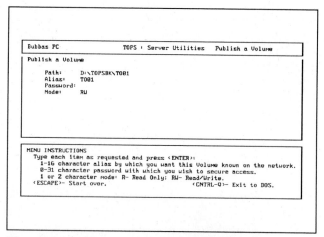

Figure 1-19. Your screen will resemble this illustration when publishing subdirectories on a PC.

TOPS/DOS has a few differences from the other versions. Because of the memory limitations of most PCs, TOPS/DOS comes in modules. To conserve memory, you load only the modules you need for your specific functions. Later chapters explain some of the strategies you can use to work more efficiently with TOPS/DOS on a PC.

■ TOPS applications

We're on the home stretch now. You've already been introduced to most of the basics you need to start planning your network. Let's finish up by taking a quick tour of the things you can do with TOPS.

File exchanging

The most basic, essential use of TOPS is to trade files between computers. Two concepts hold the key to understanding file exchanges: publishing and mounting.

Publishing

You learned earlier that a server is a disk whose files are available to the network. To make a disk into a server, you *publish* it (Figure 1-20). Publishing is like posting a message: "Hey everybody, use this disk if you want to."

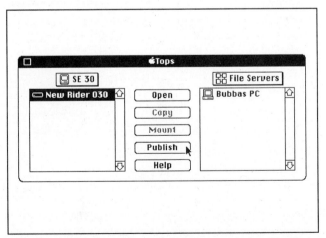

Figure 1-20. Macintosh computers use a screen like this one to mount and publish a volume.

To this point, we've talked about publishing a disk. In real life, you will usually publish only a portion — for instance, one subdirectory (if you're a PC user) or one folder (if you use the Mac). Once published, it becomes known as a *volume*. A volume is any disk (or portion) published on the TOPS network. You can publish more than one volume at a time.

Mounting

To use a volume, you must *mount* it onto your own machine (Figure 1-21).

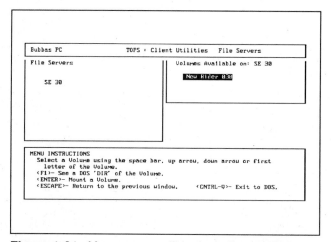

Figure 1-21. Your screen will look similar to this one when mounting a disk on a PC compatible. Once mounted, you can use it as if it were directly attached to your computer.

When you mount a volume, it's like plugging it into your machine. As far as you are concerned, when you access a volume on the network, you're using another disk on your computer — even though that disk happens to reside down the hall on someone else's computer.

You'll learn more details in later chapters. For the moment, just be sure you understand three key concepts:

• Publishing a disk makes it into a server that can be seen and used by the rest of the network.

• Once published, a disk (or a portion of a disk) is called a volume.

• To use a volume (a published disk from another machine),

you must first mount it onto your own computer. Mounting a disk makes your computer a client.

To summarize: Servers publish. Clients mount.

Translating file formats

You already know that TOPS automatically interprets between incompatible operating systems. The *TOPS Translators* can also translate between file formats. For instance, a PC WordStar file can be copied to MacWrite format (Figure 1-22).

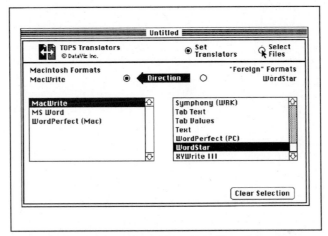

Figure 1-22. Translating from WordStar format to MacWrite format. The TOPS Translators can convert dozens of different file formats.

This is only one small example of the many possible conversions. Chapter Six, "Translating Files with TOPS," gives complete details about installing and using this valuable function.

Printing

TOPS can make it easy and simple to use any printer, thanks to two utilities called *TPRINT* and *NetPrint*.

With TPRINT, you can publish a printer just the way you publish a disk. As you recall, publishing makes a resource available to the rest of the network. When you publish a printer that is attached to your computer, you make it possible for other computers to use it. Those other clients can access the printer as if it was attached to their own computers.

TPRINT can also use printers that attach directly to the network. (Certain printers, such as the Apple LaserWriter, can hook up to the network without passing through a computer.)

PC owners who just want to print, and don't need to do anything else for the moment, can use a special standalone utility called NetPrint. NetPrint doesn't give them any of the other TOPS functions. It does, however, give them access to those printers attached directly to the network. See Chapter Seven, "Printing with TOPS," for a full explanation of all printing functions.

Print spooling

TOPS provides more than the ability to print over the network. You can use TOPS Spool to print documents in the background. That means you send your documents to TOPS Spool instead of the printer. TOPS Spool makes a temporary disk copy. Then it takes care of passing this file on to the printer. Meanwhile, you can go back to work.

This spooling capability means you don't have to wait for the printer to finish its current job before you send your document. You can send it right away. TOPS Spool will save it until the printer is ready, even if there are other documents waiting already. TOPS Spool remembers which documents were first in line and passes them to the printer in order, without intervention from you (Figure 1-23).

Electronic mail

With the addition of special mail software, you can also use TOPS to send and receive messages between workstations attached to the network. You type in a message and specify the recipient (Figure 1-24). TOPS routes it to the correct workstation. You can also attach files to your message.

Several packages support electronic mail over TOPS. Chapter Eight, "Sending Electronic Mail with TOPS," describes the leading packages and how to use them.

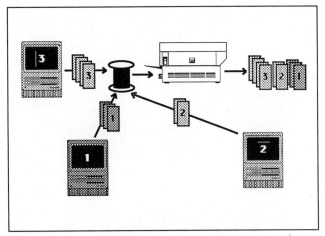

Figure 1-23. TOPS Spool lets you put documents in line for printing. Meanwhile, you can go back to work. TOPS will continue printing in the background.

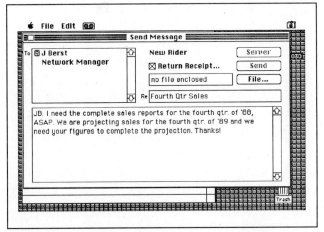

Figure 1-24. With an optional program like Microsoft Mail, you can send electronic mail to the different computers on your TOPS network.

Other applications

File exchanging, format translating, printing, electronic mail — these four applications are important, but they're not the only things you can accomplish with the versatile TOPS network. For instance, you can also implement:

• Remote operation, whereby you use the screen of one computer to control and operate a second

- Modem sharing, so a single modem can serve many computers

- Backup over the network, so you only need one tape drive or removeable hard disk

- Security, whereby you can restrict who can access which files

These functions, and others, are covered in later chapters.

Continuing on

This first chapter has given you an overview of (1) the key concepts that govern TOPS and (2) what TOPS can do for you and your business. But TOPS can't do any work until you install it. The first stage in that process is to plan the kind of network you want, as you'll learn in the next chapter.

Chapter Two

■ Planning a TOPS Network

Spending a few minutes to plan is the fastest way to get to the promised LAN — the world of efficient, hassle-free TOPS networking. And the fastest way to plan a LAN (a local area network), in our opinion, is to use this chapter together with the checklists on the next two pages.

TOPS is easy to install *provided* you decide in advance which options to use. This chapter explains your alternatives and makes recommendations. It also gives you a place to record your choices — the planning checklists, which summarize your decisions. You will use one *Overall network checklist* to plan the entire network and one *Individual device checklist* for each node on the network.

Please read through the entire chapter before you start planning. You must consider a half dozen or so factors *simultaneously* before making your final decisions. When we sat down to write this chapter, we realized we didn't know which factors to mention first. It's the old *chicken or the egg* quandary. We decided to begin with the chicken. Then we'll tell you about the egg. It's up to you, however, to read about them both before you start cooking. Otherwise, you might end with an omelet when you really wanted a chicken salad sandwich.

This chapter will step you through the decision points, following the same order as the checklist. It starts with the overall network decisions, then moves on to the individual devices. In essence, it is a series of questions about how you want to do things. Once you've answered all the questions, you've planned the network. It's that simple.

Overall network checklist

Sketch: Draw proposed layout, writing in station names and length of cable runs. Use separate sheet if necessary. Circle stations that need terminating resistors.

Total cable length: _____   Total DIN-8 interface boxes: _____

Cable type: ☐ Phone wire ☐ LocalTalk ☐ Mixed ☐ Other   Total DB-9 interface boxes: _____

Topology: ☐ Daisy chain ☐ Trunk ☐ Star

Individual device checklist

Station name: _____   Type of device: _____

Operating System/version #: _____   TOPS serial#: _____

TOPS version #: _____

AppleTalk port

☐ DIN-8   ☐ DB-9

Cable

☐ Phone wire   ☐ LocalTalk   ☐ Other _____

Interface box

Brand _____

Self-terminating: ☐ Yes ☐ No   Connector: ☐ DIN 8   ☐ DB-9

Computers

RAM: _____

Hard disk volume(s):

Size _____MB   Name _____

Size _____MB   Name _____

Floppy disk(s): (fill in number of matching drives)

Size _____MB   Name _____

| | | Size _____MB | Name _____ |

_____ 360K   _____ 1.2MB   Size _____MB   Name _____

_____ 1.44MB   _____ 400K   Size _____MB   Name _____

_____ 720K   _____ 800K

Board settings (PCs only)

Network board: IRQ _____   I/O _____ DMA _____   Serial board: IRQ _____   I/O _____

Video board: IRQ _____   I/O _____ DMA _____   Other board(s): IRQ _____   I/O _____   DMA _____

Bus mouse: IRQ _____   I/O _____   IRQ _____   I/O _____   DMA _____

Printers

Standalone network device: ☐ Yes   ☐ No

Page Description Language (PDL) or Emulation: _____

Ports: ☐ AppleTalk   ☐ DIN 8   ☐ AppleTalk DB-9

        ☐ Serial   ☐ Parallel

        ☐ Dedicated laserboard

Printer driver: ☐ TPRINT   ☐ NetPrint

Printer driver version #: _____

Auto-Publish settings

Volumes/printers _____   _____   _____

to auto-publish _____   _____   _____

                 _____   _____   _____

Volumes/printers _____   _____   _____

to auto-mount   _____   _____   _____

                 _____   _____   _____

■ Overall network decisions

This section discusses decisions you make just once for the entire network:

- choosing the network variety
- selecting a cabling option
- planning the topology

It concludes with suggestions on how — and why — to sketch your layout on paper before you start.

Which variety of TOPS should you use?

Chapter One explained that you can use TOPS with either of two popular protocols: Ethernet or AppleTalk. AppleTalk is by far the most common choice for TOPS. Although slower than Ethernet, it is quite adequate for small networks. Moreover, it's less expensive, especially when you consider that Apple-Talk circuitry is already built into Macintosh computers.

You can use AppleTalk for larger networks too, but you'll need to take steps to improve performance. You should consider using speedup boxes, dedicated servers, repeaters, and/or zones — strategies discussed in more detail later in the book.

Ethernet costs roughly three times as much per node, but it runs two to ten times faster. Ethernet is a logical selection for large networks where speed is an issue. And it's your best choice if most of your computers already have Ethernet circuitry (as with Sun workstations). Don't forget, however, that both Macintoshes and PCs need add-in boards before they can connect to Ethernet cabling.

We'll have some things to say about Ethernet in later chapters. For the most part, however, *this book assumes that you are installing an AppleTalk-compatible network.*

Which cabling option should you use?

Most Ethernet-compatible networks use some type of coaxial cable, but you can also use twisted-pair (thin Ethernet) or fiber-optic cabling. If you are installing TOPS over Ethernet, explore your cabling options with a competent dealer, or with your company's network manager. In all likelihood, you will want to match an existing Ethernet installation elsewhere in the company.

For the purposes of this book, we will assume you are installing a LocalTalk-compatible TOPS network. In that case, you have two main cabling options: LocalTalk (traditional) cable or phone wire. (A third type — fiber-optic cable — is found in specialized installations.)

Phone wire is the best choice for most installations. Still, it will pay to examine both possibilities before you decide.

LocalTalk cable

In the early days of Apple networking, there was only one cabling option. You may see it referred to as *shielded twisted-pair* or *traditional* cable. We call it *LocalTalk* cable, to reflect the fact that it was introduced when Apple brought out the LocalTalk networking scheme. You can identify LocalTalk cable by its thickness and by the round plug at the end (called a *Mini-DIN 3*). Figure 2-1 shows traditional LocalTalk cable in comparison to flat phone wire.

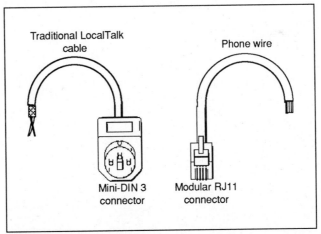

Figure 2-1. Two common cabling options: LocalTalk (left) and flat phone wire (right).

Although it works perfectly well for short distances, LocalTalk cable is more expensive than phone wire. To stretch over distances longer than 30 feet, you must buy specially made cables, or splice short lengths of ready-made cable with in-line connectors. LocalTalk cable is a good choice only if you meet two conditions: (1) you have a small network with short distances between devices and (2) you already own some of the cable. Otherwise, phone wire is a better choice.

Phone wire

Phone wire is the most popular cabling option. As you can see by referring again to Figure 2-1, it uses familiar telephone wire and *modular connectors*. Phone wire can function up to 3000 feet (depending on conditions), compared to 1000 feet for traditional LocalTalk cable. Phone wire, then, is cheaper while being capable of longer distances than LocalTalk cable.

Mixing cable types

Strictly speaking, you don't have to stick with one type of cable. If you are starting from scratch, buy phone wire. But if you have some LocalTalk cable, don't throw it away. You can link LocalTalk cable to phone wire with special adapters.

To mix cable types, group one type at one end of the network (Figure 2-2). That way, you need only one adapter to bridge the two cable types. Multiple adapters on a single network can cause loss of signals.

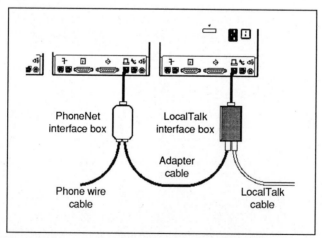

Figure 2-2. In this sample network, all the devices with LocalTalk cable have been grouped to the right. That way, the network needs only one adapter to bridge between the different cables.

Cable length requirements

The actual length of the network you can achieve depends on several conditions, including the type of cable. As a rule of thumb, try to keep LocalTalk cabling to a total length of 1000 feet, with no more than 100 feet between nodes. If you exceed 100 feet between any two nodes, you must get special cables, or splice the ready-made cables with in-line connectors.

The maximum length of a phone wire network depends on the gauge (thickness) of the wire. The *lower* the gauge, the *thicker* the wire. The thicker the wire, the better the signal.

In our discussion of phone wire so far, we've concentrated on *flat wire* (sometimes called *modular* phone wire). Flat wire is 26 gauge. Although perfectly adequate for smaller networks, it cannot carry as much as thicker wires. You can also buy 24-gauge *two-pair* phone wire or 22-gauge *round* wire.

Thicker wire permits longer cable runs. The maximum lengths you see in product brochures are based on 26-gauge round wire. If you use a thinner wire instead, you must reduce the length accordingly. Table 2-1 summarizes our recommended maximums for the most common gauges.

Table 2-1. Recommended maximum cable lengths

Cable Type	Maximum Total Length	Maximum Between Two Nodes
LocalTalk (traditional)	1000	100
26-gauge phone wire (flat)	2000	500
24-gauge phone wire (flat)	3000	1000
22-gauge phone wire (round)	3000	1000

| Note | Our recommendations are practical rules of thumb, not theoretical maximums. They may differ from what you see in ads.

Although you may be able to exceed these numbers under

certain conditions, we advise against pushing the limits. You could be setting the stage for intermittent and unexplained problems. If you need to go beyond these amounts, use repeaters to amplify the signals.

At the end of this section, we recommend sketching your layout. At the same time you draw the sketch, you should estimate the cable lengths between each station so you can keep within the guidelines. The planning checklist includes space for recording cable lengths.

Tip When estimating cable lengths, it's not enough to measure from machine to machine. You must also add the distance from the ground to the desk height (if you are running cable under the floor) or from the ceiling to the computer (if you are stringing cable through a suspended ceiling).

Which topology should you use?

Plan the topology of your TOPS network carefully before you start installing the hardware. There's no sense stringing cables or drilling holes in walls until you know exactly where things should go. As you recall from Chapter One, the three most common layout options are the daisy chain, the trunk, and the star. This section discusses all three.

The pros and cons of daisy chain layouts

Hooking up a daisy chain network is a simple matter of running the wire from one computer to the next. You connect the devices one-by-one in a row. A daisy chain is easy to install and easy to expand. And there's another, little-realized advantage. The daisy chain makes it easy to reconfigure the network. Later in the chapter we'll talk about how and where to put the busiest users so they don't clog up the rest of the network. If you are using a daisy chain configuration, you can easily connect the machines in a different order.

On the down side, a daisy chain cannot handle as much traffic or as many devices as an active star. Nor is it as convenient as a trunk layout.

Tip Use a daisy chain layout if possible. Switch to a star or trunk configuration only if necessary to get higher performance or greater flexibility.

The daisy chain topology is the logical choice for small TOPS networks, especially if they meet most of the following criteria:

- first-time users

- fewer than 12 nodes

- a total length less than 1000 feet with 22-gauge round wire, or 500 feet with 26-gauge flat phone wire.

- low-traffic network (rarely more than two or three stations active at the same time)

- you don't know yet who your heaviest users will be and you want the flexibility to reconfigure the network

- no dedicated server

If you have more than 12 nodes, you can still use the daisy chain setup. Simply divide the network into *zones* of eight devices or less. Then connect the zones with repeaters.

Planning daisy chain layouts

All you have to do to plan a daisy chain layout is decide which nodes to connect to which. The best way to do that is to sketch the layout on the planning checklist. We'll show you some examples as we go along.

Your goals should be (1) to use the least amount of cable while (2) isolating the heaviest users away from the rest of the network. Why do you want to save cable? For one thing, it costs money. In addition, the less cable, the less chance of exceeding the maximum length, the less need for repeaters, and the stronger the signals.

Obviously, you also have to consider the layout of your office. Take advantage of existing connections if possible. For instance, suspended ceilings and crawl spaces let you string cable without drilling holes or attaching cables to the outside of walls. Figure 2-3 shows a sketch of the simple, eight-node daisy-chain configuration we use in one office of New Riders Publishing.

Now suppose that we find out later that the heaviest network traffic is between computer X and laser printer Y. Figure 2-4 shows how we could rewire the daisy chain to isolate these two nodes at one end.

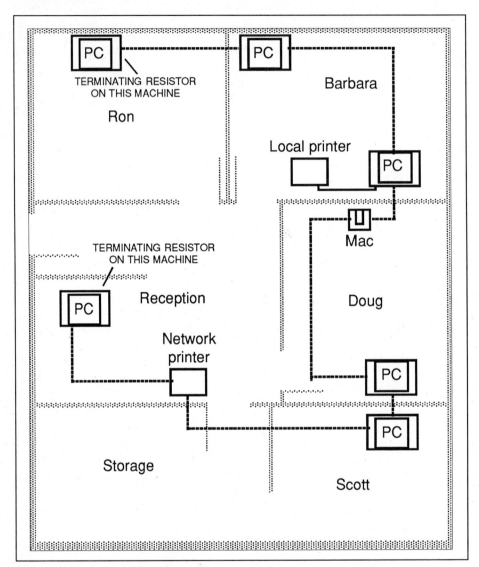

Figure 2-3. A daisy chain layout.

Look at either diagram closely. As you can see, the ends of the chain do not connect. By all means, do *not* create a loop by connecting the two ends. TOPS will not operate in a ring configuration.

Notice as well that all the interface boxes in the middle of the chain have two cables plugged into them. But the two boxes at the ends have only one cable. The extra sockets are filled with *terminating resistors*. Figure 2-5 shows a closeup.

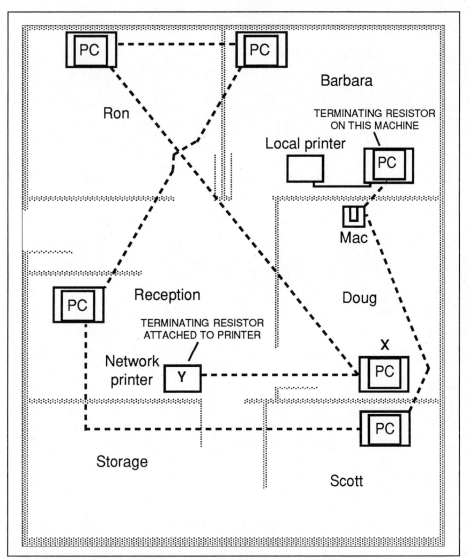

Figure 2-4. The same office rewired to isolate the heaviest users at one end. Notice that the placement of the machines has not changed, only the wiring.

And that brings us to an important rule for laying out daisy chain networks: A daisy chain must have two terminating resistors, one at each end.

You're going to encounter resistors in every type of layout, so let's define this important term. A terminating resistor absorbs excess electrical energy. It prevents excessive signal noise from confusing the network.

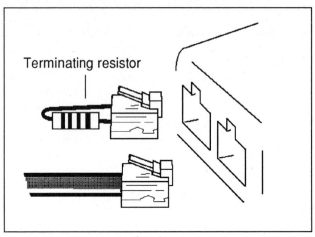

Figure 2-5. A terminating resistor fits into the empty socket of an interface box. You need one at each end of a daisy chain network.

Here's how it works. Imagine throwing a golf ball at a concrete wall. If you throw it hard, it will bounce back forcefully. Now suppose that you've covered the wall with twelve inches of foam rubber. No matter how hard you throw the ball against the wall, the foam will absorb the energy. The ball will fall harmlessly to the ground.

The terminating resistor is the electrical equivalent of foam rubber. Without it, electrical signals reach the end of the network and bounce back with enough force to cancel other signals traveling along the same wire (called *ringing*). With the resistor in place, much of the signal is absorbed.

Most interface boxes require you to physically insert a terminating resistor into an empty socket. However, some brands advertise themselves as *self-terminating*. These boxes include terminating resistors inside. Normally, those resistors do not function. But the boxes are able to detect when they are at the end of the line. When they detect that condition, they automatically activate the resistor.

Let's summarize the simple rules for planning a daisy chain layout:

• String the computers together one after another.

• Never connect the network in a loop.

- Keep the cable runs as short as possible.

- Put a terminating resistor at each end (or use self-terminating interface boxes).

- Divide larger networks into smaller zones. Set up each zone as a standalone daisy chain. You can connect the zones later with repeaters or a star controller.

That's it. We told you daisy chains were easy. Now let's explore the trunk topology, which takes a bit more planning.

The pros and cons of trunk layouts

Many functioning TOPS networks use the trunk topology. This arrangement can pose problems for a beginner, including excessive ringing, insufficient or excessive termination, signal interference, and difficulty calculating maximum cable length. These challenges are compounded if you try to use existing phone wiring to carry the network signals.

At first glance, a trunk layout resembles a daisy chain. (Advanced users: Remember that we're using *trunk* to indicate a wiring arrangement, not in its strict technical sense). But the connection does not go directly from machine to machine via the interface boxes. Instead, the central cable (the trunk) creates the connection. The interface boxes hang from the central trunk on short lengths of wire called *drop cables*.

This small difference has several ramifications. The first is an advantage. Because the trunk makes the connection, you can plug and unplug devices from the network without affecting any of the others. (By contrast, if you remove an interface box from a daisy chain, you must bridge the gap.) A trunk layout lets you prewire an office without regard to the exact placement of the devices.

But there's another consequence. Since the interface boxes connect only to the trunk line and not to each other, they do not use both outlets. Each interface box will have an empty socket. That leads to the tempation to fill those sockets with terminating resistors. Too many resistors is as bad as too few.

Perhaps the easiest way to understand a trunk layout is to picture a typical phone installation. The wires inside your home or office walls form a central trunk line. *Wall jacks* let you tap into that line to attach phones. In a TOPS network, you attach computers and printers to the wall jacks instead, but the principle is the same (Figure 2-6).

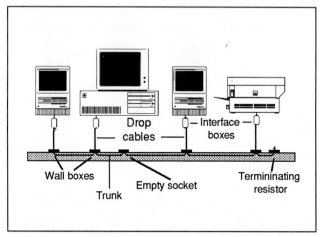

Figure 2-6. A trunk layout.

You should consider a trunk layout if you meet most of the following conditions:

- intermediate or advanced user
- total length less than 1000 feet
- already have trunk line installed in wall (or can install it inexpensively)
- want the flexibility of plugging and unplugging devices from the central line without disturbing others

Planning trunk layouts

It is possible — though not recommended — to use existing telephone lines to carry TOPS signals. If a trunk layout appeals to you, install a separate set of phone wires. In essence, you will be duplicating a typical phone system, except that the lines and wall boxes will be used by the network, not by the telephones. This is most practical in new offices before the walls go up, but you can also use this layout in existing offices with a little extra effort.

Tip If you set up a separate trunk line for TOPS, paint the outlets or mark them for network use, so co-workers don't try to plug in phones.

You'll want to use round, 22-gauge, solid-strand phone wire for the central trunk. You can buy this wire at most electronics outlets. For wall jacks, use RJ11 modular wall boxes, available at the same sources. You can use ordinary 26-gauge flat wire to hook the interface boxes to the wall jacks (Figure 2-7).

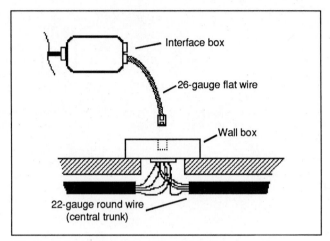

Figure 2-7. A typical trunk connection.

Figure 2-8 shows the same office as before, this time configured as a trunk layout. Take a moment to look at this sketch. Then we'll discuss some of the issues involved in building a successful TOPS trunk topology.

As with daisy chain layouts, a trunk line must have a resistor at each end. You can install these resistors in two ways. You're already familiar with the simplest way — by plugging resistors into the empty sockets of the interface boxes at the ends.

How do you tell which boxes are at the ends? Here we come to one of the problems of trunk layouts. If your office was prewired, it can be tough to judge which wall boxes are at the end. Think of your office phone system. Could you say which wall jacks are at the end of the trunk? Probably not.

WARNING Install resistors *only* in the two interface boxes at the ends of the trunk. Leave an empty socket in each remaining interface box.

Provided you have an interface box at each end of the trunk,

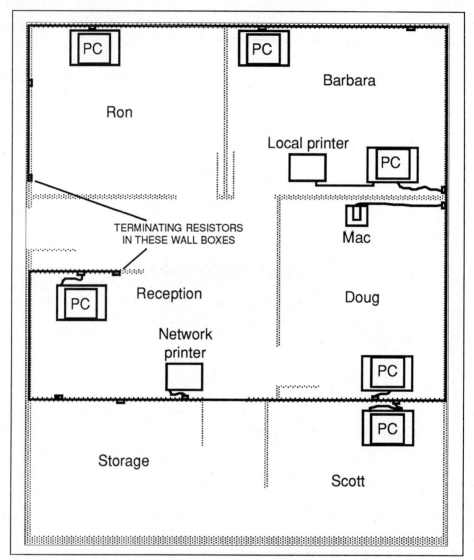

Figure 2-8. The New Riders TOPS installation as a trunk layout.

you can terminate simply by plugging resistors into the empty sockets (or by using self-terminating interface boxes). But what if you have an empty wall box at the end, as illustrated in our previous sketch of the New Riders office? In that case, you must terminate the wall box. You can do this by putting a 120-ohm resistor across the active wires that are on the back of the wall plate.

You may prefer to terminate the network by deliberately putting an unused wall box at each end. That way you don't have to remember to reterminate if you change the arrangement of the devices. You will also have an easy starting point if you need to add more length to the network in the future. Figure 2-9 shows how to wire a resistor into a wall box.

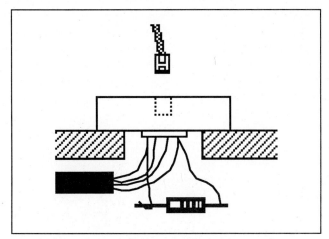

Figure 2-9. You can terminate the network by wiring a resistor into the wall boxes at both ends.

WARNING Install the terminating resistor in *either* the interface box *or* the wall box, not both.

We've already warned you of several potential problems with trunk layouts. Before we turn you loose on your own, we must warn you of some other potential pitfalls. One of these concerns the drop cable, the length of wire that runs between the wall box and the interface box.

Keep the drop cable as short as possible. When computing the maximum length of your network, multiply the drop cable by two. In other words, if you have used 100 feet of drop cable, count it as 200 feet when calculating the maximum length. This rule comes into play because nearly everyone uses 26-gauge flat wire as drop cable. However, manufacturers calculate maximum length based on the thicker 22-gauge round wire. You double the length of flat wire to approximate its lesser capacity.

A trunk layout can be as long as 1000 feet, presuming the

walls are wired with 22-gauge round wire. If you used 26-gauge flat wire inside the walls, do not exceed 500 feet.

Combining trunk lines and daisy chains

You've built your trunk layout. Because your boss is the frugal type, you installed only one wall box in each office. Now you want to put three computers and one printer into the same room. What should you do? The temptation is to daisy chain the additional devices together, then attach the nearest one to the wall box (Figure 2-10).

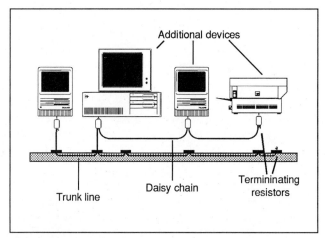

Figure 2-10. A dangerous arrangement. Do not attach a daisy chain to a trunk layout except as a last resort.

Attaching a daisy chain to a trunk layout can cause termination problems. If you *don't* terminate the daisy chain, it may experience ringing problems (signal cancellation). If you *do* terminate, you may foul up the trunk line.

A better way to add devices to a trunk is by adding wall boxes, thereby adding direct connections to the trunk (Figure 2-11).

In some offices, however, it is impossible to get inside the walls to locate and tap into the existing cables. In those cases, you might want to consider replacing the single-outlet wall box with a double-outlet box. Then you can loop the daisy chain in from one outlet and back out the other. In essence, the daisy chain becomes part of the trunk line (Figure 2-12).

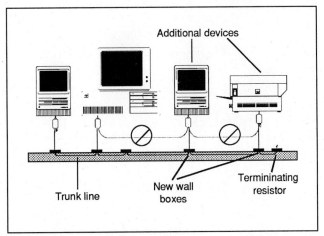

Figure 2-11. The safest way to expand a trunk layout is to add wall boxes.

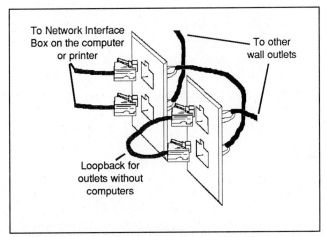

Figure 2-12. By adding a double wall box, you can safely add extra devices to a trunk installation.

Another solution recommended by some manufacturers is to attach the daisy chain with a repeater. To do this, treat the daisy chain as a separate unit. Terminate both ends, then attach the daisy chain to a repeater and the repeater to the trunk line (Figure 2-13).

If you are forced to attach a daisy chain to the trunk without a repeater, keep the chain as short as possible. If it's short enough, you may be able to get by without a resistor at the end of the chain. However, if the chain gets much longer than 20

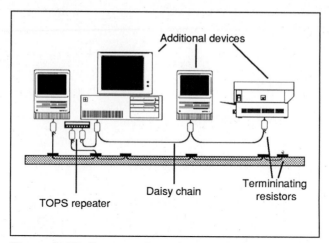

Figure 2-13. If you are forced to attach a daisy chain to a trunk, use a repeater to avoid termination problems.

feet, you may have to terminate the chain, too. Since you already have terminators on both ends of the trunk, this puts you into a dangerous situation. You may be able to get away with three or even four terminating resistors on a single trunk, but you are raising the likelihood of problems.

The dangers of existing phone lines

Typical phone wire includes four wires inside the outer sheath. Some phone systems use only two of those wires. You may have heard that you can use the remaining wires for your TOPS network without interfering with telephone calls.

At first glance it seems easy. A TOPS interface box automatically uses the outside pair of wires (usually color-coded yellow and black) in a four-wire cable. Most phone systems automatically use the inside pair (red and green). It seems logical to let the network and the phone system coexist inside the same cable. That would do away with the need to string new wires throughout the office.

But we think it's a mistake to mix phone systems and TOPS networks over the same lines. The combination intensifies the problems of termination and interference. What's more, many office phone systems use all four wires, making sharing impossible. In some cases, the extra wires are used by an alarm system.

WARNING Hooking up TOPS to your existing phone lines is not recommended.

To be fair, we're not saying you *can't* use existing phone lines for your TOPS installation. We're merely alerting you that it's probably not worth the risk. Still, the expense of stringing new cable may convince some of you to take your chances. Having warned you of the dangers, we will now give some advice to those of you who choose to ignore us.

Our first suggestion is to make absolutely sure you have two unused wires. If the phone system uses more than two wires, you should not try to run TOPS over the same cable.

Tip If the phone system has any kind of intercom, paging, or lighted buttons, it is using more than two wires.

Our second suggestion is to find out what type of wire you have inside the walls. It is probably 22-gauge round wire. If it is 24- or 26-gauge wire instead, you will have even more difficulty carrying both sets of signals (phone and network) over the same cable.

Our third suggestion is to consider carefully how you will attach both the phones and the interface boxes to the wall jacks. If you attach the phone to the interface box, you must terminate the ends of the trunk at wall jacks. (You won't have an empty socket for a resistor in the interface box, since you are using it for the phone.)

Our fourth suggestion is to follow all the other rules for trunk layouts with extra care.

The pros and cons of star layouts

So far we've examined daisy chain and trunk layouts. Now we'll look at the final alternative: the star layout. In a star layout, devices connect through a central node. (Once more for emphasis: We are not talking about star configurations as defined in high-level networking schemes like ArcNet and Ethernet. We use the term to indicate a wiring arrangement.)

Before we can give you advice about star layouts, we must distinguish between the two different types. An *active star* has a *star controller* at the center. A *passive star* does not. Figure 2-14 shows both kinds.

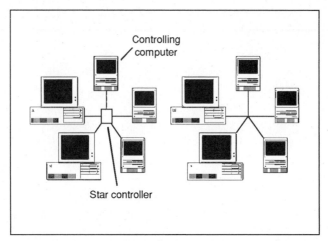

Figure 2-14. An active star layout (left) has a star
controller at the center. A passive star (right) does not.

A star controller is similar to a repeater. A repeater amplifies
signals so you can have a longer network. A star controller
does the same thing, but it can handle many lines at the same
time (Figure 2-15). Thus, a star controller makes it possible to
have a larger network with more devices.

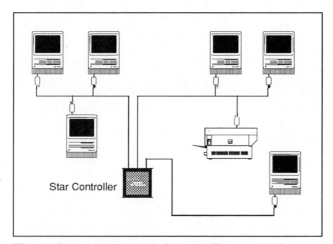

Figure 2-15. A star controller acts like a central
switchboard. When a message comes in, it
determines where it should go, amplifies the signal,
and routes it to its proper destination.

Our diagram shows each device returning to the star controller. In practice, it is more common to divide larger networks

into self-contained zones. Then you connect each zone to the star controller.

A star layout makes it easier to extend the length of a network, by connecting separate zones through the central node. But star layouts do have drawbacks. They take more cable. Passive stars create termination problems. Active stars require the extra expense of a central controller. You should consider a star layout if you match most of the following conditions:

- Intermediate or advanced user.

- The office is already prewired in a star configuration.

- You want to use a centralized star controller to increase the speed and efficiency of the network.

- You want to use a star controller to expand the network into separate zones.

Planning star layouts

We recommend against passive star layouts. Since there are no clearcut ends, it is difficult to know whether and where to terminate. However, some offices come prewired in passive star configurations. Your office probably qualifies if your telephone company tells you it has a *punch-down box*, a *phone closet*, or a *drop point*. These terms refer to standard telephone wiring — which brings up another stumbling block. Passive networks often piggy-back over existing phone lines. We've already discussed the dangers and difficulties of putting networks and phone systems on the same cable.

If you have no other choice than to use a passive star, then keep these tips in mind:

- keep branches to 100 feet or less

- limit yourself to six branches or less

- put terminators on the four longest branches

Active star networks are an advanced configuration. They are covered in later chapters along with repeaters, zones, and other power techniques.

Which advanced options do you need?

If you plan to install a small, low-traffic daisy chain TOPS network of eight devices or fewer, you should be able to complete your planning based on the information in this chapter. On the other hand, you may need to consider advanced options if you meet any of the following conditions:

- You have more than eight devices on the network.

- You need to use more than 1000 feet of cable.

- Two or three of the devices get such heavy use they slow down the rest of the network.

- You have a high-traffic network, with regular, simultaneous access by multiple users.

- You plan to use a dedicated server.

- You plan to connect your TOPS network to an Ethernet network.

Those of you in borderline situations should go ahead with a simple daisy chain installation. Only if performance suffers should you consider advanced options. In other words, don't fix it if it ain't broke. But if a simple network won't do the job, here are a few of the options at your disposal. You can mix and match these solutions to fit your individual needs:

- Relocate devices that get heavy use.

- Add repeaters to extend the network.

- Use a faster protocol to improve performance.

- Use a dedicated server.

- Break the network into zones.

We're not going to plunge into the nuances of sophisticated network configurations right now. We've saved those details for later chapters. If you know already that you'll need more sophisticated techniques, you can turn to those chapters now and integrate them into your plan. However, we recommend that you phase in larger networks. Break them into smaller, self-contained zones. When all the zones are up and running, you can connect them together into one larger network.

Sketching the network on paper

We have completed most of the decisions for the network as a whole. Now that you've read this far, some of you may be ready to create a sketch of your proposed layout. Others may prefer to do the planning for the individual devices first. In either case, you'll find space on the planning checklist to create your drawing. A separate piece of paper works just as well.

At first glance, it may seem trivial to sketch a simple network (Figure 2-16). In real life, however, it's a useful exercise. It's much easier to correct mistakes on paper than after the cable has been installed in the walls. A sketch often helps you to make key decisions, such as:

- which wiring arrangement will use the least cable

- which scheme isolates the busiest users away from the rest of the network

- where to put the network printers

- whether or not to add a repeater

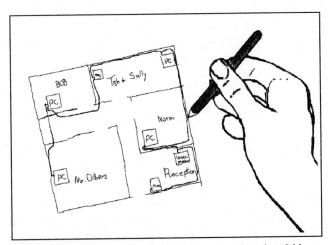

Figure 2-16. Even small, simple networks should be sketched before installation.

As you draw, jot down these four facts for each node:

1. type of device

2. type of connector it requires

3. amount of cable to run to the next station

4. station name

The station name is a unique label that identifies each node (Figure 2-17). You will use it to label the wires when you make the hardware connections, as explained in Chapter Three. You will also use the same designations when installing the software and using the network, as taught in Chapter Four.

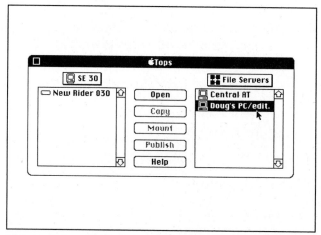

Figure 2-17. Station names identify each node to the rest of the network. Choose the names with care.

Give some thought to the names you choose. First of all, you must keep them to 15 characters or less (including spaces). You can include spaces in a name. However, you will have to remember to enclose the entire name in quotes when you tell the software about it.

Station names are your means of identifying the different devices. Don't call the boss's computer "Captain Bligh's PC" unless you're sure he'll appreciate the joke. Likewise, don't use cryptic names. You may remember that "Bozo" stands for the 80MB IBM PC in the sales department and "Granny Smith" is the Apple LaserWriter in word processing. It won't be so obvious to the new employee you hire next month.

Some companies with multiple computers use the department name followed by a number: Sales 1, Sales 2, etc. However, this scheme forces everyone to remember that Sales 1 is

Samantha and Sales 2 is Bill. In addition, they have to remember that Samantha has a Mac while Bill uses a PC.

A better strategy is to include both the type of machine and an identifying label in the station name — *Steve's PC*, for instance, or *Eng. Mac IIcx*.

■ Individual device decisions

To this point, we've focused on broad issues that affect the network as a whole. Now let's turn our attention to the individual devices. Use the hints and suggestions below to fill in a planning checklist for each node on the network. We've divided this portion of the chapter into two sections, one for hardware issues and one for software.

What hardware do I need?

This section explains which computers can run with TOPS and which ones need to be upgraded. It includes our recommended daily allowances of memory and disk space for efficient operation. It also describes printers, cables, connectors, and interface boxes — in short, all the pieces you need to put together a TOPS network.

Macintosh hardware requirements

Theoretically, you can run TOPS on any Macintosh except the early 128K models. In real life, however, TOPS is much more efficient if your hardware meets certain standards. For this reason, we've listed two requirements: (1) the theoretical minimum and (2) the practical minimum.

Theoretical minimum: You can run TOPS on a single-floppy Macintosh 512, but the Macintosh Plus is highly recommended as the bare minimum configuration.

Practical minimum: Life on a 512K single-floppy Macintosh is difficult. Much of your time will be spent swapping disks and waiting. A more realistic minimum configuration is 1MB RAM with a 20MB hard disk if you use the Finder. If you use MultiFinder, your minimum configuration should be a Macintosh Plus 2MB and a 20MB hard disk. Remember that the TOPS software remains in memory along with other desk accessories you load. If you like to use memory-hungry applications such as CAD packages, desktop-publishing packages, or HyperCard, you'll want more RAM.

PC hardware requirements

You can run TOPS on most PC compatibles, including machines compatible with the IBM PC/XT, the IBM AT, and the IBM PS/2.

Theoretical minimum: You can theoretically run TOPS on a dual-floppy PC with 512K RAM. You can install TOPS on a floppy disk, as long as you have 700K of disk space.

Practical minimum: Do not attempt serious network usage with anything less than 640K RAM. In addition, we recommend a 20MB or larger hard disk.

Network interface cards

In addition to the minimum RAM and disk requirements mentioned above, all PCs must have a network interface card. As you recall from Chapter One, the interface card contains the circuitry to connect the computer to the network.

Printer requirements

You can use virtually any printer on TOPS by connecting it to a computer that's on the network. That computer can then load TOPS and publish the printer. The process is the same as publishing a volume. In both cases, publishing lets the rest of the network see and use the device as if it were attached to their own machines. We refer to such printers as *published* or *shared*.

There's a second way to use printers: by operating them as standalone *network printers*. A network printer is one that does not have to be connected via a computer. It attaches directly to the network and is always available. Any client on the network can use it at any time (Figure 2-18).

A printer must meet two conditions to operate as a standalone network printer. It must (1) be PostScript compatible and (2) include AppleTalk circuitry with an AppleTalk-compatible connector — either a DB-9 or a Mini-DIN 8 (Figure 2-19).

Many laser printers include an AppleTalk-compatible port

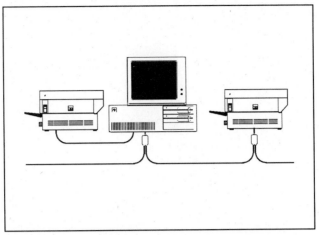

Figure 2-18. A published printer (left) connects to the network via a computer. A network printer (right) connects directly to the network.

Figure 2-19. PostScript printers can operate as standalone network printers if they have either a DB-9 (left) or a Mini-DIN 8 connector (right).

and other ports. The Apple LaserWriter Plus, for instance, includes both a DB-9 and a DB-25 serial port (Figure 2-20).

Modem requirements

Modems are similar to printers. They can operate as published devices (connected via a computer) or as standalone network modems. Network modems are still relatively rare.

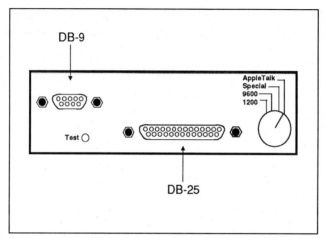

Figure 2-20. The Apple LaserWriter Plus has both an AppleTalk-compatible DB-9 port and a DB-25 serial port.

They must have both an AppleTalk interface and software that permits access by anyone on the network.

Cable requirements

We've already covered cables pretty thoroughly. At this point, suffice it to say that each device must have a sufficient length of compatible cable to stretch to the next node of the network.

Interface box requirements

Every device on the network must have one interface box (repeaters need two). A variety of different brands have appeared. Some of the most popular include:

- TOPS TeleConnector

- Belkin QuickNet

- Farallon PhoneNet

- Nuvotech TurboNet

Tip You can usually mix different *brands* of interface boxes on the network, as long as they have the correct connectors.

Be sure the interface box has the right connector (see below).

Connector requirements

Every interface box — regardless of its speed — must have

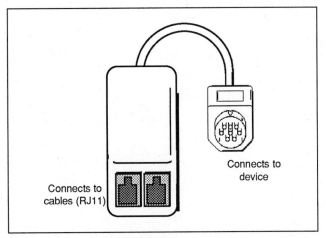

Figure 2-21. An interface box has three connectors.

connectors to link it to the computer and the cable. Each box has three connectors. Two hook to the cables running to the next nodes and one connects to the device (Figure 2-21).

Since most small TOPS networks use phone wire, our diagram shows the two connections to the cable as RJ11 modular phone jacks. You can also buy interface boxes compatible with traditional LocalTalk cable. In that case, the cable connections will be Mini-DIN 3 plugs.

The remaining connection must match the port on the back of the device. In other words, the cable coming out of the interface box must match the connector on the computer. There are two types of AppleTalk ports: *Mini-DIN 8* and *DB-9*. One way to find out what connectors you need is to inspect the back of each device. Figure 2-22 illustrates the appearance of the ports and the connectors.

The inspection method is one way to find out which connectors you need. A faster way is to consult Table 2-2. It lists the connectors for a variety of popular devices.

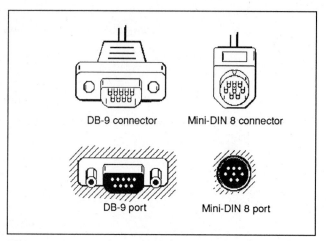

Figure 2-22. A quick look at the back of the computer or printer will tell you if it needs a Mini-DIN 8 connector (right) or a DB-9 connector (left).

Table 2-2. Connector requirements

DB-9	Mini-DIN 8
Macintosh 512K	Macintosh Plus
Macintosh 512KE	Macintosh SE
TOPS FlashCard	Macintosh SE/30
LaserWriter	Macintosh II
LaserWriter Plus	Macintosh IIx
Linotronic typesetters	Macintosh IIcx
TOPS Repeater	ImageWriter II
Apple LocalTalk board	LaserWriter IISC
DaynaTalk board	LaserWriter IINT
Hercules Network Graphics Plus	LaserWriter IINTX
TandyLink card	

What software do I need?

Before installing TOPS, make sure your computers have the proper systems software.

Tip Try to use the same Finder version for every networked Mac, and the same DOS version for every PC compatible.

Macintosh system software requirements

Use Table 2-3 to confirm that your Macintosh computers have a TOPS-compatible system. If not, get an update from an authorized Apple dealer. If you don't know which version you have, pull down the Apple menu and select About the Finder (Figure 2-23).

Table 2-3. Macintosh system recommendations

Model	System
512K	System 3.2/Finder 5.3
512KE	System 4.1/Finder 5.5
Plus	System 6.0.2 or higher
SE	System 6.0.2 or higher
SE/30	System 6.0.3 or higher, MultiFinder 6.0 or higher
II	System 6.0.2 or higher, MultiFinder 6.0 or higher
IIx	System 6.0.2 or higher, MultiFinder 6.0 or higher
IIcx	System 6.0.3 or higher, MultiFinder 6.0 or higher

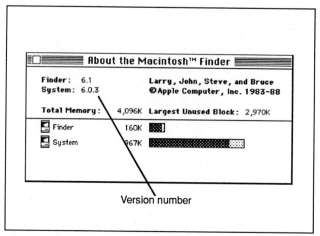

Figure 2-23. Select About the Finder from the Apple menu to see the version number for the System and the Finder.

PC system software requirements

You must have DOS 3.1 or higher to run TOPS on a PC compatible. If you don't know which version of DOS you have, examine the original system disk that came with your computer. Or exit to DOS. At the DOS prompt type: `ver` and the screen will display the version number.

Continuing on

This chapter has provided the know-how to plan a simple TOPS network. It led you through the decisions that affect the network as a whole. Then it showed you how to confirm that you have everything you need for each device on the network.

Now you are ready to set things up. That occurs in two steps. First, you hook up the cables, connectors, and computers. Second, you install the software. The next chapter takes you step-by-step through phase one: connecting the hardware.

Chapter Three

■ Connecting the Hardware

Connecting a TOPS network is so easy even a grownup can do it. This chapter will show you how. Hooking up hardware involves only three steps (Figure 3-1) — and Macintosh users can even skip the first one:

- install the network boards (PCs only)

- string the cable

- attach the interface boxes

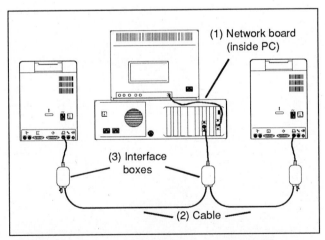

Figure 3-1. Connecting hardware involves (1) installing network boards in the PCs, (2) stringing the cable, and (3) attaching the interface boxes.

This chapter assumes that you have prepared by planning the network layout as explained in Chapter Two.

◼ Installing network boards

This first section applies only to PC compatibles. We put it up front to get the hard part out of the way. If you don't have any PCs on your network, skip this material and go straight to the section called "Stringing cable."

As you know, every device on a TOPS network must have AppleTalk circuitry. Macintosh computers have it built in, as do many PostScript-compatible printers. Unfortunately, IBM PC compatibles do not. The good news: You can buy add-in AppleTalk network boards for PCs. Once inside the computer, these boards hook up to TOPS with the same cables and interface boxes you use for other devices (Figure 3-2). Popular brands include the FlashCard from TOPS, the TandyLink card from Tandy, the DaynaTalk board from Dayna, and the Apple LocalTalk board from Apple.

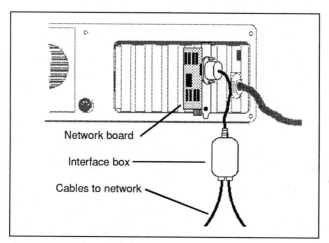

Figure 3-2. A network board fits inside a PC. It contains a port at the rear for attachment to the network via an interface box.

Some of these network boards, such as the FlashCard, can send signals faster than standard AppleTalk (provided the device at the other end is also capable of the higher speeds). In later chapters, we explain how to rev up network performance by using these faster protocols. For the moment, we will focus on the problem of installing the boards.

Now for the bad news: Be forewarned that a network board may conflict with other boards inside your PC. Fortunately, you can often spot and solve such conflicts in advance.

Spotting potential conflicts

Before you install an AppleTalk board, spend a few moments anticipating the likelihood of problems. If you fall into the high-risk category, you can save time by troubleshooting in advance. Without going into technical details, you are likely to experience board conflicts if the computer contains or is any of the following:

- any graphics adapter board other than one of the IBM standards (MDA, CGA, EGA, VGA) or Hercules' Monochrome Graphics Adapter

- two serial ports

- a bus mouse

- a printer controller board

- a memory board with an extra serial port

- a game port

- a multifunction board with a clock

- another network board

- an IBM PS/2 Model 25

- an IBM PS/2 Model 30

If you think you're at risk, read the section *Solving board conflicts* before you install the network board. Otherwise, you may have to pull the board out again to change its settings.

WARNING **You may have problems even if you are in the low-risk group. If your PC hangs when you execute the LOADTOPS command, you probably have a board conflict.**

Solving board conflicts

Read this section if you are at risk for board conflicts. It explains how conflicts occur and how to solve them. If you are in the low-risk category, skip ahead and put the board into the computer. Then install the software and try it out. If you have problems, return here for suggestions.

A conflict occurs when two boards use the same *address*. An address is a numerical designation. The computer uses it to make sure it is sending information to the right location. If two boards use the same address, the computer cannot distinguish between them.

How can you tell whether two boards have conflicting addresses? One solution — not a very good one — is trial and error. You put the network board in and try it out. If it doesn't work, you pull it out and change one setting. Then you try it again. If it still doesn't work, you pull it out and change a different setting. And so on, one at a time, until you isolate the conflict. Believe it or not, this is how many network boards get installed.

| Note | If you adopt the trial-and-error method, you may end up pulling boards in and out several times. You may also get a little irritable. Don't say we didn't warn you.

A better solution is to examine the documentation for your computer *and* the boards inside it. That way you can spot conflicts in advance, and change the AppleTalk board before you put it in.

Comparing documentation

To compare the documentation, pull out the manuals for the computer, the boards already inside, and the network board you want to install. If you have lost the manual, get the information from the manufacturer or the dealer.

No two boards can share the same addresses. Look through the manuals and compare the settings in these three areas:

1. interrupt request (IRQ)

2. input/output (I/O) address

3. direct memory access (DMA) channel

(You don't have to know what these three things mean to successfully install a PC board. For those of you who are interested, the IRQ is the way the board accesses the computer. It's a way of saying "Hey, can I have some attention over here?" The I/O address is where the computer sends information to and from the board. And the DMA is the channel the board uses if it wants to access the computer memory directly, bypassing the central processing unit (CPU). Bypassing the CPU lets it communicate at faster speeds.)

If all of the boards are *different*, everything is fine. If they are the *same* in any area, you must change one of the boards.

Changing board settings

Changing board settings takes two steps. First, you must physically alter switches on the board. Second, you must tell the software about those changes. We cover the first step in this chapter. In Chapter Four, "Installing the Software," we explain how to reconfigure TOPS software to tell it you've changed settings.

Notice that we're assuming you're going to change the Apple-Talk network board. That's the logical choice. Since you haven't put it in yet, you can easily adjust it. If you change an existing board instead, you'll probably have to pull it out to reach the switches. In addition, you may have to reconfigure some of your software to recognize the changes.

> **Note** | If you make changes, *write down the new settings*. You can't reconfigure the TOPS software without them. If you don't reconfigure the software, TOPS won't operate properly. You'll find space to jot down the board settings on the planning checklist from Chapter Two.

Let's step through a sample so you get the hang of things. We'll use the TOPS FlashCard as an example. Remember: The precise details of your board may differ, but you'll need to go through a similar process.

Let's say we're installing the FlashCard in an IBM AT compatible. Let's further assume that this computer has a board inside called the BubbaCard. Referring to the FlashCard and BubbaCard manuals, we discover these settings:

	FlashCard	BubbaCard
IRQ	2	2
DMA	1	3
I/O	398	310

As you can see, the IRQ of the FlashCard conflicts with our imaginary BubbaCard. To solve the conflict, we can reconfigure the FlashCard to use an alternate IRQ. Referring again to the FlashCard manual, we find that IRQ3 is an acceptable alternate.

So far, so good. We've identified the conflict, and we know what has to change. To make that change, we must move the jumper. A *jumper* is a small box with plastic on the outside and metal on the inside. It connects pins on the board. Referring to the FlashCard manual, we find that the FlashCard's IRQ is controlled by a jumper called *Jint* (Figure 3-3).

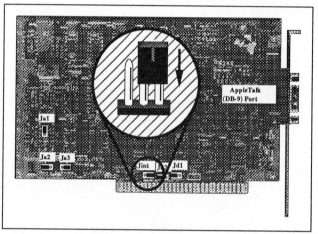

Figure 3-3. A jumper connects pins on a board. You change jumper settings by moving the jumper so it connects a different combination of pins.

To move a jumper, carefully lift it straight up until it comes off the pins. Then push it down in its new position. Usually the board includes tiny markings that show you which position is which. In our case, we must change the Jint jumper from its default setting of 2 to the new setting of 3. Look at Figure 3-4. The top part of the drawing shows the jumper in its original setting. The bottom version shows the jumper after it has been moved.

We're done changing the board. If we were doing this in real life, we would *write down the new settings* so we could tell the software about them later.

Figure 3-4. The Jint jumper in its original setting of 2 (top) and after being changed to the alternate setting of 3 (bottom).

In our imaginary example, we only had to change a single jumper. In some cases, however, you must move several jumpers to alter one address. For instance, the I/O address of the FlashCard is controlled by *three* jumpers: Ja1, Ja2, and Ja3. Refer back to Figure 3-3 to see where they are located on the board. The FlashCard manual contains more details.

Some boards use DIP switches instead of jumpers. A DIP switch works like a tiny light switch (Figure 3-5). You can change it with the tip of a ball-point pen. The positions are usually printed on the circuit board and shown on diagrams in the manuals.

WARNING Don't use a pencil to set DIP switches. Particles of lead may break off and permanently short the switch.

WARNING You cannot change board settings at random. You must change from the default (standard) setting to a permitted alternate. Consult the board manual to find permitted alternates.

Putting the board into the computer

No matter which brand of network board you use, the physical

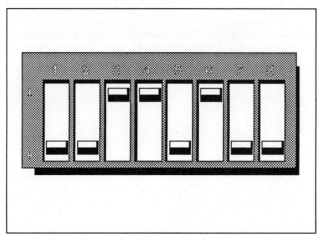

Figure 3-5. A typical DIP switch (greatly enlarged).

installation is the same. This section will show you how to install network boards.

WARNING Take precautions to avoid damage from static electricity whenever you work with a printed-circuit board, or open the cover of a computer. Static electricity can damage the computer components.

Here are five common-sense guidelines:

1. Wear shoes with rubber soles.

2. Wear cotton clothes. Avoid silk and polyester.

3. Remove all jewelry.

4. Do not work on a carpeted floor.

5. Touch a metal surface that is grounded (like a cold water pipe) to drain away any static charges before you pick up the board.

To put a board in a PC, unplug the computer and remove its cover (Figure 3-6). It is usually necessary to remove about five screws along the outside edge of the back side. Then slide the cover forward slowly, taking care to avoid snagging wires. Look for an empty slot.

You can put a network board into any empty slot *except* slot

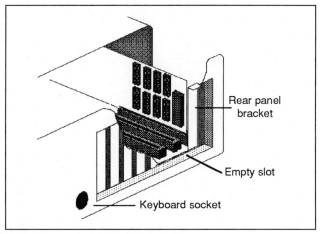

Figure 3-6. Removing the cover from a PC.

eight on an IBM XT or compatible (slot eight is OK for other models). Slot eight is the slot next to the keyboard socket.

Now remove the bracket behind the empty slot. By taking off the bracket, you create an opening for the AppleTalk port on the network board. Unscrew the bracket. Save the screw — you'll need it again in a moment.

WARNING **If you drop the screw in the computer, get it out immediately. A loose screw in a computer can cause damage and permanently ruin the main logic board.**

Carefully push the board into the slot. Check that the rear panel bracket fits into position. In other words, make sure that the bracket matches up to the opening you just created. Fasten the card's rear bracket using the same screw that formerly secured the blank bracket (Figure 3-7).

Now slide the cover back onto the computer. Notice the port that projects out the back of the computer. This is the Apple-Talk port to which you will attach the interface box.

Tip Don't screw the cover back on until you've installed the software and are sure you won't have to get inside again to resolve board conflicts.

Repeat the board installation for all the PCs on your network. When you're done, you're ready to string the cable.

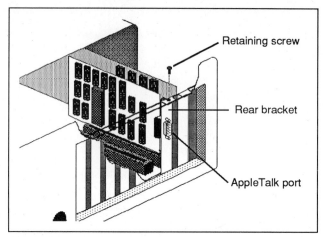

Figure 3-7. The network board after installation.

■ Stringing cable

This section assumes that you are installing phone wire cable, but many of the suggestions apply equally to other cable types.

Most companies run the wire over a suspended ceiling, through a crawl space under the floor, or through the walls by drilling holes (Figure 3-8). You can also run it along baseboards and under carpets. It takes less wire to go through walls, so the network can stretch across longer distances.

Tips for easier cable installation

Here are seven cable tips gleaned from TOPS pros:

1. Make a cable diagram in advance. Include the station names, the devices, the connectors, the terminators, and the cable lengths. Use the planning checklist from Chapter Two or any piece of paper.

2. Label every cable. Mark each end with the room number or station name of the device at the other end. Use a permanent ink pen such as a Sanford Sharpie to write directly on the wire. Or use color-coded labels. If you later add to the network, it will be easy to tell which wire to reposition.

3. Measure twice and cut once.

4. Don't forget to allow for enough cable to reach from the wall

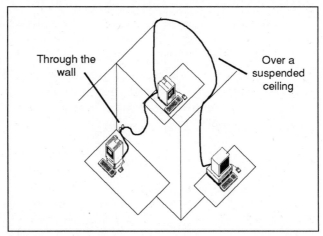

Figure 3-8. Most users run TOPS cabling from office to office through a suspended ceiling, a crawl space, or holes drilled in the walls.

to the computer. If you're coming up from the floor, you'll need an additional three feet. If you're coming down from a suspended ceiling, you should allow an extra eight to twelve feet per node.

5. To tidy up holes in walls, use plastic grommets (available from cabinet shops) or wall plates designed for cable TV installations (available at most electronics stores).

6. If you plan to add connectors to the cables yourself (as opposed to using cables with preattached connectors), do it *after* you string the cable. It's easier to get wire through tight spots without any connectors.

7. To avoid interference and possible loss of data, don't put the cable near electrical wiring or fixtures. For instance, if you're going through the ceiling, avoid running parallel to fluorescent light fixtures and power conduits.

Making extra cable

If you need extra cable, you can buy phone wire in standard lengths with modular plugs already attached. However, if you are the do-it-yourself type, you can buy wire and plugs separately and make your own cables. (Readers not wanting to assemble their own cables can skip this section.)

Phone wire cable comes in different gauges. The lower the gauge number, the higher the quality. If possible, use 22-gauge wire for your network. The maximum network length claimed by manufacturers is based on 22-gauge wire. If you substitute 26-gauge wire instead, you must reduce the maximum length by half. A network that can go up to 1000 ft. (before adding a repeater) with 22-gauge wire can stretch only 500 ft. with 26-gauge.

Nevertheless, 26-gauge, four-conductor, flat phone wire (often called modular wire) is the most readily available and the easiest to work with. It is adequate for short networks, or for short runs from the wall to the computer.

Once you get the cable, you will also need modular phone connectors for the ends. Modular telephone plugs come in different versions, so be sure to get the right type. You want the RJ11 plug designed for four leads.

WARNING   **Make sure you don't buy the four-wire modular connectors for telephone handset cords (the curly cord between the handset and the telephone). Although they look similar, they are narrower and will not work with the network interface boxes.**

Use a modular connector crimping tool to connect the plug to the wire (Figure 3-9). You can buy these tools from the same store that sold you the phone wire and plugs, including electronics stores and hardware stores.

When you're making cable, treat each length as a separate unit. Inside the sheath are four *leads*. You will use two of them to connect TOPS. You must attach a plug at each end of the cable. The leads must attach to *opposite* sides of the plug at each end. For instance, if the yellow lead is on the left side on one end, it must attach to the right side at the other end (Figure 3-10).

Tip   Rather than trying to remember whether the yellow lead was attached to the left or right side in the previous office, it helps to alternate offices. Keep the yellow lead to the left in one room and to the right in the next room. This will automatically flip the wires for you.

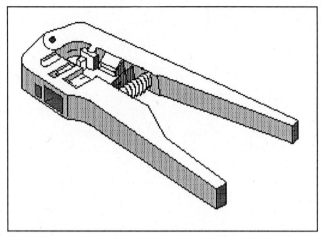

Figure 3-9. If you plan to build your own cable, you will need a crimping tool to attach the modular plugs to the ends of the wire.

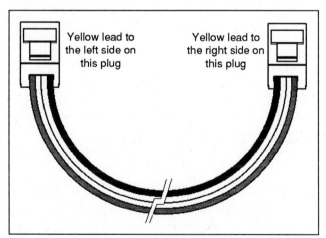

Yellow lead to the left side on this plug

Yellow lead to the right side on this plug

Figure 3-10. If you are building your own cable, the leads must attach to opposite sides of the plugs.

■ Attaching interface boxes

To this point, you've learned about PC boards and cabling. Now you're ready for the third and final step: attaching the interface boxes. Here's the procedure in brief:

1. Turn off every device on the network.

2. Plug the interface boxes into the back of each device.

3. Plug the cables into the interface boxes.

4. Put terminating resistors at the ends of the network.

To review: Every TOPS node must have an interface box. An interface box is about as big as a cigarette package. It connects to the back of the computer or other device. It also has two sockets for the cables that run to other nodes (Figure 3-11).

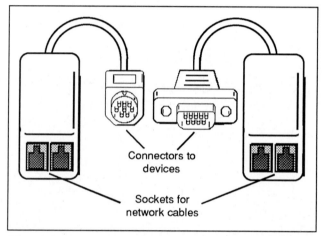

Connectors to devices

Sockets for network cables

Figure 3-11.   Typical interface boxes. The connectors attach to AppleTalk ports at the backs of computers and printers.

Daisy chain and star topologies

Attaching interface boxes varies slightly depending on the topology you've chosen. With daisy chain and star layouts, you fill both cable sockets *except* for the two boxes at the ends of the network. Those at the end have terminating resistors in the empty socket (Figure 3-12). Self-terminating interface boxes (like LocalTalk) don't require a separate resistor.

We're going to assume that you've already (1) planned the layout in advance, so you know which two devices will be at the ends of the network; (2) strung the cable between machines; (3) put network boards in the PCs; (4) acquired an interface box for each device; and (5) turned off all the devices.

Now locate the AppleTalk port on the first device. Different

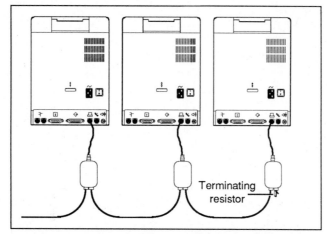

Figure 3-12. The interface boxes in the middle of a daisy chain layout must have cable in both sockets to complete the connection.

devices have the AppleTalk port in different positions. On a PC, the port is at the back of the AppleTalk network board. On a Macintosh, the box attaches to the printer port, shown by the small printer icon. On most laser printers, it attaches to a port at the side or back. Figure 3-13 shows the proper location for several common devices.

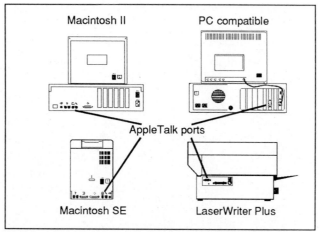

Figure 3-13. Where to attach the interface box.

Go ahead — attach the connector to the port. Now insert cables into both empty sockets (Figure 3-14). Repeat this procedure for every device in the daisy chain.

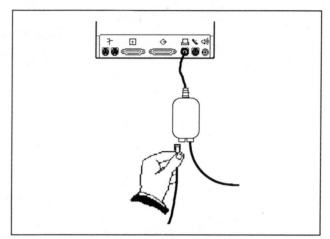

Figure 3-14. Attach the connector to the device and plug in the cables.

Tip Mini-DIN 8 connectors don't have screws to prevent accidental disconnection. You may want to use tape or Velcro to attach the interface box to the back of the computer to prevent it from being dislodged.

Adding terminating resistors

When you have finished, locate the two interface boxes at the ends of the network. They will both have an empty socket. Insert terminating resistors into the empty sockets (Figure 3-15). The resistors should have come with the interface box when you originally purchased it. You can skip this step if you are using self-terminating interface boxes.

Trunk layouts

Trunk layouts differ slightly from daisy chains. As you recall from the previous chapter, a trunk layout has a central cable and wall boxes. The interface boxes plug into the wall boxes via single lengths of cable. As a result, you fill only one of the sockets in each interface box (Figure 3-16).

Do *not* fill the empty sockets with resistors. *Only the two wall boxes at the ends of the trunk should have resistors.* If you prefer, you can terminate the wall box instead of the resistor, as explained in Chapter Two.

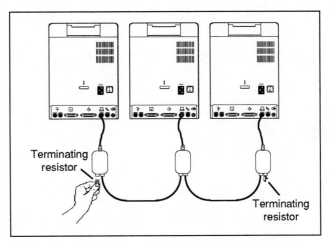

Figure 3-15. Insert terminating resistors into the empty sockets of the two interface boxes at the ends of the network.

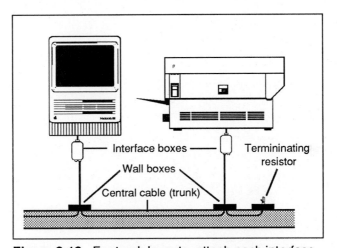

Figure 3-16. For trunk layouts, attach each interface box to the wall box with a single length of cable. Leave the other socket empty.

Continuing on

This chapter has shown how to connect the devices on a TOPS network by (1) installing network boards, (2) stringing the cable, and (3) attaching the interface boxes. Once that's out of the way, you can install TOPS software on the computers. Chapter Four explains how to make this software installation as painless as possible.

Chapter Four

Chapter Four

Installing TOPS Software

This chapter will get you up on TOPS in a hurry. It provides complete instructions for installing TOPS software on Macs and PCs.

There are different roads to the TOPS. This chapter will show you a straightforward method for standard installations. It's only one of the possible paths, but we think it's the simplest and the safest. Along the way, we'll steer you around some pitfalls that have tripped up previous users. At the end of each section, you'll find suggestions on alternate routes — when, why, and how to do things differently.

Installation varies between Macs and PCs, so this chapter has separate sections for each type of computer. Both sections include several useful aids:

- no-frills *Speed Start* instructions for advanced users

- illustrated, step-by-step directions for beginners

- suggestions for custom installations

- tips on testing to make sure you got things right

To get the most out of this chapter, you need to understand basic TOPS terminology (Chapter One). You should have planned the network (Chapter Two) and connected the hardware (Chapter Three). Now you're ready to put the software onto the computers. Once you've finished, you'll have the full power of TOPS at your disposal.

Tips for TOPS

Keep the following tips in mind as you install TOPS:

1. Don't mix different versions of the same operating system.

Make sure all the Macs have the same version of the System, Finder, and LaserWriter driver. Make sure all the PCs have the same version of DOS.

2. Don't mix different versions of TOPS. If you're updating from a previous version, update the entire network.

3. If you haven't already done so, use the planning checklist from Chapter Two to confirm that all the computers meet the minimum hardware and software requirements.

4. In a combined Mac and PC environment, install the Macs first. Then you can use them to test the PC installations.

5. If you changed any board settings when installing network boards in the PCs, keep the new settings handy for quick reference. You'll need to enter them during the PC software installation.

6. Backup the hard disk(s) before installing TOPS on any computer.

7. Recheck all the connections to make sure they're tight before you test the network.

■ Installing TOPS on a Mac

Installing TOPS on a Macintosh is simple and straightforward, thanks to the Installer program that comes on the TOPS distribution diskettes. This section will explain how to:

- install TOPS on a MAC

- customize the installation

- test the installation

Before you start

Our instructions assume you are putting TOPS onto a hard disk. If you are installing on floppies instead, refer to the tips for custom installations.

When you invoke the installation program, the first thing it wants to know is the destination — that is, where you want to install the software. It checks the destination to make sure there's enough room. If so, the Installer copies files to that destination.

Once it has copied the files, the Installer changes the System. To be more specific, it installs a desk accessory called TOPS DA. This desk accessory loads TOPS automatically every time you start the Macintosh and keeps a software kernel resident in memory at all times.

WARNING **If you use a virus protection program such as Vaccine, remove it from your System Folder and restart before installing TOPS. Leaving the program active while TOPS is loading could cause unexpected problems later on. When you are through installing TOPS you can move the virus-fighting program back into the System Folder and restart the computer again.**

Tips for Mac installations

Don't install TOPS using the original disks. Make a working copy of the TOPS disks and store the originals in a safe place. Use the working copies to install the software.

Make sure AppleTalk is active in the Chooser. If not, select Chooser from the Apple menu and click on the Active button next to AppleTalk.

WARNING **Do not install TOPS with either MultiFinder or Switcher active.**

TOPS consists of small files, or *modules*. Table 4-1 lists these files and their functions. If you plan to install everything, it's not crucial to know what they all do. But if you're short on space and have to install a minimum configuration, you'll want to know each file's job. That way, you can choose which ones to keep and which ones to do without. The table shows optional files in normal type and essential files in bold.

Table 4-1. TOPS/Macintosh software modules

Module	Function	Approx. Size
TOPS	Network operating software	68K
SoftTalk	Network driver software	26K
TOPS DA	Desk accessory that starts TOPS and keeps various functions memory resident	68K
TOPS Key	Contains serial number (cannot have two stations with the same serial number on the same network)	2K
TOPS Help	Contains the text for the tutorial help controlled by TOPS DA	36K
TOPS Prep	Contains name and startup information for each station	2K
Start TOPS	Loads TOPS if it was not loaded automatically at startup (will not work with MultiFinder)	3K
Interbase	Translates Macintosh files names to names a PC can understand	24K
PC Icon	Creates an icon on the Mac desktop for PC files	2K
Unix Icon	Creates a Mac icon for Unix files	2K
VMS Icon	Creates a Mac icon for VMS files	2K
Total File Size		235K

Speed Start for Macs

If you're experienced with the Macintosh, follow the quick procedure explained below. If you're unsure about any of the steps, refer to the full instructions that follow.

■ Insert TOPS Disk 1. Double-click on the Installer icon.

■ When the Installer screen appears, click on the Drive button. Select the disk on which you wish to install TOPS.

■ Click on Install.

■ When the Installer has finished copying, click on Quit. Then click on Continue.

Installing TOPS on a Macintosh

This section includes step-by-step, illustrated instructions for putting TOPS on a Macintosh.

■ Start the Macintosh as usual. When you see the Desktop, insert TOPS Disk 1 into a floppy disk drive.

If the Macintosh does not automatically open a window for the floppy disk, double-click on it to do so.

■ Double-click on the Installer icon in the TOPS Disk 1 window (Figure 4-1).

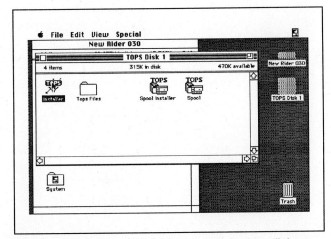

Figure 4-1. Insert TOPS Disk 1 and double-click on the Installer.

The TOPS Installation screen appears (Figure 4-2).

■ Click on the Drive button until you see the System disk on which you want to install TOPS. Normally, this will be a hard disk. Then click on Install.

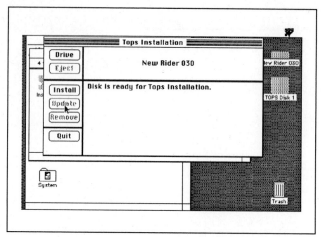

Figure 4-2. Use the Drive button to find the destination for the software, then click on Install.

The Installer first checks to see how much space is available on the destination disk. Then it reads all the files that are absolutely necessary for TOPS to run. You'll see a blur of files as they are installed by TOPS. Provided there's enough room on the destination disk, the Installer will also read the other files. The Installer then writes all the files to the destination.

When the Installer is finished, it tells you that you must restart before the TOPS installation takes effect (Figure 4-3).

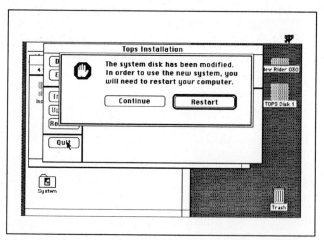

Figure 4-3. When the Installer has finished copying files for TOPS itself, you can quit, or you can continue and install TOPS Spool.

■ If you are *not* going to install the TOPS Spool or the TOPS Translators, click on Restart.

■ If you are going to install the TOPS Spool and the TOPS Translators, click on Continue.

You can install TOPS Spool and TOPS Translators at the same time you install TOPS, or later, at your preference.

Custom installations

The instructions we just gave you covered a standard setup. Some of you may have special needs that require a custom installation. This section explains some of your options:

• installing on a floppy

• installing a minimum configuration

• updating from a previous version

• installing manually (without the Installer)

• creating a version that does not start up automatically

• removing TOPS

Note | If you have a standard configuration, you can skip this portion and go directly to the section on testing.

Installing on a floppy

If you are not planning to install TOPS Spool or TOPS Translators for the time being, simply install TOPS as described above for a hard disk, but substitute a system floppy disk as the destination disk.

If you plan to add TOPS Spool and/or the TOPS Translators, the ideal strategy is to put them all together on a single system floppy disk. That way you can start up TOPS automatically, and you can have all the TOPS functions available without disk swapping. However, this is not possible unless you have an HDFD floppy drive and a high-density 1.44MB system diskette. You will also have to leave off some of the ancillary files.

If you use 800K floppies instead, we recommend that you put TOPS and TOPS Spool on a single system floppy disk. Then put the TOPS Translators on a second, non-system floppy. A system floppy disk is any floppy that contains a bootable System Folder. To create a system disk, format a blank diskette and use the Installer macros that came with your original Macintosh system diskettes.

Note When creating system floppy disks, be sure to copy the same version of the system in use by the other Macs on the network.

Installing a minimum configuration

If space is at a premium, you should be able to find one or more strategies you can use to delete unneeded files in Table 4-2. You may also want to turn back to Table 4-1, which lists all the TOPS/Macintosh files and their approximate sizes. Remember — the ideal situation is to have all of TOPS available. Take these steps only if it is essential to conserve room.

Table 4-2. Space-saving strategies

Condition	Strategy
The System is taking too much space on a floppy	Use Font/DA Mover to remove unneeded fonts and desk accessories
There are no PCs on the network	Delete Interbase and PC Icon
There are no Unix or Vax computers on the network	Delete UNIX Icon and VMS Icon
You can do without tutorial help	Delete TOPS Help
You always start up TOPS automatically	Delete Start TOPS
TOPS has already been installed	Delete Installer

Updating from a previous version

If you are updating from version 2.0, follow the same installation instructions. The TOPS Installer will sense the presence of the previous version and give you the option of updating it.

Tip You can update over the network by copying TOPS Disk 1 to any folder. Then publish the folder. Any Macintosh workstation on the network can then mount the folder and use it to update the workstation.

WARNING Don't try to update by simply copying files. Use the Installer instead, to preserve your serial number.

Installing manually

If you are installing TOPS for the first time, you can do so manually without the Installer by (1) copying all the files to the System Folder of the destination disk and (2) installing the TOPS DA (desk accessory) in the System Folder. You should not, however, try to update manually. Use the Installer to update from a previous version.

To install TOPS manually:

■ Copy all the files from TOPS Disk 1 to the destination disk's System Folder.

■ Run the Font/DA mover by double-clicking on the TOPS DA icon that you just copied to the System Folder.

■ When the Font/DA mover dialog box appears, click on the Desk Accessory button. Then hold down the Option key and click on Open.

■ Click on Drive. Then select TOPS Disk 1.

■ Select TOPS DA. Then click on Copy to install the desk accessory in the System Folder.

■ After the installation is complete, click on Quit.

■ Restart the Macintosh to make your changes take effect.

Note You can also use this method to install TOPS Spool. You can delete TOPS Spool and Spool Installer if you prefer.

Creating a non-startup version

The previous instructions create a version of TOPS that loads automatically every time you start the Macintosh. If you prefer, you can modify the setup so TOPS does not load unless you specifically request it.

Normally, you install the TOPS Desk Accessory in the System

Folder. The Macintosh will automatically load two *init* files upon startup: SoftTalk and TOPS. Like all init files, these two stay resident in memory, even if you load other programs later. Together they require about 100K of RAM.

In most cases, tying up that 100K does not cause any problems. However, if you are extremely short on memory, you may prefer to load TOPS only when you actually need it.

To change the setup so TOPS does *not* load automatically, create another folder called TOPS and drag the SoftTalk and TOPS files from the System Folder to the TOPS folder.

WARNING **You cannot use Switcher or Multi-Finder if you are using the Start TOPS application.**

Follow these instructions to use the Start TOPS application.

- Starting TOPS. Since TOPS will no longer be memory resident, you must now start it manually. To load TOPS, open the System Folder and double-click on Start TOPS.

- Ending TOPS. To end a TOPS work session and free up RAM for other programs, restart your Macintosh.

- Cancelling the startup routine. In some cases, you may want to cancel the startup routine on a one-time basis. In other words, you want TOPS to load automatically most of the time, but not this particular time. To cancel automatic loading, press and hold the Option key as you start up the Macintosh. When the Install TOPS? dialog box appears (Figure 4-4), click on No.

Removing TOPS

To remove TOPS, use the Installer as previously instructed. When the Installer screen appears, click on Remove instead of Install. The Installer will automatically delete the files and remove the desk accessory. When the Installer has finished, click on Quit and restart the Macintosh.

Testing TOPS on the Mac

Now that you have copied the TOPS software to the Macintosh, you should test it to see if the installation was successful.

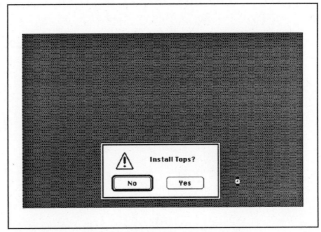

Figure 4-4. The Install TOPS? dialog box.

At the same time, you can check to see that the computer is wired to the network correctly.

Tip Test each computer as soon as you install it. That way you can easily isolate problems. If you wait to test them all at once, you may have trouble pinpointing where the trouble lies.

You must have TOPS installed on at least one other computer. To check the installation you will:

1. Publish a volume on the Macintosh and check that it can be seen by the other computer.

2. Publish a volume on the other computer and check that it can be seen by the Macintosh.

■ Start by selecting TOPS from the Apple menu. If this is the first time you've used TOPS on this machine, a dialog box appears asking for your station name (Figure 4-5).

Note Choose the name with care. It will automatically apply to this Macintosh from now on unless you change it. See Chapter Two, "Planning a TOPS Network," for naming suggestions. (To change a station name on a Macintosh, click and drag on the TOPS DA's Open button. A dialog box will prompt you for the station name change.)

■ Type in the station name. Click on OK.

The TOPS DA dialog box appears (Figure 4-6).

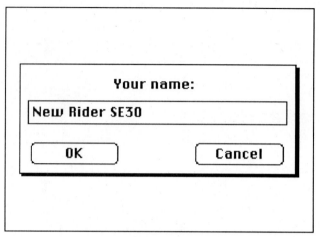

Figure 4-5. You must enter the station name the first time you use TOPS on a Mac.

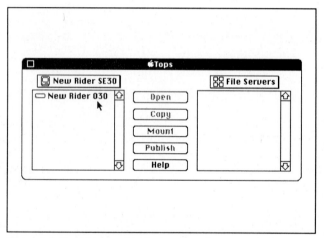

Figure 4-6. After typing in your station name the first time, the TOPS DA dialog box appears.

Now you will publish a volume on the Macintosh. (Beginners: Just follow along. You'll get full instructions on using TOPS in later chapters.) As an example, let's say we're testing a Macintosh with the station name New Rider SE30. We decide to publish the volume New Rider 030. We'll give you step-by-step instructions, with our example names shown in parentheses.

■ Select the disk, folder, or file you want to publish from the local window (in our example, New Rider 030). Click on Publish (Figure 4-7).

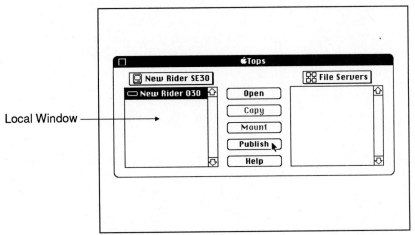

Figure 4-7. Publishing a volume on the Macintosh.

■ Go to a second computer on the network. Load TOPS.

■ Check to see that the Macintosh station name (New Rider 030) appears on the network. On a Macintosh, you check by looking at the right window of the TOPS DA dialog box. On a PC, you check by selecting File Servers from the Client Utilities menu (Figure 4-8).

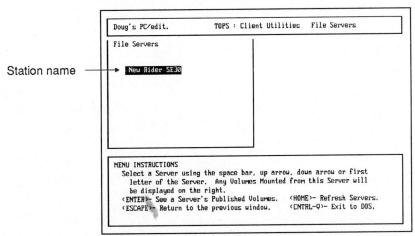

Figure 4-8. Check to see if the Macintosh station is visible on a PC. You could also check with a second Macintosh.

■ While still on the second computer, publish a volume (a disk, folder, subdirectory, or file).

On a PC, you publish by selecting Publish a Volume from the Server Utilities menu, then entering the volume path and characteristics. For the purposes of our example, we have published the volume D:\TO\PIX. (Figure 4-9).

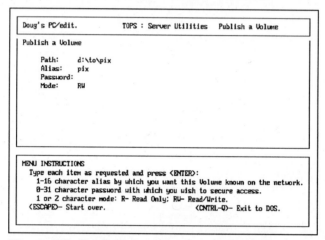

```
┌─────────────────────────────────────────────────────────────┐
│ Doug's PC/edit.        TOPS : Server Utilities   Publish a Volume │
│                                                             │
│ Publish a Volume                                            │
│                                                             │
│     Path:     d:\to\pix                                     │
│     Alias:    pix                                           │
│     Password:                                               │
│     Mode:     RW                                            │
│                                                             │
│                                                             │
│                                                             │
│                                                             │
├─────────────────────────────────────────────────────────────┤
│ MENU INSTRUCTIONS                                           │
│   Type each item as requested and press <ENTER>:            │
│     1-16 character alias by which you want this Volume known on the network. │
│     0-31 character password with which you wish to secure access. │
│     1 or 2 character mode: R- Read Only; RW- Read/Write.    │
│   <ESCAPE>- Start over.                    <CNTRL-Q>- Exit to DOS. │
└─────────────────────────────────────────────────────────────┘
```

Figure 4-9. Publishing a volume on the second computer. You could use a Macintosh instead.

■ Return to the original Macintosh (New Rider SE30). Check for the station name of the second computer in the network window (Figure 4-10).

■ Select the station name (Doug's PC/edit) and click on Open.

The published volume from the second computer should appear in the network window (Figure 4-11).

If the Macintosh fails any part of this test, check the wiring connections and try again. If it still fails, reinstall the software.

■ Installing TOPS on a PC

We might as well admit it right up front: It's harder to set up TOPS on a PC than on a Macintosh. The process is longer, and there are more ways to go wrong. Fortunately, you only need

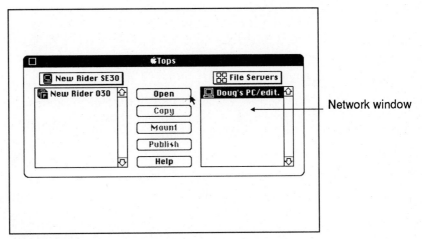

Figure 4-10. Check to make sure you can see the
second computer's name on the original Macintosh.

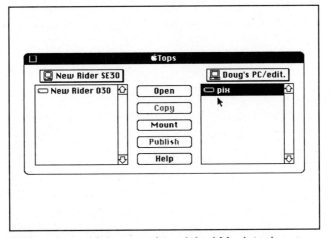

Figure 4-11. Make sure the original Macintosh can
see the volume published on the second computer.

to install the software once. From then on, TOPS is at your
disposal. This section explains how to:

- install TOPS software on a PC (both the network driver and
  the network operating software)

- customize the installation

- test the installation

Beginners: Please don't get impatient or discouraged. Tens of thousands of people have successfully set up TOPS on their own, without help. You have it easier, because you have step-by-step, illustrated instructions and advice.

Incidentally, just because we tried to make life easier for beginners doesn't mean we ignored advanced users. They can skip our detailed instructions in favor of our short, to-the-point *Speed Start* guide.

Because PCs vary widely, you are likely to need a custom installation. We recommend skimming this entire section before you start. Check to see if you can safely use the standard installation or if you need a custom installation instead.

Before you start

TOPS comes with a program called SETUP that handles installation for you. Still, the process will go more smoothly if you understand what's going on. TOPS software comes in *modules*. These modules fall into four general categories:

1. *The network driver* takes care of talking to the rest of the network.

2. *The network operating software* interacts with the computer's operating system, handling the user interface.

3. *Customization files* tailor TOPS to your computer and your preferences.

4. *Utilities* perform special functions.

The great thing about TOPS on the PC is that you can load as few or as many modules as you need. Tables 4-3 and 4-4 summarize most of the files and their functions (we left out a few esoteric files). We realize the lists are fairly long. Nevertheless, we recommend that you spend a few minutes becoming familiar with them. Pay special attention to Table 4-3, which explains the most important modules.

| Note | We are assuming that you are installing a LocalTalk-compatible network with a TOPS FlashCard. If you are installing an Ethernet-compatible network instead, or if you are using a different network board, the names of the network drivers will be different.

Table 4-3. TOPS/DOS software modules

Category	Module	Function	Approx. File Size
Network driver	ALAP.EXE	Low-level LocalTalk driver for the TOPS FlashCard network board	17K
	PSTACK.EXE	Protocol stack driver for the TOPS FlashCard network board	28K
Network operating software	TOPS.EXE	Main program	65K
	TOPSTALK.EXE	AppleTalk protocols for a PC that is both a server and a client	20K
	TOPSTALC.EXE	AppleTalk protocols for a PC that is a client only	14K
	TOPSKRNL.EXE	Network software for a PC that is both a server and a client	74K
	TOPSCLNT.EXE	Network software for a PC that is a client only	46K
	TOPSMENU.EXE	An optional menu interface for TOPS functions	66K
	TOPSPRTR.EXE	Lets you publish a local printer so other computers on the network can share it	16K
	TPRINT.EXE	Network printing services from the DOS prompt when TOPS is loaded	37K
	NODEINIT.EXE	Initializes AppleTalk driver	5K
	NODEKILL.EXE	Kills all AppleTalk activity	5K
	ATALKERR.EXE	Displays AppleTalk error information	6K

Table 4-4. TOPS/DOS Customization files and utilities

Category	Module	Function
Customization	ALAP.CFG	Saves configuration settings for the FlashCard network board
	LOADTOPS.BAT	Batch file that loads TOPS server and client modules into memory
	LOADCLNT.BAT	Batch file that loads TOPS client-only modules into memory
	TOPSTART.BAT	Stores the volumes you wish to publish and mount automatically each time you start TOPS
	TOPSKRNL.DAT	Saves information about the computer such as station name, nonstandard disk drives, and memory usage
	TOPSPRTR.DAT	Saves information about printing parameters, who can access printers you publish, whether to delete spool files, and which port to use for local printers
	TPRINT.DAT	Saves information about which printer you prefer to use if there are several on the network
Utilities	NETPRINT.EXE	Printing to network printers from within an application
	INITPRIN.EXE	TOPS version of the DOS background print queue, used when printing with TPRINT to a local printer
	TOPSPAP.EXE	Printer protocols to access a network printer with non-TOPS software
	SETUP.EXE	Installation program
	TUPDATE.EXE	Installation if you are updating from a previous version
	TCOPY.EXE	Copies files over the network from the DOS prompt
	TDEL.EXE	Deletes hidden files from the DOS prompt, one at a time

Category	Module	Function
Utilities	TDIR.EXE	Gets a directory, including hidden files, from the DOS prompt
	TEXTEND.EXE	Special utilities for the multi-user version of dBase
	TNETBIOS.EXE	Special routines for multi-user network applications such as database managers and electronic mail
	XDEL.EXE	Deletes all hidden files in a subdirectory
	XDIR.EXE	Views contents of TOPS extended directory
	XSYNC.EXE	Keeps TOPS extended directory up-to-date when changes have occurred while TOPS was not running

Tips for PC installations

Don't install TOPS using the original disks. Make a working copy of the TOPS disks and store the originals in a safe place. Use the working copies to install the software.

Backup the hard disks. Then copy the AUTOEXEC.BAT and CONFIG.SYS files to a floppy if they are located in the root directory. We recommend naming the copies AUTOEXEC.PRE and CONFIG.PRE to denote that they are pre-TOPS versions. Do *not* name them AUTOEXEC.BAK and CONFIG.BAK. The TOPS installation routine makes its own backups with those names, and yours will be overwritten. Don't rely on the backup copies created by the TOPS installation program. It is best to be safe in case you need to restore the computer to its previous condition.

In addition, if you are updating from a previous edition of TOPS, make separate copies of the files TOPSKRNL.DAT and TOPSTART.BAT if they exist in your TOPS subdirectory. Call them TOPSKRNL.PRE and TOPSTART.PRE. You may want to refer to these previous files after updating TOPS.

Most people put their TOPS files in the subdirectory C:\TOPS. You can put them somewhere else if you prefer, but keep them together in one place. Exception: If you keep all your batch files in one subdirectory, you will want to locate your TOPS batch files in the same place.

We will use C:\TOPS for our examples. If you've chosen a different location instead, substitute that subdirectory whenever you see C:\TOPS in our samples. For instance, if you plan to put the TOPS files in D:\NETWORK, substitute that name wherever you see C:\TOPS.

We recommend installing the network driver first, then the network operating software (NOS).

Our instructions cover hard disk installation. If you are installing on a floppy instead, turn to the customization section that follows.

Speed Start for PCs

If you're experienced with PCs, follow the quick procedure explained below. If you're unsure about any of the steps, refer to the full instructions that follow.

Installing TOPS involves two steps: 1) installing the network drivers and 2) installing the network operating software. In addition, certain situations may require some customization:

- reconfiguring the network driver
- customizing for nonstandard disks
- updating

To install the network driver software:

■ Copy the driver software from the floppy disks that come with the network board to the TOPS subdirectory.

To install the network operating software:

■ Put TOPS disk 1 into drive A: and load the Setup program.

■ At the opening menu, press *I* to install.

■ Press Enter to accept the default location of C:\TOPS or type in a different destination and press Enter.

■ Press *Y* to confirm your choices. Setup will copy the files. Load disk 2 into A: when the screen prompts you.

■ Type *Y* to add C:\TOPS to the path.

■ Type *Y* to modify the files and buffers in CONFIG.SYS if asked.

If you changed any of the settings on the network card when you put it inside the PC, you must reconfigure the network driver software to match the new settings. The following instructions apply to the FlashCard. If you used a different card instead, refer to its manual.

■ Press *C* from the main Setup menu to configure the network driver.

■ Move the menu highlight to each configuration setting and confirm that it matches your card. If it does, press Enter. If it does not, select the alternate setting that matches your card and press Enter.

If you have disk drives other than A:, B:, and C:, you must tell TOPS about them:

■ Add the new drives to line 13 of the TOPSKRNL.DAT file using an ASCII text editor.

To update from a new version:

■ Press *U* from the main Setup menu. Then follow the same steps as for a first-time installation.

To test TOPS after installation:

■ Load TOPS and publish a volume on the PC. Go to a second computer, load TOPS, and check to see that the published volume is visible on the second computer.

■ Publish a volume on the second computer. Go back to the first PC. Check to see that the volume from the second computer is visible on the first PC.

Installing the network driver software

This section covers the network driver for the TOPS Flash-Card network board. Even if you are installing a different driver for a different board, you may want to review this information for tips and suggestions that could apply to your situation.

Note If you are using a board other than the FlashCard, you must install its network driver in a separate procedure, as outlined in the manual for that board.

Network driver software identifies the board to the network and tells the network the user's name, the board's FlashTalk capabilities, and the network protocol (such as AppleTalk). Without the proper driver, the network won't recognize the board, and the computer cannot communicate with the rest of the network.

Copying the driver software

To install the network drivers, you need the diskette labelled *TOPS FlashCard Driver* that comes with the FlashCard. You must copy all the disk's files to the TOPS subdirectory.

You will begin by creating the TOPS subdirectory:

■ With your PC turned on, go to the root directory on the C: drive. At the C:\ prompt, type:

```
md \TOPS <Enter>
```

Note Make sure you are at the root directory. If you are not sure of your current subdirectory, type `prompt $p$g <Enter>` at the DOS prompt. This will display your subdirectory name.

■ To change the current directory to the TOPS directory, type:

```
cd \TOPS <Enter>
```

■ Insert the FlashCard diskette in floppy drive A:.

■ To copy the FlashCard files, type:

```
copy A:*.* <Enter>
```

This copies every file on the FlashCard diskette to the hard drive. Driver installation is complete.

Note You have just installed driver software for the standard, default settings. If you changed any of the settings when you put the board in the computer, you must *reconfigure* the driver to match, as explained later in this chapter.

Installing the network operating software

Now that the network driver is on the hard disk, you're ready to install the network operating software (NOS).

TOPS provides a program called *Setup* that makes installation a breeze. You can also use Setup to customize your installation (as described in the next section). All you need are your working copies of the TOPS software diskettes. The procedure will not interfere with the existing TOPS directory and network driver files.

While running Setup, you can press the Esc key to abort at any time. Your system will be left exactly as it was before you started Setup. You can restart Setup at any time to install, update, or configure your TOPS network software.

We assume that you've already created a C:\TOPS subdirectory and copied the network driver, as described previously. (If you haven't created a TOPS subdirectory yet, don't worry — Setup will do it for you.) With the computer still on:

■ Insert TOPS disk 1 DOS Version in drive A:.

■ Change your active drive to A: by typing:

```
A: <Enter>
```

■ Start the Setup program by typing:

```
setup <Enter>
```

The opening menu appears (Figure 4-12). As you can see, you have the option to install, update, or configure.

■ To install the TOPS network operating software, press *I*.

A warning message appears, explaining that Setup will modify your AUTOEXEC.BAT and CONFIG.SYS files (Figure 4-13). Existing files with these names (if any) will be renamed with a .BAK extension. Let's take a brief time-out to discuss these two important files.

As the name implies, DOS uses the CONFIG.SYS file to *configure* the *system*. Each time the computer starts up, it reads CONFIG.SYS to learn, for instance, how many memory buffers are allowed, how many open files are allowed, and whether or not any nonstandard devices are attached to the

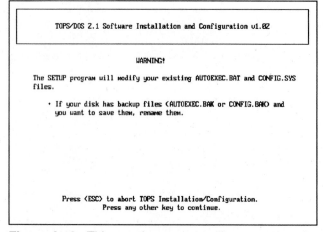

```
┌─────────────────────────────────────────────────────────┐
│ ┌─────────────────────────────────────────────────────┐ │
│ │  TOPS/DOS 2.1 Software Installation and Configuration v1.02 │ │
│ └─────────────────────────────────────────────────────┘ │
│                                                         │
│       Welcome to TOPS/DOS 2.1 installation and configuration! │
│                                                         │
│    Press:   ┌───┐                                       │
│             │ I │    to install TOPS/DOS 2.1            │
│             └───┘                                       │
│             ┌───┐                                       │
│             │ U │    to update  TOPS/DOS 2.0  to  TOPS/DOS 2.1 │
│             └───┘                                       │
│             ┌───┐                                       │
│             │ C │    to configure driver for network card │
│             └───┘                                       │
│                                                         │
│        Press <ESC> to abort TOPS Installation/Configuration │
└─────────────────────────────────────────────────────────┘
```

Figure 4-12. The opening Setup menu.

```
┌─────────────────────────────────────────────────────────┐
│ ┌─────────────────────────────────────────────────────┐ │
│ │  TOPS/DOS 2.1 Software Installation and Configuration v1.02 │ │
│ └─────────────────────────────────────────────────────┘ │
│                                                         │
│                       WARNING!                          │
│   The SETUP program will modify your existing AUTOEXEC.BAT and CONFIG.SYS │
│   files.                                                 │
│         • If your disk has backup files (AUTOEXEC.BAK or CONFIG.BAK) and │
│           you want to save them, rename them.           │
│                                                         │
│                                                         │
│         Press <ESC> to abort TOPS Installation/Configuration. │
│             Press any other key to continue.            │
└─────────────────────────────────────────────────────────┘
```

Figure 4-13. This warning appears after you press *I* to install TOPS.

system. (If DOS doesn't find a CONFIG.SYS, it uses the standard defaults.)

During TOPS installation, Setup checks CONFIG.SYS to make sure there are enough files and memory buffers for TOPS. If it finds less than 20 files or 20 buffers, it modifies CONFIG.SYS and increases them. If it finds no CONFIG.SYS at all, it creates one with these statements:

FILES=20

BUFFERS=20

Now let's take a moment to look at AUTOEXEC.BAT, which is a special kind of batch file — one that is *automatically ex-ecuted* each time you start up the computer. When you turn on the machine, it looks first at CONFIG.SYS. Then it looks for AUTOEXEC.BAT in the startup disk's root directory. If it finds the file, DOS automatically executes all the commands inside.

During the installation routine, Setup gives you the oppor-tunity to add a command to AUTOEXEC.BAT (or to create one if you don't have one already). This command creates a *path* to the TOPS subdirectory. By adding C:\TOPS to the path, you can load TOPS from any subdirectory.

| Note | If you have not yet backed up CONFIG.SYS and AUTOEXEC.BAT, exit the Setup program by pressing the Esc key and do so now. Do not use the .BAK extension, since it conflicts with the backups made by Setup. Then restart Setup and return to this point.

Back to our installation. At this point, you've seen the warning message about AUTOEXEC.BAT and CONFIG.SYS.

■ Press any key to proceed.

The Software Transfer display appears (Figure 4-14). You use this screen to choose the startup drive and a location for the TOPS files.

The default path specifies C:\TOPS, the typical location for TOPS files. If you accept this default recommendation, Setup will install the files in C:\TOPS.

■ Press Enter to accept C:\TOPS as the destination.

| Note | To enter a new directory name, backspace to erase the default name and enter the name of your choice. Don't worry about whether or not that name already exists. If Setup doesn't find the directory, it will create it for you.

■ To accept C: as the startup drive, press Enter.

A message appears asking you to confirm your choices.

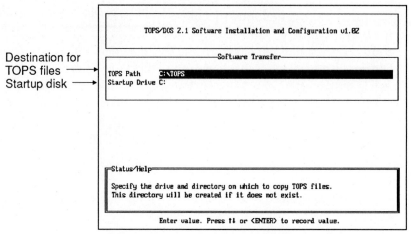

Destination for
TOPS files ⟶
Startup disk ⟶

Figure 4-14. The Software Transfer screen.

■ Type *Y* to confirm you want the startup drive and destination shown on the screen.

| Note | Type *N* to change either one before continuing.

Setup now copies all files from the floppy disks to the hard disk. After finishing with disk 1, Setup prompts you for disk 2 (Figure 4-15).

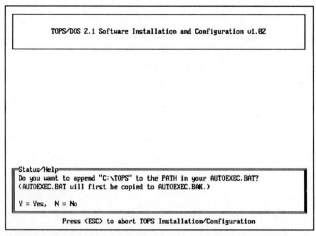

Figure 4-15. This screens lets you add the TOPS subdirectory to the path in your AUTOEXEC.BAT file.

■ Remove disk 1 from drive A: and insert disk 2. Then press any key to continue.

Setup copies the files from disk 2 to the TOPS subdirectory. When finished, it lets you decide whether or not to add C:\TOPS to the AUTOEXEC.BAT path (Figure 4-16).

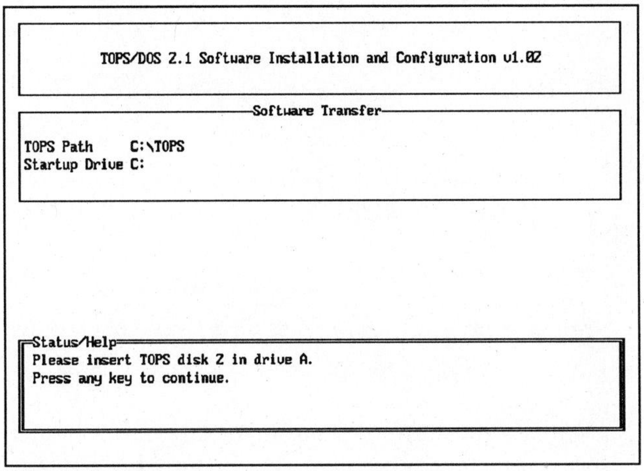

```
┌─────────────────────────────────────────────────────────────┐
│   ┌───────────────────────────────────────────────────────┐ │
│   │   TOPS/DOS 2.1 Software Installation and Configuration v1.02  │ │
│   └───────────────────────────────────────────────────────┘ │
│   ┌────────────────────────Software Transfer────────────────┐ │
│   │ TOPS Path      C:\TOPS                                   │ │
│   │ Startup Drive C:                                         │ │
│   │                                                         │ │
│   │                                                         │ │
│   │                                                         │ │
│   │ ┌─Status/Help─┐                                         │ │
│   │ │ Please insert TOPS disk 2 in drive A.                 │ │
│   │ │ Press any key to continue.                            │ │
│   └─┴─────────────────────────────────────────────────────┘ │
└─────────────────────────────────────────────────────────────┘
```

Figure 4-16. Setup tells you when to insert the next disk for copying.

■ Type *Y* to add C:\TOPS to the default PATH setting in your AUTOEXEC.BAT file. (An AUTOEXEC.BAT file is created if you did not have one before.)

| Note | If you do *not* add the TOPS directory to PATH, you can only load and run TOPS from the TOPS directory.

You can modify AUTOEXEC.BAT manually if you prefer. This screen simply asks Setup to do it for you.

At this point, you may see another screen (Figure 4-17).

You will see this screen only if the files and buffer settings in your system configuration file (CONFIG.SYS) are not high enough for TOPS to operate properly (minimum of 20 files and 20 buffers). If you do not see the screen, it means that your settings are already high enough.

■ If you see the screen, type *Y* to modify CONFIG.SYS (or create one if you did not have one before).

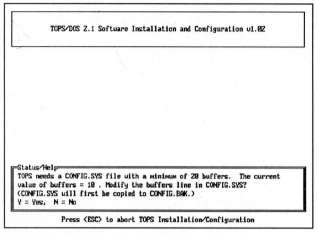

Figure 4-17. This screens lets you decide whether or not to have Setup modify your CONFIG.SYS file.

| **Note** | You can manually modify CONFIG.SYS if you prefer. However, don't forget to do so before running TOPS. Otherwise, it may not run properly.

You're almost finished with Setup. A final message appears (Figure 4-18).

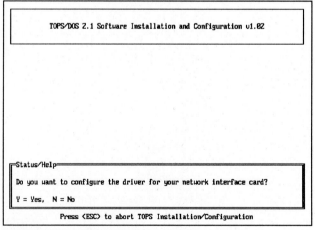

Figure 4-18. This screen asks if you want to reconfigure the network driver.

This option applies only to the TOPS FlashCard driver. You cannot use it if you have a different brand. Instead, you must use the configuration routines that come with that board.

■ If you did *not* change any of the Flashcard settings when you installed it inside the computer, press *N*. You are finished with Setup.

■ If you *did* change any of the board settings, press *Y*.

Pressing *Y* takes you directly to the configuration session, covered separately below in the section titled "Custom installations."

> **Note** After you run the Setup program and install the TOPS network software, you *must* restart your computer before loading TOPS. The changes don't take effect until you do.

■ If you have finished the installation, press Ctrl-Alt-Del to restart your computer.

■ If you plan to configure the network driver, do not restart yet. Continue on to the next section.

Custom installations

The instructions in the preceding section took you through a standard installation. Lucky people who fall into that category can skip straight to the section called *Testing TOPS on the PC*. But if you have anything different from the norm, you'll need to read through the following advice. It explains how to customize your installation in several ways:

• reconfiguring the network driver

• customizing for nonstandard disks

• installing on a floppy

• updating from a previous version

• installing for automatic startup

Reconfiguring the network driver

Read this section if you changed any of the settings for the network board when you installed it in the PC. It explains how to reconfigure the driver software to recognize those changes. These instructions apply to the TOPS FlashCard. If you have another brand instead, you must go through similar procedures using the software supplied by the board manufacturer.

Make sure you have your new board settings written down. You will need to refer to them during this procedure. See Chapter Three, "Connecting the Hardware," for information on when, why, and how to change board settings.

You can get to the configuration routine in two ways. One is to choose *C* from the opening Setup menu (Figure 4-19).

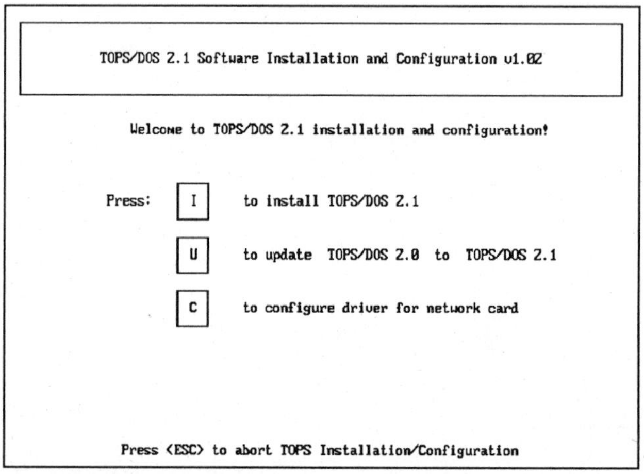

```
┌─────────────────────────────────────────────────────────────┐
│ ┌─────────────────────────────────────────────────────────┐ │
│ │   TOPS/DOS 2.1 Software Installation and Configuration v1.02 │ │
│ └─────────────────────────────────────────────────────────┘ │
│                                                               │
│        Welcome to TOPS/DOS 2.1 installation and configuration! │
│                                                               │
│                                                               │
│     Press:    ┌───┐                                          │
│               │ I │    to install TOPS/DOS 2.1               │
│               └───┘                                          │
│               ┌───┐                                          │
│               │ U │    to update  TOPS/DOS 2.0 to  TOPS/DOS 2.1 │
│               └───┘                                          │
│               ┌───┐                                          │
│               │ C │    to configure driver for network card  │
│               └───┘                                          │
│                                                               │
│                                                               │
│          Press <ESC> to abort TOPS Installation/Configuration │
└─────────────────────────────────────────────────────────────┘
```

Figure 4-19. Choose *C* from the opening Setup menu to reconfigure the driver software.

You can also reach this point directly from the installation procedures described above. At the end, the program asks if you wish to configure the driver software. Press *Y* to proceed directly to the card selection screen (Figure 4-20).

Since these instructions deal with the FlashCard, you can accept the default by pressing Enter:

■ Press Enter to confirm that you want to modify the Flash-Card driver.

The FlashCard Configuration menu appears (Figure 4-21).

The first driver setting — the Board IRQ — is highlighted. Next to the line you see the current setting. The small box to the right shows the two possible choices. For the IRQ, you can use either *2* or *3*.

■ If the highlighted IRQ value *does* match your board setting, press Enter to record it.

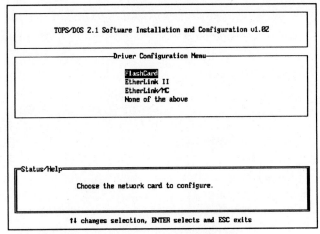

Figure 4-20. The card selection screen.

Current setting

Setting choices

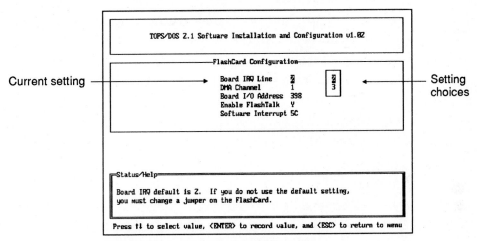

Figure 4-21. The Configuration menu.

■ If the highlighted IRQ value of *2* does *not* match the setting on your board, use the down arrow key to select the other IRQ value of *3*. Then press Enter to record the new setting.

When you record the setting, the highlight moves to the next setting, the DMA Channel. As before, the current setting shows to the left, and the possible alternates to the right.

■ If the highlighted DMA value *does* match your board setting, press Enter to record it.

■ If the highlighted DMA values does *not* match your

setting, use the arrow keys to select the alternate value
that matches. Then press Enter to record this new setting.

After recording the DMA value, the highlight moves to the
Board I/O Address.

WARNING **If you have a 286 or 386 class machine, you will
get better FlashTalk performance if you set the DMA value to
3 and adjust the FlashCard jumpers accordingly.**

Note If you choose a value of *none*, you will disable direct
memory addressing. Although this will eliminate any possible
DMA conflicts with other boards, it will also make it impossible for
the board to communicate at higher FlashTalk rates. It will still,
however, be able to communicate at standard AppleTalk rates.

- If the highlighted value *does* match your board setting,
  press Enter to record it.

- If the highlighted value does *not* match your setting, use
  the arrow keys to select the address you want. Press
  Enter.

The final two settings do not relate to hardware changes on
the board. Most users can simply press Enter to accept the
default values. The first is Enable FlashTalk. FlashTalk is a
way of communicating faster over an AppleTalk network.

- Press Enter to accept the default of *Y* to enable FlashTalk.

The highlight moves to the final setting: Software Interrupt.

- Press Enter to accept the default interrupt.

Now that you have recorded all the settings, the program asks
you whether to save them or not (Figure 4-22).

- Press *Y* if the settings are correct.

- Press *N* if you need to redo any of the settings.

When you press *Y*, the Setup program copies the new settings
to the batch files that load TOPS (LOADTOPS.BAT and
LOADCLNT.BAT). Batch files are covered later in the book.

This completes the FlashCard driver configuration:

- The Setup program will automatically exit to DOS.

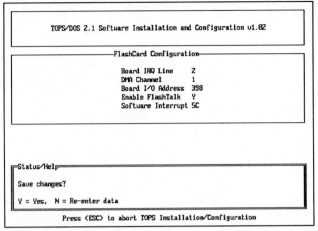

Figure 4-22. This message gives you the chance to redo the settings if you made a mistake.

Note You must restart your computer before your changes will take effect.

Customizing for nonstandard disks

TOPS assumes that you are using only drives A:, B:, and C:. If you are using other drives, you must tell TOPS by modifying the TOPS Data File (TOPSKRNL.DAT). Do this if you have more than one hard disk, a single hard disk with more than one partition, a RAM disk, a Bernoulli backup, and so on.

In brief, you must modify the drive map in line #13 of TOPSKRNL.DAT to reflect the additional drives. Use any ASCII text editor.

Installing on a floppy

Most of the procedures for installing on a hard disk apply to a floppy installation as well. You will, however, need to make the changes and consider the points listed below.

First, you must create a blank system disk to hold TOPS. A system disk contains the operating system kernel, IO.SYS, MSDOS.SYS, and COMMAND.COM, so the computer can be started from that disk. Be sure to use the same version of DOS as the other PCs on the network. To create a system disk, format a diskette with the /s command. For instance, format b:/s would format a diskette in drive B: and copy the system files (hidden files, IO.SYS and MSDOS.SYS, and visible file COMMAND.COM) to that floppy.

You'll also need to create a TOPS subdirectory on the blank system floppy to store the network driver and the network operating software. To do this, move to the B: drive and type md \TOPS <Enter>. To move to the new directory from the B:\ prompt, type cd \TOPS <Enter>.

Perform the installation with the FlashCard and TOPS diskettes in drive A: and the blank system disk in drive B:.

First you should copy the network driver files from the TOPS FlashCard Driver diskette to the TOPS directory on B:.

That takes care of the network driver. Next you should use the Setup program on TOPS disk 1 to install the network operating software. Put disk 1 into drive A: and type Setup <Enter> to start.

When the Software Transfer display appears, change the defaults (which are set up for a hard drive system). Enter B:\TOPS for the destination and A: as the startup drive.

Follow the previous instructions for hard disk installation to complete the rest of the floppy disk installation. Remember to restart your computer before loading TOPS.

Updating from a previous version

If you already have an older version of TOPS on your PC, you can use the Setup program to update it. The procedure is similar to a hard disk installation.

If you've customized TOPS in any way, you'll want to save those parameters before updating. You should either save them under a new name, or jot down the information on paper so you can reenter it after the update.

To save your parameters, make copies of the following four files *under different file names*:

- CONFIG.SYS, which may contain configuration settings for the ATALK.SYS device driver. Although version 2.1 does not use ATALK.SYS, you can reuse the same parameters to customize its replacement, ATALK.EXE.

- AUTOEXEC.BAT, which may contain instructions to start

up TOPS automatically and to include the TOPS subdirectory in the path.

- TOPSKRNL.DAT, which may contain configuration settings for the TOPS software.

- TOPSTART.BAT, which may contain instructions to publish and/or mount volumes automatically.

To update, follow the instructions for a hard disk installation to load Setup and move to the opening menu. Then choose *U* (for update) instead of *I* (for install). Then follow the instructions given above for a standard installation.

| Note | Following the update procedure preserves your TOPS serial number. To avoid losing this number and creating an unusable version of TOPS, do not attempt to install the software as if it were new. Update it instead.

Testing TOPS on the PC

Once you have installed the TOPS network software and the FlashCard driver software, you should test them both to see if TOPS has been installed correctly and to check your hardware connections. Beginners should follow along, even if they are unfamiliar with some of the commands. They will get full instructions on operating TOPS in later chapters.

To run a test, you need to have TOPS installed on at least one other computer. To check the installation you will:

1. Publish a volume on the PC and check that it can be seen by the second computer.

2. Publish a volume on the second computer and check that it can be seen by the PC.

Tip Test each computer in turn as soon as you install it. That way you can easily isolate problems. If you test them all at once, you may have trouble pinpointing problems.

■ Turn on the PC. Move to the disk containing TOPS. At the DOS prompt, move to the TOPS directory by typing:

```
cd \tops <Enter>
```

■ Load TOPS by typing:

```
topsmenu <Enter>
```

A message appears asking for the station name (Figure 4-23).

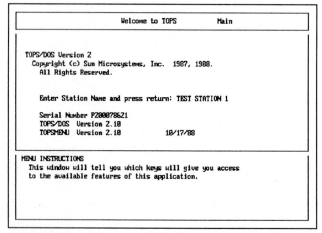

```
                        Welcome to TOPS          Main


 TOPS/DOS Version 2
    Copyright (c) Sun Microsystems, Inc.  1987, 1988.
    All Rights Reserved.


    Enter Station Name and press return: TEST STATION 1

    Serial Number P200078621
    TOPS/DOS  Version 2.10
    TOPSMENU  Version 2.10              10/17/88

 MENU INSTRUCTIONS
    This window will tell you which keys will give you access
    to the available features of this application.
```

Figure 4-23. Use this screen to enter the station name.

■ To enter the name, type:

```
TEST STATION 1 <Enter>
```

The Main menu appears (Figure 4-24). The highlight appears on the selection Client Utilities.

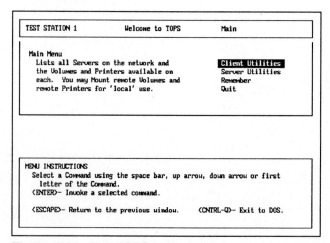

```
 TEST STATION 1          Welcome to TOPS          Main

 Main Menu
    Lists all Servers on the network and      Client Utilities
    the Volumes and Printers available on     Server Utilities
    each.  You may Mount remote Volumes and   Remember
    remote Printers for 'local' use.          Quit




 MENU INSTRUCTIONS
    Select a Command using the space bar, up arrow, down arrow or first
      letter of the Command.
    <ENTER>- Invoke a selected command.

    <ESCAPE>- Return to the previous window.     <CNTRL-Q>- Exit to DOS.
```

Figure 4-24. The TOPS Main menu.

■ Use the down arrow key to move the highlight to Server Utilities. Press Enter.

The Server Utilities menu appears (Figure 4-25), with the highlight on the selection Publish a Volume. Press Enter.

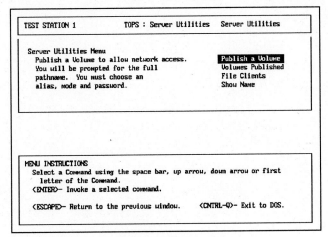

Figure 4-25. The Server Utilities menu.

The Publish a Volume menu appears.

■ Type C:\TOPS as the volume to be published (Figure 4-26). Press Enter.

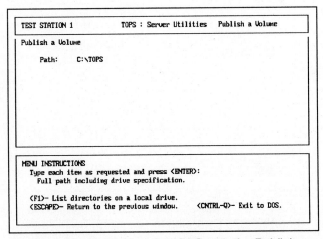

Figure 4-26. Publishing C:\TOPS with the Publish a Volume menu.

■ Press Enter three times to step through the volume alias, password, and access mode options.

TOPS displays a message, telling you that it is working. Once the volume has been successfully published, you will see a blank Publish a Volume menu.

■ Press [ESC] twice to return to the Main menu.

Now you will go to another TOPS station to make sure it can see the volume you just published. We will assume you are using another PC, but you could use a Macintosh.

■ Go to the second PC. Repeat the procedures above to load TOPS and get to the Main menu. Use TEST STATION 2 as the station name.

■ From TEST STATION 2's Main menu, use the down arrow key to highlight Client Utilities. Press Enter.

The Client Utilities menu appears.

■ Use the down arrow key to highlight File Servers. Press Enter.

You should see the name TEST STATION 1 at the top of the window in the File Servers section (Figure 4-27).

Station name ———

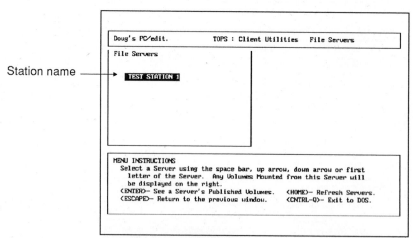

Figure 4-27. Checking to see if TEST STATION 1 is visible to the network.

■ While still on the second computer, publish a volume (a disk, folder, subdirectory, or file).

As you recall, to publish a volume on a PC you select Server Utilities, select Publish a Volume, and then type in the name of the disk, folder, file, or subdirectory you want to publish.

■ Return to the original PC (TEST STATION 1). Check for the second computer by selecting Client Utilities and File Servers (Figure 4-28).

Station name

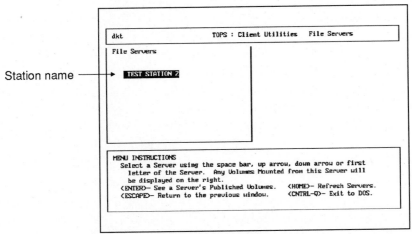

Figure 4-28. Check to make sure you can see the second computer's name on the original PC.

■ Now make sure you can see the published volume from the second computer by highlighting the File Server's name and pressing return (Figure 4-29).

If the PC fails any part of this test, check the wiring connections and try again. If it still fails, reinstall the software.

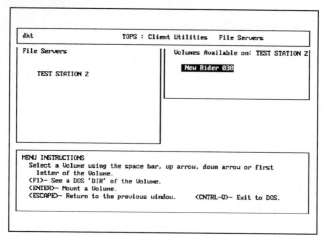

Figure 4-29. Make sure the original PC can see the volume published on the second computer.

Continuing on

This chapter took you step-by-step through a standard TOPS installation for both a Macintosh and a PC. It also covered some ways to customize your installation. Despite our efforts to cover custom installations, we didn't have the space to cover all the options in one chapter. TOPS is extremely flexible. By design, this chapter focused on a straightforward, plain-vanilla installation.

Those of you who want to experiment with advanced configurations will find advice in later chapters. Don't worry, you won't need to redo your installation. We will show you how to take a basic TOPS setup and fine-tune it to your needs and preferences.

But you don't need an advanced setup to start putting the power of TOPS to work. Once you've got a basic TOPS installation up and running, you're ready to explore its many capabilities. You'll get started in the next chapter.

Part Two

Learning TOPS

TOPS is easy to learn and use. The next five chapters provide all the essentials you'll need to operate a TOPS network.

Chapter Five

Loading and Starting TOPS

Learning the correct ways to load and start TOPS will make life with TOPS easier and more efficient. For example, you can have TOPS automatically publish disks at startup time, so they're ready for use. Or, if you're a PC user, you can load only the TOPS modules you need, thereby conserving memory for other applications.

This chapter will show you all the options at your disposal. It is divided into three sections:

- fundamentals
- loading TOPS on a Mac
- loading TOPS on a PC

Mac and PC Speed Start sections are included for experienced users, plus step-by-step instructions for novices. This chapter assumes that you've already hooked up the network and installed the software, as described previously.

Fundamentals

In a moment, we'll show you how to start TOPS. But first, you need to understand how TOPS works. You also need a clear grasp of five key terms:

- servers
- clients
- publishing
- mounting
- volumes

How the software works

When you load TOPS software, it becomes *memory resident*. It remains in the computer's memory even after you load other programs (Figure 5-1). In the Mac world, this capability is called a *desk accessory* (DA). PC users sometimes refer to it as *terminate-and-stay-resident* (TSR) software.

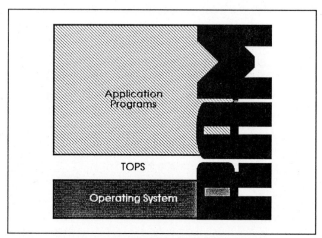

Figure 5-1. Because TOPS software is memory resident, it can coexist with other programs.

The memory-resident approach has advantages. It lets you access TOPS functions while running other software. However, TOPS does use up some of the available memory. Macintosh users have an easy solution — buy more memory. Many PCs, however, are limited to only 640K of memory. Since TOPS requires more than 200K for itself in certain configurations, there may not be enough left for memory-hungry applications like Ventura Publisher or Paradox.

Because of these limitations, it's important to conserve memory on PCs. One way to conserve is to load only the portions of TOPS you really need. We'll show you how in the PC section of this chapter.

Servers and clients

Beginners, this would be a good time to review the definitions in Chapter One, "Getting Started with TOPS." In particular, you need to understand the terms *server* and *client*. PC users must be especially clear on the distinctions. A PC can join the network either as a server or as a client. You can't choose between them until you understand the differences. (Mac users always join as both.)

A server makes files available to the network. A client uses them. To use the analogy from Chapter One, a server makes all or part of its information warehouse (its disk) available to the network. A client can access the warehouse to take or leave information.

The terms can be confusing because they overlap. A server is automatically a client. The reverse is not true. A client is not necessarily a server. To make the distinctions more obvious, we will use the terms *server/client* and *client only* in this chapter.

Publishing and mounting

The two terms you will encounter most often when using TOPS are *publishing* and *mounting*. These two procedures are the heart and soul of TOPS. You use them to grant or gain access to just about anything on the network.

In brief: Servers publish. Clients mount. To extend the previous analogy, when a server publishes a disk, it is like unlocking the warehouse and telling the other stations they can use it if they want. Once you publish, all the other stations can see the disk on their TOPS screens. And all the other stations can use it if they want (unless you restrict access with a password).

When a client mounts a disk, it is like opening the warehouse door. Once the door is open, the client can take information in or out. You may find it easier to understand mounting if you think of it as a way of attaching a new disk to your computer. Once you mount a disk, your computer treats it like any other (Figure 5-2). For instance, the new disk gets its own icon on the Mac desktop. In the PC environment, the new disk becomes drive D:, E:, or F: (depending on how many drives you have already).

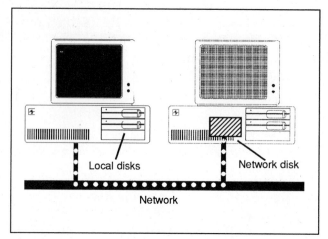

Figure 5-2. Mounting a disk is like attaching it to
your computer. From that point on, you can access it
as you would any other disk.

The Mac version of TOPS always loads as a *server/client*. PC
users, however, can choose different modes. If they have files
that others on the network need, they must publish the directories containing these files. Only a server can publish. Therefore, they must load TOPS as a *server/client*. If all they want
to do is mount, PC users can load TOPS as a *client only*.

Volumes

A *volume* is any disk or portion of a disk. On a PC it can be an
entire disk, a disk partition, a directory, or a subdirectory. On
a Mac it can be either a disk or a folder. The word *volume* is
just a convenient shorthand description. Instead of saying
"publish the disk or any portion thereof," we say "publish the
volume."

Here's a key concept: When you publish a volume, the other
computers on the network see it as if it were a disk. That holds
true even if you are only publishing a small portion of your
physical disk. In the eyes of the other computers, that small
portion is treated like a separate disk (albeit a small one). On
a PC, the volume gets its own disk drive letter. On a Mac, it
gets its own desktop icon.

Key concept #2: When you publish a PC directory, you automatically publish all its subdirectories (Figure 5-3). To put the

same phrase into Mac terminology, when you publish a folder, you automatically publish all the folders inside (Figure 5-4).

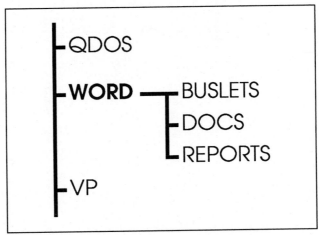

Figure 5-3. This tree depicts a typical PC subdirectory structure. Notice that if you publish the directory WORD, you automatically publish the subdirectories BUSLETS, DOCS, and REPORTS.

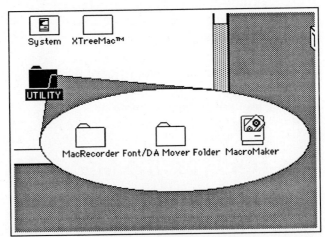

Figure 5-4. Here is a typical Mac desktop. Notice that if you publish the folder UTILITY, you automatically publish the folders MacRecorder, Font/DA Mover Folder, and MacroMaker inside.

Tip To save time, PC users should put all the subdirectories they want to publish under one directory. Then they can publish everything in a single step (Figure 5-5). Mac users should put all the folders into one folder, and then publish that one folder.

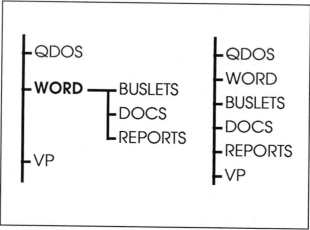

Figure 5-5. The tree on the right shows an inefficient directory structure. You would have to publish the subdirectories WORD, BUSLETS, DOCS, and REPORTS in separate steps. The tree on the left shows a better way. You can publish everything you want by publishing the directory WORD.

Note | Be careful where you store confidential information. If you want to keep it off the network, don't put it in a parent directory or folder that might be published.

■ Loading TOPS on the Mac

This section explains how to load and start TOPS on a Macintosh, and how to unload it if necessary. It also explains how to customize the startup routine — for instance, how to ask TOPS to publish a volume automatically whenever it loads.

Speed Start for Macs

Experienced users can follow the quick instructions below. If you are unsure about any of the steps, use the full explanations that follow.

To start TOPS the first time:

■ Turn on your computer.

■ Type in the station name of the computer when requested by the dialog box.

From this point on, TOPS will remember your station name and enter it automatically at startup time. TOPS is automatically loaded each time you turn on the computer.

To change a station name:

■ Go to the main TOPS dialog box.

■ Unpublish all volumes and folders.

■ Click and hold on the Open button and drag down to the Open... option.

■ When the dialog box appears, type in the new name and click on OK.

To unload TOPS temporarily:

■ Hold down the Command key and the Option key while turning on the computer.

To unload TOPS permanently:

■ Remove the TOPS applications from the System Folder.

To auto-publish (or auto-mount):

■ Publish (or mount) the volume as normally, except that you press and hold on the Publish button.

■ Drag down to the Publish... option on the secondary menu.

■ When the dialog box appears, click on the Remember box and then click on OK.

To remove a volume from the auto-publish (or auto-mount) list:

■ Unpublish (or unmount) the volume as usual, except that you press and hold on the Unpublish button.

■ Drag down to the Unmount... option on the secondary menu.

■ When the dialog box appears, click on the Remember box to remove the check mark and then click on OK.

Loading TOPS

Loading TOPS on the Mac is easy and automatic. When you installed the TOPS software on the Mac, you also installed an *init*. An init is a software program that loads itself whenever you start the computer (whenever you *initi*alize the computer). This particular init loads TOPS into memory. Thus, just by turning on the Mac, you have automatically loaded TOPS. About the only change you will notice is that your computer takes longer to start up. That's because it takes a few moments to load the TOPS software into memory.

Identifying yourself to the network

If this is the first time you have signed on to the network, a dialog box shows up and prompts you for the name of your station (Figure 5-6). From then on, the TOPS software will remember this name, so you won't have to type it again.

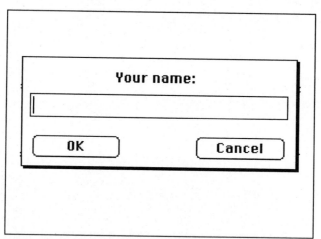

Figure 5-6. If you have never signed onto the network, TOPS asks you to identify the name of your station.

If the name already exists on the network, a second dialog box alerts you to the conflict. Click the Continue button to return to the previous dialog box to try a different name.

Opening the TOPS dialog box

We already mentioned that TOPS is memory resident. In Mac terminology, it is a desk accessory (DA). That means it is waiting for you no matter what other programs are active. Since TOPS is installed as a DA, you can access its power as easily as calling up the calculator.

To bring the TOPS dialog box to the screen:

■ Select the TOPS desk accessory from the Apple menu (Figure 5-7).

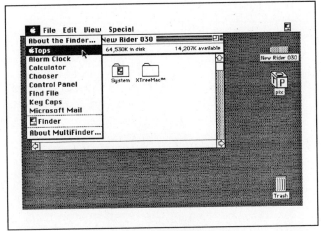

Figure 5-7. Pull down the Apple menu in the upper left-hand corner to select the TOPS DA.

| Note | There is no need to exit your current application. You can leave it open and on the screen while you work with TOPS. When you exit TOPS, you will return to your original application.

When you select the DA, the TOPS dialog box appears (Figure 5-8). The dialog box is divided into 3 sections.

1. the Local Window (left)

2. the Network Window (right)

3. the Command Buttons (center)

For the moment, we are only concerned with how to load and start TOPS. In later chapters, you will work extensively with this main dialog box and its elements.

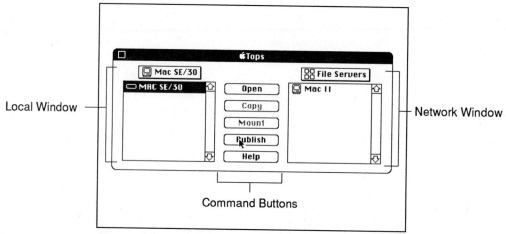

Local Window

Network Window

Command Buttons

Figure 5-8. The main TOPS dialog box.

Changing a station name

After you name your station the first time, TOPS uses that name from then on. If you need to change the name, you can do so easily:

■ Go to the main TOPS dialog box.

■ Highlight the title bar above the local window (on the left-hand side of the TOPS window.)

■ Click and hold on the Open button until a secondary pull-down menu appears. Drag down to the Open... option on the secondary menu.

The dialog box in Figure 5-9 appears.

■ Type in your new station name.

> Note You must unpublish all volumes and folders before you can change the station name.

Unloading TOPS temporarily

What if you don't want TOPS to load? Let's say you want to run a memory-intensive application like PageMaker on a 512K Macintosh. In that case, you'd want to reserve all the memory for PageMaker. You can keep TOPS from loading by holding down the Command and Option keys as you turn on the computer (Figure 5-10).

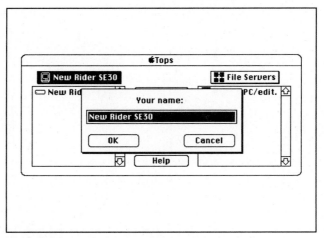

Figure 5-9. Use this dialog box to rename the station.

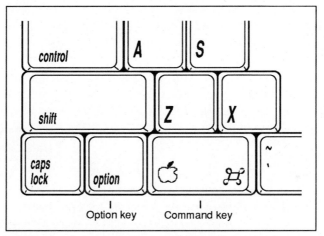

Figure 5-10. To prevent TOPS from loading, hold down the Command key and the Option key as you switch on the Macintosh.

Be patient. Hold down the keys until you see a dialog box asking whether or not you want to load TOPS (Figure 5-11). If you click on No, TOPS will not load.

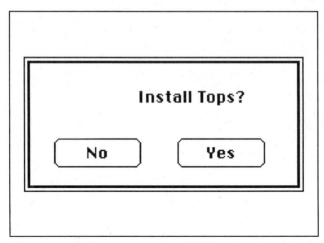

Figure 5-11. If you don't want TOPS to load, hold
down the command and option keys until you see this
dialog box, then click on No.

Unloading TOPS permanently

We recommend that most Mac users allow TOPS to load automatically at startup. That's the most convenient way to have
the power of TOPS available whenever you want it. In most
cases, the memory-resident TOPS DA (desk accessory) has no
effect on the operation of other programs.

Still, some users may be short on memory or have other
reasons for not wanting TOPS to be loaded at all times. For
instance, perhaps they are tied to the network mainly to use a
remote printer. Perhaps they only use TOPS to transfer files a
few times a month. In that case, they might not want to keep
TOPS in memory. If they prefer, these users can remove the
init that loads TOPS on startup. To remove the init:

- Open the System Folder.

- Drag the TOPS init out of the folder.

- Restart the computer.

If you remove the init, TOPS will no longer load automatically.
To use TOPS, you will have to start it up using the Start TOPS
utility. This utility is placed in your System Folder when you
install TOPS.

To start TOPS using the utility:

■ Open the System Folder.

■ Click on the Start TOPS icon (Figure 5-12).

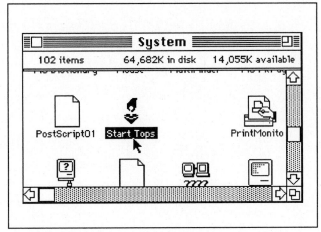

Figure 5-12. If you've chosen *not* to have TOPS load automatically, then you must click on the Start Tops icon to load it.

> Note | Mac users can print to a network printer without TOPS. However, to transfer files they must load the TOPS software.

Auto-publishing and auto-mounting

We're almost through describing how to load TOPS on a Mac. Before we finish, we want to explain how to customize the loading process. With a few quick steps, you can instruct TOPS to automatically publish and/or mount the volumes you use most often.

Auto-publishing and auto-mounting have a variety of time-saving uses. For instance, let's say your computer is the message center for your electronic mail system. You'll need to auto-publish the volume containing the mail files. Otherwise, you'll have to remember to publish it each day before the others can start leaving messages. Likewise, if a workgroup stores its files in one particular volume, that volume should be published and mounted by all the stations in the workgroup.

In a medium-sized workgroup, it's possible to have a dozen or more volumes that need to be published and mounted before the network can function normally. But there's no need to remember to do all that when TOPS can do it for you.

Auto-publishing

You auto-publish with TOPS's Remember function. Start by going to the main TOPS dialog box (select TOPS from the Apple menu). You will use a slight variation of the normal publishing routine. (Publishing is covered in detail in Chapter Six, "Exchanging Files with TOPS.")

Normally, you would select the disk or folder you want to publish from the TOPS dialog box, then click on the Publish button (Figure 5-13).

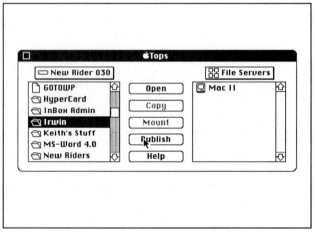

Figure 5-13. To publish the folder Irwin, you would click on Irwin, then click on the Publish button.

To instruct TOPS to publish that volume automatically, you use a secondary dialog box available through the Publish button:

■ Select the volume you want to publish from the list at the left of the dialog box.

■ Click *and hold* the Publish button. A secondary menu drops down. Drag the mouse down to the Publish... option and release the button.

The Publish... dialog box appears (Figure 5-14).

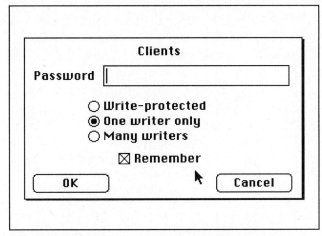

Figure 5-14. With the Publish dialog box, you can
tell TOPS to remember to auto-publish a volume
every time it starts up.

We'll cover all the options in this dialog box in the next chapter. For now, we're only concerned with the last option:
Remember.

■ Click on the Remember box. Make sure that a check mark
appears to confirm your choice. Then click on OK.

TOPS now publishes the volume as it would normally. And
because you clicked Remember, it will automatically publish
this volume whenever you start the computer.

You can auto-publish up to 12 different volumes. Auto-
publishing also works with floppy disks and partitioned
volumes. If the floppies or the partitions are not present
during startup, TOPS will simply bypass them and finish
starting up the computer. As soon as you put in the floppy
disks or bring up the partitioned volume, TOPS will automatically publish the volume onto the network.

If TOPS encounters a problem auto-publishing a particular
volume, it brings up a dialog box. You have two choices: Continue or Forget. Both choices bypass the automatic publishing
of that folder so you can continue with startup. However, the
Forget choice permanently removes the volume from the list,
so TOPS will not attempt to auto-publish it again.

Tip During the course of a work session, you may unpublish
some or all of the auto-published volumes. To republish them

in one step, hold down the Option key while selecting the TOPS Desk Accessory from the Apple menu. This same trick works for remounting auto-mounted volumes.

Removing a volume from the auto-publish list

If you no longer want a volume auto-published, simply follow the same procedure. Go to the main TOPS dialog box. Click on the volume. Click and hold the Unpublish button. When the secondary menu appears, click and drag the mouse down to the Publish... option to bring up the Publish dialog box. Click on the Remember box. This time, the check mark will disappear. Click OK. The volume has now been unpublished and removed from the auto-publish list.

Auto-mounting

Auto-mounting is very similar to auto-publishing. You set it up with a variation of the normal mounting procedure. Normally, you mount a disk from the main TOPS dialog box by selecting it, then clicking on Mount. To put this volume on the auto-mount list instead, you click *and hold* the Mount button. When the secondary menu appears, you drag down to the Mount... choice and release the button. The Mount dialog box appears (Figure 5-15).

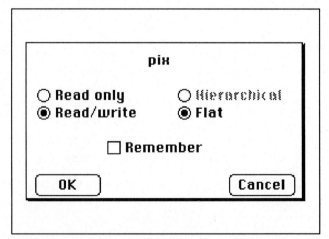

Figure 5-15. The Mount dialog box.

Click on the Remember box if you want TOPS to auto-mount this volume every time you start up the Macintosh. A check mark appears to confirm your choice. Then click OK.

Note You can't mount or use the Remember option until the volume has been published by the server workstation.

TOPS will try to auto-mount all the volumes you asked for when you start up the computer every morning. However, if some of your colleagues have forgotten to publish those volumes, they won't be available to TOPS. In that case, TOPS offers you three choices: Continue, Try Again, and Forget (Figure 5-16).

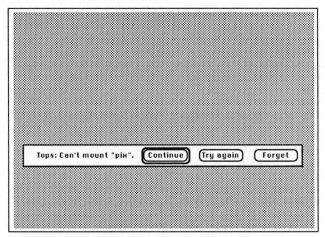

Figure 5-16. TOPS brings up this dialog box if it is unable to auto-mount all the volumes you asked for.

Choose Continue if you want TOPS to skip that volume and do the rest of the ones on your list. You can then mount that volume manually later. Choose Try Again if you've just yelled down the hall and reminded your colleague to publish the volume. And choose Forget if you not only want to continue, but also to remove that volume permanently from the auto-mount list.

Removing a volume from the auto-mount list
To remove a volume from the auto-mount list, click on the mounted volume in the TOPS dialog box. Then click and hold the Unmount button. Drag down to the secondary menu option and release the button to bring up the Mount dialog box. Click on the Remember box, thereby removing the check mark. Once you click OK, the volume will be both unmounted and removed from the auto-mount list.

■ Loading TOPS on the PC

Loading TOPS on the PC is more complicated than on the Mac. That's because you must choose among different ways to join the network. This section will explain how to:

- choose which way you should join the network

- use the right commands to load TOPS

- understand what's happening when you issue the TOPS loading commands

- automate loading with batch files

- auto-publish and auto-mount at the same time you load

Speed Start for PCs

Experienced users can use the abbreviated instructions in this section. Beginners will want to follow along with the full instructions that follow.

To load and start TOPS:

- ■ To publish and mount volumes, join as a server/client by typing LOADTOPS <Enter> at the DOS prompt.

- ■ To publish and mount volumes *and* publish printers, join as a server/client plus printer server by typing LOADTOPS <Enter> and TOPSPRTR <Enter> at the DOS prompt.

- ■ To mount only, join as a client only by typing LOADCLNT <Enter> at the DOS prompt.

- ■ To use the menuing system with any of these modes, type TOPSMENU at the DOS prompt *after* the other commands.

To identify yourself to the network:

- ■ Type in the station name when prompted by TOPS.

To automate the station name:

- ■ Type the station name into line two of the batch file TOPSKRNL.DAT.

To change the station name:

- ■ Load TOPS.

■ At the DOS prompt, type `TOPS STATION newname` and then press Enter.

To load TOPS automatically:

■ Add the correct TOPS command(s) to your AUTOEXEC.BAT file. The precise commands depend on which mode you wish to load (server/client, printer server, or client only). You can also add the TOPSMENU command if you want the menu system to come up.

To unload TOPS:

■ At the DOS Prompt, type `TOPS UNLOAD /A` to unload everything. Type `TOPS UNLOAD /modulename` to unload one or more modules.

To auto-publish (or auto-mount):

■ Publish (or mount) the volumes or printers you want to have active at startup.

■ Choose Remember from the Main menu and press Enter; or type `TOPS REMEMBER` at the DOS prompt and press Enter.

Choosing how to join the network

Let's define the three main options, so you can decide which way you should load TOPS:

• If you need to publish and mount volumes, you must join as a *server/client*.

• If you need to publish printers as well as volumes, you must join as a server/client *plus* as a *printer server*.

• If you only need to mount, you can join as a *client only*.

• If you want to work from a menu, you can load TOPSMENU along with any of the three modes.

    | Note | TOPS has additional modules for three special situations: (1) NETBIOS, (2) multiuser dBASE, and (3) printing from the DOS prompt.

Why the different ways to load TOPS? Many PCs have memory limitations. TOPS software is constructed so you can minimize those limitations. By loading only the modules you need, you can preserve RAM for other applications. Remember — TOPS is memory-resident. It remains in memory along with other applications. Figure 5-17 shows how this can lead to an overflow condition when running TOPS together with several other programs.

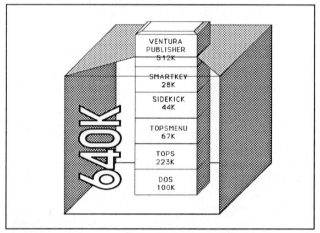

Figure 5-17. It's not hard to go through the 640K ceiling of many PCs. Fortunately, TOPS lets you load only the modules you really need.

If you plan to use TOPS together with several other applications, you'll want to make sure you have enough memory left over. You can usually find the memory requirements of an application in its documentation, or on the back of the original packaging. Table 5-1 gives the memory requirements for different ways of loading TOPS. By adding them together, you can find out in advance if you have sufficient memory. If not, you'll have to eliminate an application, or load TOPS in one of its other modes.

Using the loading commands

Your first decision, then, is how each PC should join the network. Once you know that, you can use Table 5-1 to figure out which loading commands to use.

TABLE 5-1. TOPS loading commands

Mode	Command(s) to use	Approx. Memory Requirement
Server/Client	LOADTOPS	187K (including network drivers)
Server/Client plus Printer Server	LOADTOPS TOPSPRTR	223K (187 for server/client plus an additional 36K)
Client Only	LOADCLNT	121K (including network drivers)
Optional menuing system for all three modes	TOPSMENU	67K

You enter these commands at the DOS prompt. For instance, to load TOPS as a server/client plus the printer server plus the menuing system, you would enter the following three commands:

```
LOADTOPS <Enter>

TOPSPRTR <Enter>

TOPSMENU <Enter>
```

> **Note** Make sure the TOPS subdirectory is in the path command of your AUTOEXEC.BAT batch file, so you can type these commands from any subdirectory. Otherwise you must enter these commands from the TOPS subdirectory.

Understanding the loading function

In the previous section, we explained which commands load different flavors of TOPS. Although it's not strictly required, it may be helpful to understand what goes on when you issue those commands.

The loading commands are nothing more than batch files that call up one or more software modules. TOPS creates these batch files during installation. You can also create or modify them on your own. Table 5-2 summarizes these modules and their functions. The two DAT files (TOPSKRNL.DAT and TOPSTART.DAT) are not modules, but configuration files that TOPS reads to get the startup information it needs.

TABLE 5-2. TOPS software modules

Command	Modules	Function
LOADTOPS	ALAP.EXE and PSTACK.EXE	Network drivers
^	TOPSTALK.EXE and TOPSKRNL.EXE	Server/client versions of network operating system
^	TOPSTART.DAT	Configuration information including volumes to auto-publish and auto-mount
TOPSPRTR	TOPSPRTR.EXE	Print server capability plus background print queue
LOADCLNT	ALAP.EXE and PSTACK.EXE	Network drivers
^	TOPSTALC.EXE and TOPSCLNT.EXE	Client-only versions of network operating system
TOPSMENU	TOPSMENU.EXE	Menuing system

| Note | As usual in this book, Table 5-2 assumes that you are using a FlashCard. If you are using an Ethernet card instead, the names of the network driver modules will be different.

Loading TOPS as a server/client

Using TOPS as a server/client requires only one command: LOADTOPS. At the DOS prompt (usually C: for hard disk users), type:

```
LOADTOPS <Enter>
```

You'll now see several messages as TOPS loads four software modules one after another (Figure 5-18).

```
TOPS FlashCard FlashTalk Driver, Version LAP 2.102 Installed: Flash = E
Board Address = 390, Board Interrupt = 3, Board DMA = 3, Access Interrupt = 5C


Copyright (c) 1987 Sun Microsystems, Inc.
All Rights Reserved.

TOPS AppleTalk Protocol Stack, Version TSR 2.102 Installed:

Copyright (c) 1988 Sun Microsystems, Inc.
All Rights Reserved.
TOPSTalk - SoftTalk Module for TOPS/DOS Version 2
Copyright (C) Sun Microsystems, Inc.  1987, 1988.  All rights reserved.
TOPSTalk       Version 2.10     10/17/88
TOPSTALK loaded.
TOPS/DOS Version 2
Copyright (C) Sun Microsystems, Inc. 1987, 1988. All rights reserved.
TOPSKRNL       Version 2.10     10/17/88

TOPSKRNL Serial Number:  PZ00078621
Reading TOPSKRNL.DAT file....
```

Figure 5-18. The LOADTOPS batch file calls up separate modules that turn a PC into a TOPS server/client.

These modules take up about 187K when loaded. In addition, you may see a message that TOPS is reading TOPSKRNL.DAT or TOPSTART.DAT. These files contain startup information for TOPS.

When the modules have finished loading, you can run TOPS, either via the DOS prompt, or with TOPS's special menu utility. Later in this chapter, you'll learn how to make TOPSMENU come up automatically if you prefer.

Loading TOPS as a printer server

Loading TOPS as a server/client lets you publish or mount any volume. If you also want to publish local printers, you must load another module. It's important to realize that this module works together with the server/client module. You cannot load it on its own.

In brief, TOPS has three kinds of printers. A *local printer* attaches to a computer, and can be used only by that computer. A *shared printer* also attaches to a computer, but it has been published so any workstation can use it. And a *network printer* can attach directly to the network on its own (Figure 5-19).

If you want to publish a printer so it can be shared by the rest

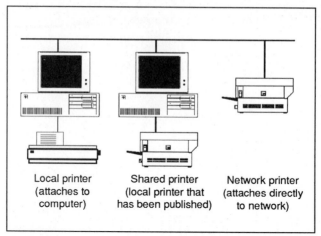

Local printer   Shared printer   Network printer
(attaches to   (local printer that (attaches directly
computer)   has been published) to network)

Figure 5-19. TOPS permits three different kinds of printers.

of the network, you must enter the command TOPSPRTR after entering LOADTOPS:

```
LOADTOPS <Enter>

TOPSPRTR <Enter>
```

You are now ready to use TOPS as a server, as a printer server, as a client, or any combination.

Loading TOPS as a client only

Using TOPS as a client only requires one command. At the DOS prompt type:

```
LOADCLNT <Enter>
```

You'll see several messages as TOPS loads the client-only modules (Figure 5-20).

These modules require 121K of memory when loaded. In addition, you may see a message that TOPS is reading TOPSKRNL.DAT or TOPSTART.DAT. These files contain startup information for TOPS.

When the modules have finished loading, you can use any of TOPS's client facilities. In other words, you can mount volumes or printer. You cannot, however, perform any server functions.

```
TOPS FlashCard FlashTalk Driver, Version LAP 2.102 Installed: Flash = E
Board Address = 390, Board Interrupt = 3, Board DMA = 3, Access Interrupt = 5C

Copyright (c) 1987 Sun Microsystems, Inc.
All Rights Reserved.

TOPS AppleTalk Protocol Stack, Version TSR 2.102 Installed:

Copyright (c) 1988 Sun Microsystems, Inc.
All Rights Reserved.
TOPSTALC - SoftTalk Client Module for TOPS/DOS Version 2
Copyright (C) Sun Microsystems, Inc. 1987, 1988. All rights reserved.
TOPSTALC      Version 2.10    10/17/88
TOPSTALC loaded.

TOPSCLNT - Client Only Module for TOPS/DOS Version 2
Copyright (C) Sun Microsystems, Inc. 1987. All rights reserved.
TOPSCLNT      Version 2.10    10/17/88

TOPSKRNL Serial Number: PZ00078621
Reading TOPSKRNL.DAT file....
```

Figure 5-20. LOADCLNT loads the software modules that turn a PC into a TOPS client.

Loading TOPSMENU

Once you've loaded TOPS, you can run it in one of two ways. The first is from the DOS command line. In this mode, you issue special TOPS commands at the prompt. For instance, the command to publish is TOPS PUBLISH.

The second way to run TOPS — and the one we recommend to beginners — is via its special menu facility. The menu is easier to use than the DOS command line and saves the trouble of remembering complicated commands.

To use the menu, you simply load the utility TOPSMENU *after* loading TOPS itself. You can use TOPSMENU no matter which variety of TOPS you have loaded. Thus, to use the menu with the server/client mode of TOPS, you would type:

    LOADTOPS <Enter>

    TOPSMENU <Enter>

To use it with the printer server mode, you would type:

    LOADTOPS <Enter>

    TOPSPRTR <Enter>

    TOPSMENU <Enter>

Once you type the TOPSMENU command and press enter, the intro screen appears (Figure 5-21).

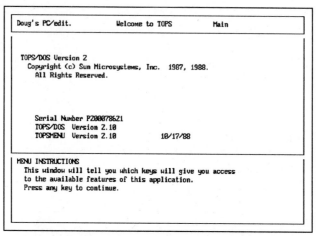

```
┌─────────────────────────────────────────────────────────────┐
│ ┌───────────────────────────────────────────────────────────┐
│ │ Doug's PC/edit.          Welcome to TOPS           Main    │
│ └───────────────────────────────────────────────────────────┘
│ ┌───────────────────────────────────────────────────────────┐
│ │ TOPS/DOS Version 2                                          │
│ │    Copyright (c) Sun Microsystems, Inc.  1987, 1988.       │
│ │    All Rights Reserved.                                     │
│ │                                                             │
│ │                                                             │
│ │                                                             │
│ │    Serial Number P200078621                                 │
│ │    TOPS/DOS  Version 2.10                                   │
│ │    TOPSMENU  Version 2.10              10/17/88             │
│ └───────────────────────────────────────────────────────────┘
│ ┌───────────────────────────────────────────────────────────┐
│ │ MENU INSTRUCTIONS                                           │
│ │   This window will tell you which keys will give you access │
│ │   to the available features of this application.           │
│ │   Press any key to continue.                                │
│ │                                                             │
│ └───────────────────────────────────────────────────────────┘
└─────────────────────────────────────────────────────────────┘
```

Figure 5-21. Type the TOPSMENU command and press Enter to see the TOPSMENU intro screen.

You'll learn to use this menuing system in the next chapter. For now, we will spend only enough time to learn how to automate the loading process.

The intro screen gives you copyright and version information. Instructions appear in the lower window. If you have not previously set your station name, TOPS asks you to do so now (Figure 5-22). The station name uniquely identifies the computer to the rest of the network. It must be no longer than 15 characters.

Tip Your station name should be meaningful to the other people using the network. While you may like "PC Packin' Mama," "Lisa's 386 Server" will be more helpful to your colleagues.

Automating the station name

Unless instructed otherwise, TOPS will ask you for the station name each time you start up. If you've chosen a permanent name for each station (a practice we recommend) you can instruct TOPS to remember it and enter it automatically.

Creating this automatic log on requires you to modify a configuration file called TOPSKRNL.DAT. For those of you al-

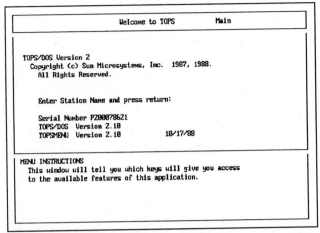

Figure 5-22. You must enter the station name before beginning your TOPS work session.

ready conversant with editing files, the process is very easy. Simply type in the station name on line two of the file. Do not exceed 15 characters.

Changing the station name

You can change your station name from the DOS command line. First load TOPS as instructed earlier in this chapter. Do not load TOPSMENU.

To view the current station name, move to the subdirectory containing TOPS (usually C:\TOPS) and type:

```
TOPS STATION <Enter>
```

To change the name, type:

```
TOPS STATION newname <Enter>
```

Substitute your actual station name for *newname*.

Loading TOPS automatically

So far you've learned how to load different versions of TOPS by typing different commands. You've also seen how to bring up the TOPS menuing system. Now we'll discuss how to automate the procedure.

You may find it easier to have TOPS load automatically as soon as you turn on your computer each day. This requires placing the TOPS command(s) in your AUTOEXEC.BAT file. AUTOEXEC.BAT is a special type of batch file. When DOS starts up, it looks first for AUTOEXEC.BAT. If it finds this file, it proceeds to execute all the commands it finds inside.

Consequently, you can start TOPS automatically by typing its commands into AUTOEXEC.BAT. Use the same commands you would have typed from the DOS prompt. Put each command on a separate line. Thus, if you want to load TOPS as a server/client with the menus, you would type:

```
LOADTOPS <Enter>

TOPSMENU <Enter>
```

If you wanted to load TOPS as a client only without the menus, you would type:

```
LOADCLNT <Enter>
```

We've mentioned putting a command series in the AUTOEXEC.BAT file for automatic startup. You could also type the commands into a standard batch file. For instance, you might create a batch file called TOPS.BAT to automatically load TOPS and its menuing system.

Unloading TOPS

Use the TOPS UNLOAD command to remove TOPS from memory. If you do not use this command, TOPS remains in memory until you turn off the computer.

You can unload all or part of TOPS. You must leave the menuing system and go to the DOS prompt to do so. To unload everything, go to the DOS prompt and type:

```
TOPS UNLOAD /A <Enter>
```

It doesn't matter whether you use upper or lower case. Notice that there is a space between each word, and that the slash is a *front* slash.

Table 5-3 lists the abbreviations you use to unload various portions of the TOPS software. All of these entries must be preceded with the TOPS UNLOAD command.

WARNING Unload modules in the reverse order of loading, or you may crash your machine.

Table 5-3. TOPS unloading commands

Module	Function	Entry
TNETBIOS	NetBios routines for TOPS	/TNETBIOS
TOPSPRTR	Printer server	/PRTR
TOPSKRNL	Part of network operating system for server/client	/KRNL
TOPSCLNT	Part of network operating system for client only	/CLNT
TOPSTALK	Part of network operating system for server/client	/TALK
TOPSTALC	Part of network operating system for client only	/TALC
ATALK and PSTACK	Network drivers	/ATALK

You can unload portions of TOPS by typing in a space and the name of that module after the unload command. You might do this to free up memory for another application. For instance, to unload the printer server, you would type:

```
TOPS UNLOAD /PRTR <Enter>
```

To unload TOPSKRNL and TOPSTALK (the network operating system), you would type:

```
TOPS UNLOAD /KRNL <Enter>

TOPS UNLOAD /TALK <Enter>
```

You can reload modules after unloading, using the loading commands explained earlier in the chapter.

Auto-publishing and auto-mounting

With a few quick steps, you can instruct TOPS to automatically publish and/or mount the volumes you use most often. These activities will occur as part of the loading process — you won't have to do anything except watch it happen.

The process is very simple. You publish and/or mount the volumes manually. Then you tell TOPS to remember what you just did. You can tell TOPS to remember with the menu system, or with a command from the DOS prompt. Here's how it works with the menus:

■ Publish and/or mount the volumes you want to have available every day when you start up. You can also publish or mount the printer(s) you use most often.

■ Return to the Main menu.

■ Select Remember from the Main menu and press Enter (Figure 5-23).

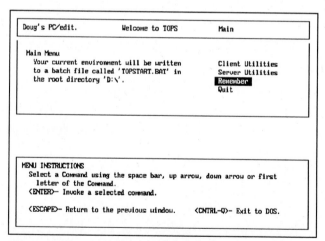

Figure 5-23. Use the Remember option from the Main menu to ask TOPS to publish or mount volumes automatically at startup time.

You can accomplish the same thing with a command from the DOS prompt. First publish and/or mount the volumes or printers you want to have available every time you start up. Then go to the DOS prompt and type:

```
TOPS REMEMBER <Enter>
```

Whether you use the menu or the command line, TOPS takes the same actions. It lists all the publishing and mounting you've done in the current session in a special batch file called TOPSTART.BAT and writes this file to the root directory of your startup disk. From that point on, TOPS will read this file and follow its instructions each time it loads. This process is automatic; you do not need to issue any new commands. When you use the LOADTOPS or LOADCLNT commands, TOPS routinely checks for the TOPSTART.BAT file and uses it if it exists.

| Note | Because TOPS merely remembers what you've done, you should be careful not to do any unnecessary publishing and mounting before using the Remember function.

For instance, suppose you publish a volume and then un-publish it because you changed your mind. If you used Remember at this point, TOPS would automatically publish and unpublish this volume every time you start it. A better strategy is to end the TOPS session, then reload TOPS. After starting fresh, you should publish and mount only the volumes and printers you want active at startup.

■ Continuing on

This chapter has shown you how to load and start TOPS from a Mac or a PC. In addition, it has explained how to customize and automate the process to make it as easy and fast as possible.

Now you're ready to go to work with TOPS. The next few chapters show you how.

Chapter Six

▌Exchanging Files with TOPS

With the techniques from this chapter, you can move files from one computer to another without leaving your chair. And you can transfer files between computers that are otherwise incompatible. This chapter assumes that you already know how to load and start TOPS. It explains:

- the differences between Mac and PC files
- how to exchange files on a Mac
- how to exchange files on a PC

▌Mac versus PC files

You don't have to master the theoretical differences between Macs and PCs to operate TOPS. Still, if you plan to exchange files between the two machines, it will pay to have a basic understanding. Otherwise, you're likely to make mistakes. This section explains what you need to know to safely transfer files between the two platforms. It covers differences between:

- the terminology
- the file structures
- the naming systems
- the operating systems

Mac versus PC terminology

Mac and PC users often use different words for the same concept. Table 6-1 lists some of the terms you may encounter as you switch between platforms:

Table 6-1. Mac versus PC terms

Mac term	PC term	Meaning
Chooser	(none)	A memory resident accessory for selecting and configuring printers and other devices.
(none)	CONFIG.SYS	A special file in the root directory of a PC that contains information about the computer's setup if it deviates from the plain vanilla default settings.
(none)	AUTOEXEC.BAT	A special file that instructs the computer what to do automatically when first turned on or rebooted.
Desk Accessory (DA)	Terminate-and-stay-resident program (TSR)	Program that remains in memory after loading, thereby coexisting with other programs.
Desktop	Root directory	The highest level of the disk organization. All folders (subdirectories) branch from here.
File	File	Data stored together on the disk as a logical unit.
Finder	(none)	Portion of the operating system devoted to file management.
Folder	Subdirectory	A subdivision of a disk roughly analogous to a manila folder. Can contain files or other folders (other subdirectories).
Icon	Drive letter	Means of identifying a disk.
System	Operating system	Software that runs the computer itself and provides the user interface.
(none)	DOS prompt (or command line)	Where PC users type in their commands to the system. Mac users perform the same functions with the mouse, or by typing into a dialog box.

Mac versus PC file structures

The differences between the Mac and PC have definite consequences when you start exchanging files. A Mac file is not a single entity, but two file entities linked together: the *resource fork* and the *data fork*. The data fork contains the bulk of the information — the numbers you type into a spreadsheet, the text you type into a word processor, and so on. The resource fork usually contains formatting. (Note to advanced users: We've chosen to ignore the exceptions.)

PC files, on the other hand, don't have this dual structure. When a Mac file is sent to a PC, TOPS has to figure out what to do with the the resource fork. Its solution is to send *two* files. The first is the data fork. It gets the original file name. The second is the resource fork. It gets the original name preceded by *R-*. Then, since DOS can't use it anyway, TOPS makes the resource file *hidden*. This keeps it from cluttering up your PC directories, yet leaves it available if you decide to send the file back to the Macintosh again. It also allows you to see the files as Macintosh application-specific files on a Macintosh as shown in Figure 6-1. In other words, if a Macintosh loads a file from PC, the resource fork lets the Macintosh treat it as a normal Macintosh file. Without the resource fork, the Macintosh would treat it as a PC file.

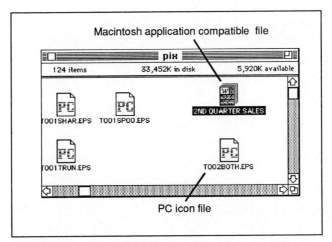

Figure 6-1. The Macintosh desktop displays files on a PC with a PC icon unless they have a Macintosh resource fork attached.

You can't see these hidden resource files on a PC with the normal PC-DOS directory command. This has two important consequences. First, you should use TOPS's XDIR command if you want to view the resource files along with the data files.

The XDIR command shows the hidden files. (Many commercial utilities also allow you to view hidden files, including XTree for the PC, QDOS, and Norton Commander.)

Second, you shouldn't use normal DOS commands to delete Macintosh files. Since DOS can't see the hidden resource files, you'll remove only the data file portions. Instead, you should use TOPS's TDEL command (covered in Chapter Eleven "Customizing TOPS on the PC"). You can also remove them by mounting the PC volume on a Macintosh, and using the Macintosh to move the files into the trash. Either method will delete both forks.

Mac versus PC file names

Macs and PCs have different naming systems. These differences can cause big headaches when you start moving files back and forth. Fortunately, all it takes is planning to avoid the problems.

We're going to give you the details below, but we can sum it all up in a single sentence: *Use DOS naming conventions if you have a mixed network.* The PC naming system is the lowest common denominator, so the names will survive transfer without getting garbled. PC names will always be acceptable to the Macintosh, *but the reverse is not true.* Here are the four things a Mac user needs to keep in mind to avoid creating names a PC won't be able to understand:

- length
- illegal characters
- use of the period
- illegal extensions

The first thing to remember is to use shorter names. Macintosh file names can have up to 31 characters. PC names, by contrast, can only be eight characters long. They can optionally have a three-character *extension*. An extension is marked by a period (Figure 6-2).

The next thing a Mac user must learn is to use characters the PC can accept. Macintosh names can use any character except the colon. The PC, however, has a longer list of excluded characters, as shown in Table 6-2. Be sure to avoid these characters in your Macintosh file names.

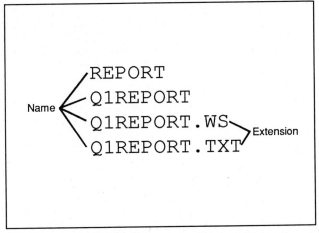

Figure 6-2. Valid PC file names. Mac users must conform to the PC system if they want their file names to survive the transfer.

When TOPS makes a transfer, it strips out illegal characters. It converts spaces to underlines, and shortens the name to the PC's eight character limit (Figure 6-3).

Table 6-2. Excluded characters in PC file names

Allowed	Excluded
Any letter	spaces
Any number	*
!	?
@	:
#	;
$	"

Allowed	Excluded
%	\
&	|
(	?
)	/
-	=
—	[
~	]
'	<
{	>
}	

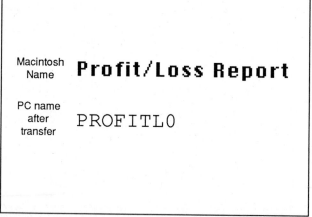

Macintosh
Name

Profit/Loss Report

PC name
after
transfer

PROFITLO

Figure 6-3. TOPS strips out illegal characters when it transfers to the PC.

Although the period is not excluded, it has a special meaning: to set off an *extension*. The extension is the optional three-character string that follows a period. Macintosh files don't need an extension. They contain a *header* that identifies the type of file and the application to which it belongs. Because PCs don't have this header information, the extension is often used to identify the file type.

You need to understand extensions for several reasons. First, if you type a period into your Mac file name, TOPS assumes that you want to create an extension. Usually, it treats the first eight letters as the name and the three letters after the period as the extension. It throws the rest away (Figure 6-4).

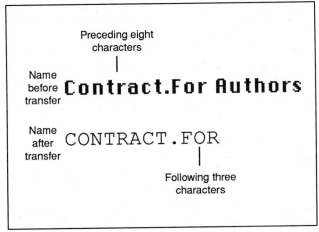

Figure 6-4. If you type a period into a Mac file name, TOPS assumes that you wanted to create an extension when it transfers the file to a PC.

If the Mac file name has more than eight characters before the period, TOPS will prune the filename down to seven characters and a numeral that denotes the file's order during the transfer. For instance, the file 2ND QUARTER.SALES would transfer to the PC as 2NDQUAR0.SAL. If you did not remove the file 2NDQUAR0.SAL from the PC and transfered a file named 2ND QUARTER FINAL.SALES to the PC, the new file would be called 2NDQUAR1.SAL.

Mac users must also be careful with the three-letter extensions they use. DOS itself has several reserved extensions. In addition, many DOS programs have special extensions. For instance, Lotus 1A spreadsheets use the .WKS extension. And many DOS programs prefer that you use a given extension, even though they don't absolutely require it.

Table 6-3 lists some PC extensions in common use. Life will be simpler if you *stick to these conventions*. Use the reserved extensions only for their intended purpose. For instance, don't name a business letter LETTER.BAT, because DOS treats anything with the BAT extension as a batch file (a special sequence of commands).

| Note | Although Table 6-3 lists the most common extensions, there are dozens of others in widespread use. In addition, most workgroups develop their own extension codes. Check with the other people on your network, then use this table as a starting point to build a list specific to your business.

Table 6-3. PC file extensions

Category	Extension	Purpose
Reserved by DOS	.AUX	Don't use
	.CON	Don't use
	.NUL	Don't use
	.PRN	Don't use
	.BAS	Basic programs
	.BAT	Batch files containing executable DOS commands
	.COM	Command files — programs in a specific structured format
	.EXE	Executable files — programs in a specific structured format

Category	Extension	Purpose
Text file extensions reserved by common agreement	.DCA	Document Content Architecture format text files
	.DOC	Microsoft Word document
	.RTF	Rich Text Format
	.TXT	ASCII text files
Graphics file extensions reserved by common agreement	.CGM	Computer Graphic Metafile
	.DWG	AutoCAD drawing file
	.DXF	AutoCAD drawing exchange file
	.EPS	Encapsulated PostScript
	.GEM	GEM format object-oriented graphics
	.HPG	Hewlett-Packard Graphic Language (plotters)
	.IMG	GEM format bitmap graphics
	.PCT	Macintosh PICT
	.PIC	Lotus 1-2-3 graphics
	.PCX	PC Paintbrush bitmap graphics
	.PLT	AutoCAD plot file
	.SLD	AutoCAD slide file
	.TIF	Tagged Image File Format

Category	Extension	Purpose
Spreadsheet file extensions reserved by common agreement	.DIF	Data Interchange Format
	.SYL	Multiplan Excel 1.5
	.WK1	Lotus 1-2-3 Version 2
	.WKS	Lotus 1-2-3 Version 1A Symphony
Database file extensions reserved by common agreement	.DBF	dBASE
Desktop publishing extensions reserved by common agreement	.CHP	Ventura chapter file
	.CIF	Ventura chapter information file
	.STY	Ventura style sheet
	.VGR	Ventura graphics file
	.PUB	PageMaker 1.0 layout file
	.PM3	PageMaker 3.0 layout file
	.PT3	PageMaker 3.0 template file
Other extensions reserved by common agreement	.DAT	Data files for TOPS on the PC
	.INI	Initialization file for application programs
	.INF	Initialization file for application programs
	.TPS	hidden desktop files for TOPS on the PC

Tip If you don't want to give up longer names on the Mac, try this trick. Use the first 11 characters to create a PC-compatible name — seven characters, one period, three more characters. (TOPS will use the eighth character for a number as discussed earlier.) Follow the DOS-compatible name with a space. Then use the rest of the Mac's 31-character limit to create a longer name. Only the PC portion will survive the transfer, but you will still have the benefit of the longer name on the Mac (Figure 6-5).

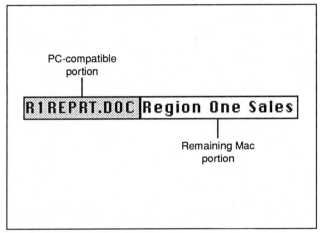

PC-compatible
portion

R1REPRT.DOC Region One Sales

Remaining Mac
portion

Figure 6-5. The first part of this file name is PC compatible for transfer over TOPS. The second part is for the benefit of Mac users.

Mac versus PC operating systems

We told you earlier that Macintosh files have both a data fork and a resource fork. MS-DOS can't handle the resource fork. TOPS takes care of this problem by creating a hidden file called XDIRSTAT.TPS. It puts this file into every PC directory you publish. XDIRSTAT.TPS has several functions, not the least of which is to link Macintosh data files with their hidden resource file.

WARNING If you delete XDIRSTAT.TPS, you will not be able to access Macintosh files stored on a PC. DOS does not have any way to link the data file to the hidden resource file.

There's another important difference that affects TOPS users.

In theory, when you publish a subdirectory, you automatically publish all the subdirectories within it. (In Mac terms, when you publish a folder, you automatically publish all the folders inside.) However, this does not hold true in one case. When you publish a PC subdirectory and view it from a Macintosh, you cannot see the subdirectories beneath it.

This problem does not exist when going from a Mac to a Mac, from a PC to a PC, or from a Mac to a PC. But if you publish a directory on a PC and mount it from a Mac, you cannot see or access the subdirectories. If you need information from a subdirectory of a subdirectory, the only solution is to publish and mount that subdirectory separately.

| Note | You cannot publish a subdirectory of a directory that is already published.

A similar problem arises if you copy nested folders from a Mac to a PC. The hierarchy is lost. All the files and folders will appear on the same level.

■ Exchanging files on the Macintosh

To this point, we've explained some of the differences between the Macintosh and the PC. You need to understand these differences to avoid confusion and mistakes when transferring files on mixed (Mac and PC) networks.

Now you're ready to get to work. This section explains how to exchange files with a Macintosh:

- how to publish

- how to mount

- how to copy

- how to use the Help button to get more information about your files

TOPS on the Macintosh follows the Mac interface as closely as possible. Because TOPS is a DA (desk accessory), you can work with it whenever you want, from any program. Chapter Five, "Loading and Starting TOPS," explained how to load

TOPS and open the TOPS DA. Once you've done that, the main dialog box appears (Figure 6-6).

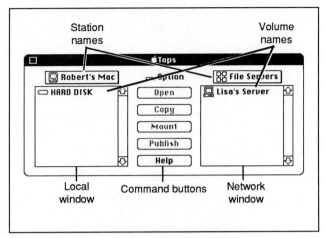

Figure 6-6. The main TOPS dialog box.

Some of you may be PC users who have never worked with Macs before. Let's spend a moment to make sure you are familiar with the parts and features of this dialog box.

The *local window* shows what's on your computer. The *network window* shows what's available from other computers on the network. The main TOPS dialog box also controls several other secondary dialog boxes. You'll learn about these as we go along. You use the main dialog box in one of three ways:

1. to publish and unpublish

2. to mount and unmount

3. to see what's going on

We'll explore all three uses in this section.

Speed start for Macs

Experienced users can use the abbreviated reminders in this section. Beginners should refer to the detailed instructions that follow.

You exchange files by publishing and mounting the volumes that contain those files. Then you can use normal copying functions to transfer the information.

To publish a volume:

■ Highlight the volume in the local window and click on the Publish button.

To restrict access by publishing with options:

■ Highlight the volume. Click and hold on the Publish button, then drag down to the Publish… option and release the button.

■ When the Publish… dialog box appears, click on the options you wish to activate. Type the password you want to assign (if any) into the Password box. Then click OK.

To unpublish a volume:

■ Highlight the volume in the local window.

■ Click on the Unpublish button.

To mount a volume:

■ Highlight the volume in the network window.

■ Click on the Mount button.

■ If the volume is protected, type in the correct password when the Password dialog box appears and click OK.

To restrict access by mounting with options:

■ Highlight the volume. Click and hold on the Mount button, then drag down to the Mount… option and release the button.

■ When the Mount… dialog box appears, click on the options you wish to activate. Then click OK.

To unmount a volume:

■ Highlight the volume in the network window.

■ Click on the Unmount button.

To see a list of the volumes you have mounted:

■ Click on the label bar above the network window, then click on the Help button.

To get information about a volume or view a file's contents:

■ Highlight the volume or file and click on Help.

To copy a file without mounting or publishing a volume:

■ Highlight the source file in one of the windows.

■ Highlight the destination in the other window.

■ Click on the Copy button.

Publishing

One way to exchange files is to publish the volumes that contain them. Then your clients can copy the ones they want to or from their machines. When you publish, you are operating as a server. (At any given time, you can act as both server and client; this is where TOPS really shines. We will show you how to operate as a client later in this chapter.)

Finding the volume(s) you want

The first step in publishing is to find and highlight the volume you want. Since it will be all or part of a local drive, you work in the local window. When you first open the TOPS DA, the label above the local window shows your computer's station name. The list below it shows the active disk drives. If you click on a drive name and then click on the Open button, you open the drive. The drive name now appears in the label at the top and the list shows all the folders on the drive (Figure 6-7).

You can open a folder just the way you opened a disk. Click on the folder name, then click on Open. Now the list shows the folders and files inside that folder. And so on down the hierarchical file structure.

To move back up the directory tree, click and hold on top of the label. A secondary menu drops down, showing you the path back up. Drag the mouse to the level you want and release the button (Figure 6-8). You return to that level.

Using the Publish button

TOPS allows you to publish floppy disks, RAM disks, hard disks, or folders. Once published, we refer to them all as *volumes*. Volumes appear to other workstations as if they are separate disk drives, even if they are only a small portion of a disk in reality.

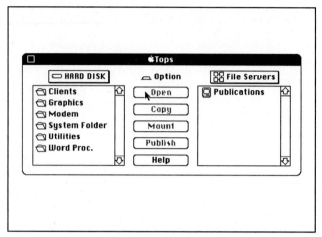

Figure 6-7. You use the local window to find the folders you want to publish.

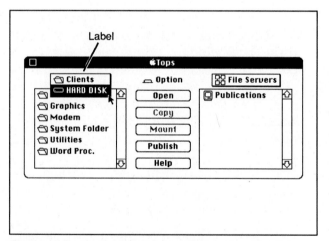

Figure 6-8. To move back to previous levels, click and drag down on the label. Highlight the level you want and release the button.

Tip Avoid publishing RAM disks or floppy disks. RAM disks are volatile. Because not all programs are compatible, a RAM disk can be accidentally purged. Floppy disks are slow and can bog down the entire network.

To publish an entire disk:

■ Highlight the drive name in the local window.

■ Click on the Publish button.

Once published, the icon in the local window changes to the TOPS icon (Figure 6-9).

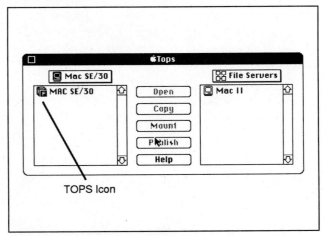

Figure 6-9. After publishing, the icon for this disk changed to TOPS's small cube icon.

WARNING **It is usually not advisable to publish an entire disk. You are giving access to the everything on your disk to everyone on the network. However, if you have a dedicated server, you will want to publish the whole disk.**

It's much more practical to publish only that portion of the disk your clients actually need to use. To publish a folder:

■ Find the folder by navigating through the disk with the local window.

■ Once the folder appears on the list, highlight its name by clicking once with the mouse.

■ Click on the Publish button.

Note It is not possible to publish files. To publish a file, put it into a folder and publish the folder.

Once you publish a volume, its icon is replaced by the TOPS icon. In Figure 6-10, the folders HyperCard, Irwin, MS Word 4.0, and New Riders have been published.

TOPS lets you publish up to 12 volumes.

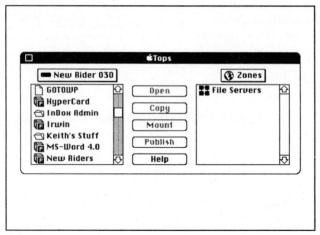

Figure 6-10. Published volumes receive a TOPS icon.

[Tip] If you really need to publish material from many different folders, you would be wise to consolidate them into one folder first. It doesn't make sense to publish 12 different volumes when you can accomplish the same thing by publishing a single folder that contains all the other folders you need.

After publishing, you may notice a performance decrease in day-to-day operations. The degradation occurs because you are now sharing your disk with other users. The extent of the slowdown depends on how many active clients you have.

Publishing with options

So far, we've introduced you to basic publishing. This mode may suffice for many users. But for additional safety, you should consider publishing with options. This function lets you control access to important files.

To publish normally, you click on the Publish button, as you saw above. To publish with options, you click *and hold* on the Publish button. A secondary menu drops down, containing only the Publish... option. If you drag down to the Publish... option and release the mouse button, the dialog box in Figure 6-11 appears.

Obviously, the best way to restrict access to files is not to publish them on the network. Still, you may want to make

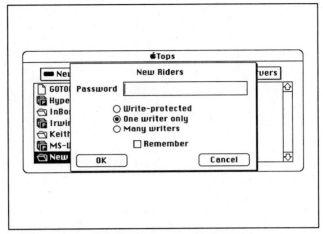

Figure 6-11. The Publish... dialog box lets you restrict access to your files.

files available to certain people while protecting them from others. Or you may want to allow people to view your files, while protecting them against accidental changes. The Publish dialog box lets you accomplish this.

Assigning a password

To restrict access to designated individuals, assign a password to the volume:

■ Highlight the volume.

■ Open the Publish dialog box by clicking and holding on the Publish button, and dragging down to the Publish... option.

■ Type in the password (Figure 6-12).

From now on, when clients try to mount this volume, they will be asked for a password. They will be denied access unless they enter the password exactly as you did.

Consider using passwords for sensitive information. For instance, you might want to publish the payroll information, but restrict access to the payroll clerk and the company treasurer. Passwords are the ideal way to accomplish this. If you don't want to assign a password but you do want to use the other restricted access features, simply leave the space blank.

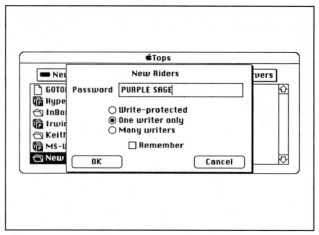

Figure 6-12. Typing a password into the Publish dialog box.

Write protecting a volume

Passwords are the best way to restrict *who* can use files. Write protection controls *what* they can do. More specifically, it lets users look at files but keeps them from changing them. (You can use passwords and write protection together if you want.) These options are controlled by the three buttons in the center of the Publish dialog box.

To select one of these options, click on the button next to the choice. If you do not select an option (or if you don't even open the dialog box), TOPS will automatically publish the volume as One writer only without a password.

The *Write-protected* button prevents anyone from changing the file. This option gives the maximum amount of security. Not only does it keep people from changing your files, it also prevents them from saving their own files onto this volume. This option is useful for sharing information that you don't want people to change. For instance, you might use it to send the quarterly sales information to other managers. And workgroup publishers can use it to protect the integrity of style sheets and formats. Other users can read and use these templates, but they cannot change them. That ensures that all the documents in the company have the same look, and that formatting changes are made only by the designated in-house designer.

The *One writer only* button lets only one person change the file at a time. The first person who mounts the volume can change it. Anyone else who mounts it later can read the files, but not alter them. They are warned of this condition by a padlock icon. This is a useful option for applications such as workgroup editing, where you don't want two people changing the same file at the same time. The One writer only option prevents simultaneous access. If a second author wants to change a text file, he or she must wait until the first user unmounts the volume. The second author can then mount the volume and gain access.

The *Many writers* button allows unlimited, simultaneous access to files. This option is only for special purpose multi-user applications. It is dangerous to allow more than one user to write to the same file. You can corrupt or lose important data. Do not use the Many writers option except with multi-user applications specifically designed for this feature.

> | Note | The Remember button at the bottom of the Publish dialog box lets you auto-publish volumes at startup time. This feature is covered in Chapter Five, "Loading and Starting TOPS."

Unpublishing

Once you have published a volume, it is available to other users on the network. To take it off the network, you must unpublish it.

> **WARNING** You must unpublish all volumes before turning off your computer or unloading TOPS from memory. Turning a computer off with files published could cause client system crashes and loss of files.

To unpublish:

■ Highlight the volume you want to unpublish in the local window.

The Publish button changes to Unpublish (Figure 6-13).

■ Click on the Unpublish button.

The TOPS cube icon reverts to the original file icon and the volume is now unavailable to the TOPS network.

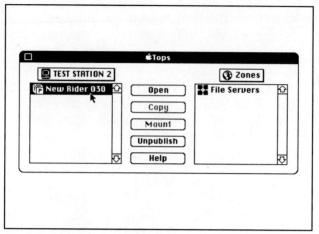

Figure 6-13. Clicking on a published folder changes the Publish button to Unpublish.

| Note | Unpublishing a volume unpublishes all the folders inside.

You cannot unpublish a volume if it is mounted on another machine. If you try to unpublish a volume while clients are using it, a warning box appears (Figure 6-14). The warning also appears if you try to shut down the system or eject published floppy disks.

WARNING If you have a non-Apple hard disk that uses a nonstandard shutdown procedure, you and your clients may not receive the warning boxes. It is always a good idea to make sure all your clients know when you are planning to shut down, eject a published disk, or unpublish a volume.

Mounting

So far you've learned to exchange files by publishing them on the network. That makes all or part of your disk available to other network users. Those users can then take information to or from your disk.

You can also exchange files by mounting a volume from someone else. Subject to certain restrictions, you can treat a mounted volume as if it were one of your own disks. You can copy files to or from it; or you can delete files.

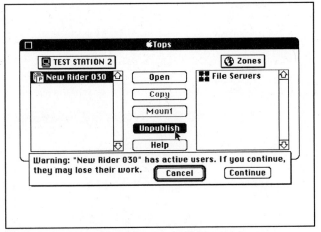

Figure 6-14. TOPS warns you if you try to shut down while a client has a volume mounted.

When you mount, you are operating as a client. Obviously, you can't mount a volume until somebody else has published it. Likewise, you won't always have unlimited access. The server might choose to publish with options, thereby limiting what you are allowed to do.

Finding the volume(s) you want

When you publish (when you act as a server), you work in the local window. That's where you select which volumes to make available to others. When you mount (when you act as a client), you work in the network window. That's where you choose which of the published volumes you want to use.

Through the network window you can see all the volumes available on the network. (Remember, though, that you can't always use everything you see. Some of the volumes may be password-protected.)

When you first bring up the TOPS DA, the network window lists all the file servers on the network. If your network is divided into zones, the label bar shows the name of your zone. If not, it reads "File Servers." Note that the list shows servers, not volumes. In other words, the list shows the name of every station that has published something, whether it published a single volume or twelve.

These servers are represented by a name and an icon. As

shown in Figure 6-15, a Mac station is represented by a Mac icon and a PC station by a PC icon.

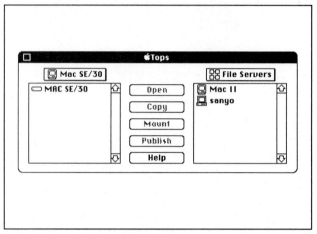

Figure 6-15. PCs and Macs have different icons in the network window.

In a zoned network, you can venture into other zones by first going back to the network level and then entering another zone. To return to the network level, position the cursor on the label bar. Click and drag down (Figure 6-16).

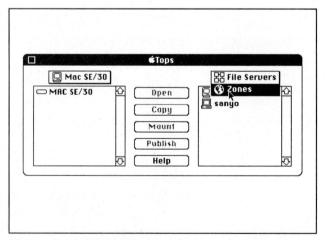

Figure 6-16. Click-drag to go back to the network level from a zone.

Most small networks don't have zones and, therefore, don't need to worry about navigating between them. Whether or not your network has zones, you move around the network window just as you do in the local window.

Tip When you first call up TOPS, it searches the network for all published volumes. If you suspect a new server has been added since you started, update the server list by double-clicking on the right label bar.

You must open a server to see which volumes have been published. To do so:

■ Highlight the name of the server.

■ Click on the Open button.

As a shortcut, you can simply double-click on the server name.

The label changes to show the name of the server. The list changes to show all the published volumes on that server. To search for a particular folder or file within a volume, you use the same procedure: You highlight the name and click Open. The list will change to show you the contents of that volume. You can continue in this fashion to move down the hierarchical tree by selecting and opening volumes and folders.

To move back up the file tree, click and hold on the label. A secondary menu drops down, showing you a list of the levels above the one you are on now. To move up, drag the mouse to highlight the level you want, and release the button.

Using the Mount button

Once you've found the volume you want to mount, all you have to do is hit the Mount button. To review:

■ Open the TOPS DA.

■ When the TOPS dialog box appears, find the volume you want in the network window. Click on it once to highlight its name.

The Mount button darkens as soon as you click on a published volume.

■ Click on the Mount button.

If the volume is password protected, the dialog box in Figure 6-17 appears. Type in the correct password. Be sure to use the exact spelling. To provide added security, the characters you type are replaced by a graphic element, so other people in the room can't see what you've typed.

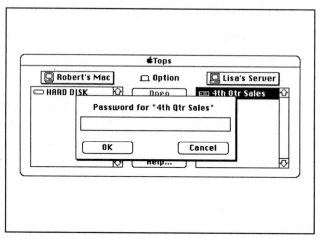

Figure 6-17. The Password dialog box gives you access to protected volumes.

If you enter the wrong password, you're returned to the password dialog box for another try.

If the volume is not password protected, you won't see the dialog box. The volume's icon is replaced by the TOPS cube icon (Figure 6-18). Once the volume is mounted, you can treat it as if it were a disk drive. You can copy and delete files and folders using standard Macintosh techniques.

If you mount a PC volume, TOPS assigns it a generic PC icon, as shown in Figure 6-19.

| Note | Just because you can access a file on a PC doesn't mean that your Mac applications will be able to use it.

A Macintosh can make use of PC files in two ways. First, you can use these files with *cross-platform* software. Such programs have versions for both the Mac and the PC. They either use the same file structure for both versions or they have a built-in translation utility. For example, Microsoft Word on the Mac can open files from the PC version of Word (and vice versa).

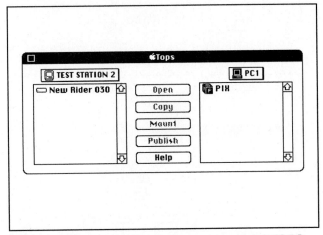

Figure 6-18. Mounted volumes get a special TOPS icon.

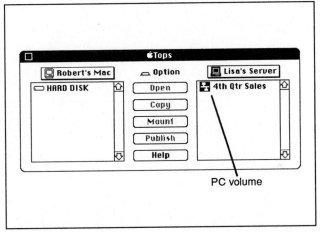

Figure 6-19. Mounted PC volumes have a special icon.

If your software is not cross-platform compatible, you can translate the PC files into a Mac file format with TOPS's built-in translators. Refer to Chapter Seven, "Translating Files with TOPS," for instructions.

Listing mounted volumes

You can mount up to six different volumes at a time. To see which volumes you've already mounted:

■ Click once on the label bar above the network window.

■ Click on the Help button.

The Mounted Volumes dialog box appears (Figure 6-20).

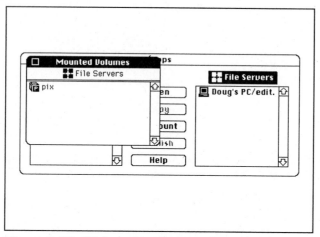

Figure 6-20. Click on the label bar and the Help button to view the Mounted Volumes dialog box.

Mounting with options

You saw earlier how to limit the access of others by publishing with options. You can also limit your own access by mounting with options. By limiting your access to published volumes, you can prevent accidental changes or deletions.

To mount with the normal default settings, you click on the Mount button. To mount with options, you click *and hold* on the Mount button. When the secondary menu appears, drag down to the Mount... option. The dialog box in Figure 6-21 appears.

You cannot use this dialog box to override the settings of the server. In other words, if the server published the volume as write-protected, you cannot unprotect it here. But you can use this dialog box to add additional protection if the server did not. The *Read only* option mounts the volume as write protected. The *Read/write* option gives you full access to the volume.

The right side of the dialog box contains two little-used options. The *Flat* setting refers to MFS volumes from early

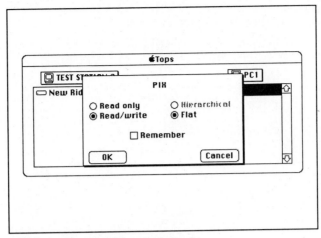

Figure 6-21. The Mount dialog box.

versions of the Macintosh. They are rarely used today. Most users will choose the default *Hierarchical* setting.

The Remember button at the bottom of the dialog box activates auto-mounting, as explained in Chapter Five, "Loading and Starting TOPS."

Unmounting

Whenever possible, unmount volumes as soon as you are finished using them. Servers cannot shut down their machines until all their clients unmount. If the servers forget and shut down anyway, you could lose data and experience other problems.

Before you can unmount a volume, you must close all the files. The best way to unmount is to drag the volume into Trash from the Finder. This is identical to the procedure you use to eject a floppy disk.

You can also unmount from within the TOPS Desk Accessory. The procedure is the same as unpublishing. You locate and highlight a mounted volume. The Mount button changes to Unmount. Click on the button to unmount the selected volume.

If you left any files open, a warning appears (Figure 6-22). Click on Continue or hit the Return key to go back to the TOPS DA. This message may come up even though you are not able to locate any opened files. Macintosh applications frequently write invisible files. If you unmount by dragging to the Trash, the Macintosh will save and close all files for you.

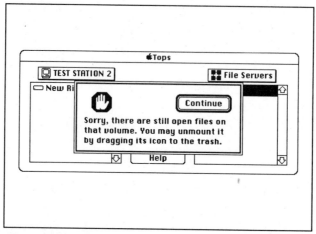

Figure 6-22. This message appears if you try to unmount a volume with open files.

Getting more information

We've already touched on some of your viewing options while explaining how to publish and mount. For instance, we showed you how to look for files and folders with the local and network windows in the TOPS DA. And we demonstrated how to list all the volumes you have mounted.

You have several other viewing options available through the Help button. To find out more about a volume, folder, or file, select it and click on the Help button. This action brings up one or more dialog boxes, depending on what you select.

If you select a volume, you see an Info dialog box like the one to the left in Figure 6-23. If you select an application, you see a dialog box like the one on the right.

If you select a document, two dialog boxes appear. The Info box gives file information. The Filtered Sample box (Figure 6-24) displays the document's contents.

Listing your clients

You can also use the Help button to get a list of your clients —

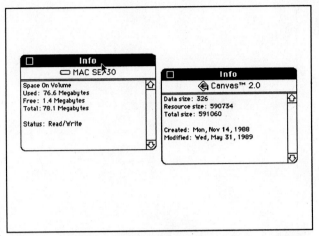

Figure 6-23. Clicking the Help button bring up details on volumes (left) or applications (right).

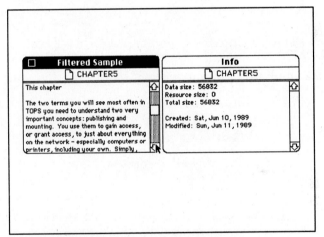

Figure 6-24. You can view the contents of a document with the Filtered Sample box.

that is, a list of the stations using a particular volume. First select the volume in the local window. Then click on the Help button. If the volume has been published, Dialog boxes like the one shown in Figure 6-25 appear.

Tip By moving the two overlapping windows away from each other, you can have a better view of their contents.

The user window gives you a list of the names of the stations that are accessing your system. In this example, a client Mac II is logged on to the Mac SE/30.

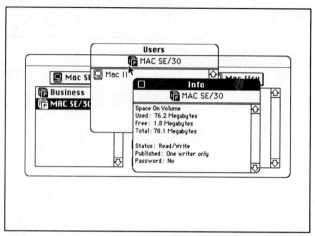

Figure 6-25. Select a published volume and click on Help to see these two windows.

Copying

The Macintosh version of TOPS has a utility not available on its PC counterpart — the ability to copy files to and from a published volume *without mounting that volume*.

To use the copy function, start the TOPS Desk Accessory. Then 1) locate the file, 2) locate its destination, and 3) copy it with the Copy button in the TOPS dialog box.

If the file is on your computer, look for it in the local window. If it's on another station, look for it in the network window. Select the file. Then open the destination. Once you have selected both a file and a destination, the Copy button darkens. Arrows show the file transfer direction (Figure 6-26).

Click on the Copy button to complete the file transfer. You must copy files one at a time if you are using the TOPS DA.

Copying with options

If you simply click on the Copy button, TOPS copies the file in its original form. However, if you click, hold, and drag down to the Copy... option, you can perform some limited file translation as you copy.

For more thorough and useful file translation, you will want to use the TOPS Translators, as covered in Chapter Seven. However, the translating option described below can be helpful for

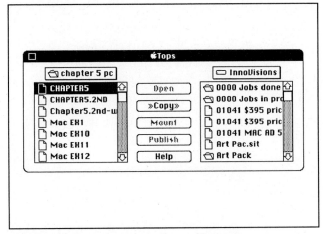

Figure 6-26. Once you select a file and a destination, the Copy button darkens and points the direction of the transfer.

moving text files for limited word processing between PCs and Macintoshes. Use it for files where the imbedded formating is not important.

When you click and drag to the Copy... option, the dialog box shown in Figure 6-27 appears. *Copy All Data* is the normal default choice. There's no need to click this button, or even to open this dialog box if this is the choice you want. It transfers the file complete with all its formatting commands. *Copy Text Only*, however, copies only the text data. All other information will be lost.

| Note | Whether the original file is a Mac file or a PC file, this copying function creates a Macintosh-format text file. It does not create a PC-style ASCII text file.

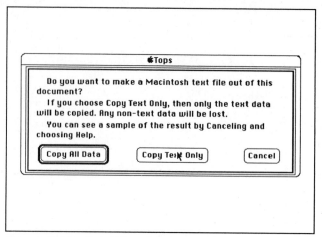

Figure 6-27. Copy Text Only strips out formatting codes while transferring the file.

■ Exchanging files on the PC

This section explains how to exchange files with a PC. You have two options. First, you can publish a volume from your own computer, and let someone else on the network mount the volume and copy the files. Or you can mount a volume that someone else has published. Once you mount a volume, you can treat it like a disk drive; that is, you can copy or delete files from it (unless the server has restricted access).

In this section, you will learn how to publish and how to mount. You will be using TOPS's optional menuing system. Please note, however, that you don't have to use menus to operate TOPS. If you prefer, you can run it from the command line (from the DOS prompt). Running TOPS from the command line is an advanced procedure that is covered in Chapter Eleven, "Customizing TOPS on the PC."

If you're using a PC, the TOPS menu program (TOPSMENU) has several benefits. It makes it simple to learn TOPS without having to remember a bevy of commands or complicated parameters. We recommend it for beginners. Once you feel comfortable running TOPS with the menus, you can experiment with the command line, using the tips in Chapter Eleven.

Speed start for PCs

Advanced users can use the quick tips in this section. Beginners will want to use the step-by-step instructions that follow instead.

You exchange files by publishing and mounting volumes so you can copy information to and from them.

To publish a volume:

■ Load TOPSMENU and go to the Main menu.

■ Select Server Utilities and press Enter.

■ Select Publish a Volume and press Enter.

■ Type in the full path name of the volume you wish to publish and press Enter.

■ Type in the alias and press Enter.

■ Type in the password (if any) and press Enter.

■ Accept the default Read only access by pressing Enter. Or type *W* and press Enter to change the access to Read/Write.

To list the published volumes:

■ From the Server Utilities menu, highlight Volumes Published and press Enter.

■ Highlight the volume and press Enter.

To list the clients:

■ From the Server Utilities menu, highlight File Clients and press Enter.

To unpublish a volume:

■ From the Server Utilities submenu, highlight Volumes Published and press Enter.

■ From the Volumes Published display, highlight the volume you want to unpublish and press the Del key.

To mount a volume:

■ Highlight Client Utilities from the Main menu and press Enter.

■ From the Client Utilities menu, highlight File Servers and press Enter.

■ Highlight the name of the server you want and press Enter.

■ Highlight the volume you want and press Enter.

■ Accept TOPS's drive designation by pressing Enter, or type in a different drive letter and press Enter.

■ Press Enter to accept the default access privileges of Read only. Or highlight Read and Write and press Enter to choose Read/write instead.

■ Type in the password (if any) and press Enter.

To list the mounted volumes:

■ From the Client Utilities submenu, highlight Volumes Mounted and press Enter.

To unmount a volume:

■ From the Main menu, highlight Client Utilities and press Enter.

■ From the Client Utilities submenu, highlight Volumes Mounted and press Enter.

■ From the list of mounted volumes, highlight the volume you want to unmount and press Del.

Using the Main menu

Chapter Five, "Loading and Starting TOPS," explained how to load TOPS into your computer's memory and how to bring up TOPSMENU, the optional menuing system. As you will recall, TOPSMENU is a separate module. You can load it by typing TOPSMENU from the DOS prompt each time you want to use it. Or you can put the TOPSMENU command into a batch file so it automatically appears each time you load TOPS.

After you see the intro screen (and enter your station name, if necessary), the TOPS Main menu appears (Figure 6-28).

Tip The different TOPS menus and submenus look similar

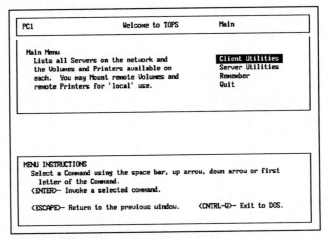

```
┌──────────────────────────────────────────────────────┐
│ ┌────────────────────────────────────────────────┐   │
│ │ PC1              Welcome to TOPS        Main     │   │
│ │                                                  │   │
│ │ Main Menu                                        │   │
│ │   Lists all Servers on the network and   │Client Utilities││
│ │   the Volumes and Printers available on    Server Utilities │
│ │   each. You may Mount remote Volumes and   Remember │
│ │   remote Printers for 'local' use.         Quit    │
│ │                                                  │   │
│ └────────────────────────────────────────────────┘   │
│                                                        │
│ ┌────────────────────────────────────────────────┐   │
│ │ MENU INSTRUCTIONS                                │   │
│ │   Select a Command using the space bar, up arrow, down arrow or first │
│ │     letter of the Command.                       │   │
│ │   <ENTER>- Invoke a selected command.            │   │
│ │                                                  │   │
│ │   <ESCAPE>- Return to the previous window.    <CNTRL-Q>- Exit to DOS. │
│ └────────────────────────────────────────────────┘   │
└──────────────────────────────────────────────────────┘
```

Figure 6-28. The TOPS Main menu.

at first glance. You can tell where you are by checking the upper right-hand corner of the top window.

The options are listed on the right side of the screen. An explanation of the currently selected/highlighted option appears to the left.

From this point you can select any options to begin using TOPS. With *Server Utilities* you publish. With *Client Utilities* you mount. With the *Remember* option, you tell TOPS which volumes to auto-mount or auto-publish (as explained in Chapter Five). *QUIT* does exactly what it says: It exits the menuing system and returns you to DOS.

| Note | Choosing the QUIT option unloads *only* the menuing system from memory. It does *not* unload the rest of the TOPS software. After quitting TOPSMENU, you can still run TOPS from the command line. You can also restart the TOPS menus at any time by typing TOPSMENU at the DOS prompt and pressing Enter. To remove TOPS from memory, use the TOPS UNLOAD command, as explained in Chapter Five.

To select an option from any TOPS menu, move the highlight from one option name to the next. You have three ways to select a menu option:

• Use the up and down arrow keys.

• Press the space bar to move the highlight down one item.

- Enter the first letter of the option's name. Some menus have more than one option name beginning with the same letter. If this is the case, entering a letter highlights the first menu item starting with that letter.

After highlighting the option you want, press Enter.

Publishing

To exchange files by publishing, you go to the Server Utilities submenu. Then you select and publish the volume you want to make available to the rest of the network.

Moving to the Server Utilities submenu

To view this submenu and its options, choose the Server Utilities from the Main menu:

■ Highlight Server Utilities and press Enter.

The Server Utilities menu appears. It displays either four or seven options, depending on whether or not you loaded the printer server module when you loaded TOPS. If you did not load the printer server, the submenu shows four options (Figure 6-29).

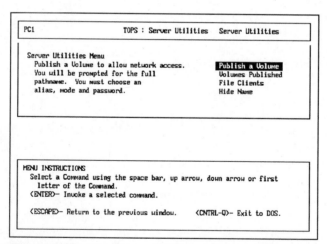

Figure 6-29. The Server Utilities submenu without printer options.

If you loaded the printer server module when you loaded TOPS, you will see an additional three options (Figure 6-30).

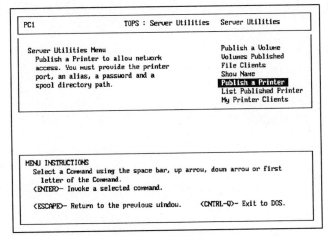

```
┌─────────────────────────────────────────────────────────────────┐
│ PC1                    TOPS : Server Utilities   Server Utilities │
│                                                                   │
│  Server Utilities Menu                    Publish a Volume        │
│   Publish a Printer to allow network      Volumes Published       │
│   access. You must provide the printer    File Clients            │
│   port, an alias, a password and a        Show Name               │
│   spool directory path.                   Publish a Printer       │
│                                           List Published Printer  │
│                                           My Printer Clients      │
│                                                                   │
│                                                                   │
│                                                                   │
│                                                                   │
│  MENU INSTRUCTIONS                                                │
│   Select a Command using the space bar, up arrow, down arrow or first │
│      letter of the Command.                                       │
│   <ENTER>- Invoke a selected command.                             │
│                                                                   │
│   <ESCAPE>- Return to the previous window.   <CNTRL-Q>- Exit to DOS. │
└─────────────────────────────────────────────────────────────────┘
```

Figure 6-30. The Server Utilities submenu with printer options.

This chapter explains the file utilities (the first four options). The Printer Server Utilities are explained in Chapter Eight, "Printing with TOPS."

This submenu gives you complete control over what to share with the rest of the network. With passwords, you can let some people use your directories (by giving them the password), while locking out those who shouldn't have access. Or, you can set a volume as read only, so others can look at the files, but not change them.

You must publish a directory to make its contents available to others on the network. Those other users mount the volume to gain access. You can publish any directory you like. All its subdirectories are automatically published along with it. You can even publish your entire disk, making every directory and subdirectory available.

The Publish a Volume submenu lets you see what directories you have on your disk. Publishing a volume requires you to:

1. find the volume you want to publish

2. select the volume

3. create an alias (or use the default name)

In addition, you can optionally:

1. assign a password

2. define access privileges

Finding the volume you want to publish

To locate the volume you want to publish from the Server Utilities submenu:

■ Highlight Publish a Volume and press Enter.

The Publish a Volume display appears (Figure 6-31).

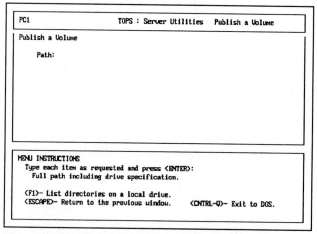

```
┌─────────────────────────────────────────────────────────────────────┐
│ PC1                        TOPS : Server Utilities   Publish a Volume │
├─────────────────────────────────────────────────────────────────────┤
│ Publish a Volume                                                      │
│                                                                       │
│      Path:                                                            │
│                                                                       │
│                                                                       │
│                                                                       │
│                                                                       │
│                                                                       │
│                                                                       │
├─────────────────────────────────────────────────────────────────────┤
│ MENU INSTRUCTIONS                                                     │
│    Type each item as requested and press <ENTER>:                     │
│       Full path including drive specification.                        │
│                                                                       │
│    <F1>- List directories on a local drive.                           │
│    <ESCAPE>- Return to the previous window.      <CNTRL-Q>- Exit to DOS.│
│                                                                       │
└─────────────────────────────────────────────────────────────────────┘
```

Figure 6-31. You'll see this display when you select Publish a Volume from the Server Utilities submenu.

The Path prompt appears in the upper left portion of the screen. TOPS is waiting for you to tell it where to find the directory you want to publish. You must enter a drive letter to identify its location:

■ Enter the drive designation. For instance, you would type *C:* if the directory was located on the C: drive, or *D:* if it was on the D: drive.

WARNING Do not press Enter yet, unless you want to publish the entire disk.

Tip If you are running a dedicated file server, publishing the root directory is the easiest way to give network users access to the server's files. Refer also to Chapter Five, "Loading and Running TOPS," for information on automatically publishing the root directory of a dedicated file server.

■ If you know the name of the directory you want to publish, type it in after the drive designator. For instance, to publish the \SALES subdirectory on the C: disk, you would type:

```
C:\SALES <Enter>
```

■ If you don't remember the name of the directory, display the directory listing by pressing the F1 function key. (Remember, do *not* press Enter yet.)

The directory listing appears in a window to the right side of the screen (Figure 6-32).

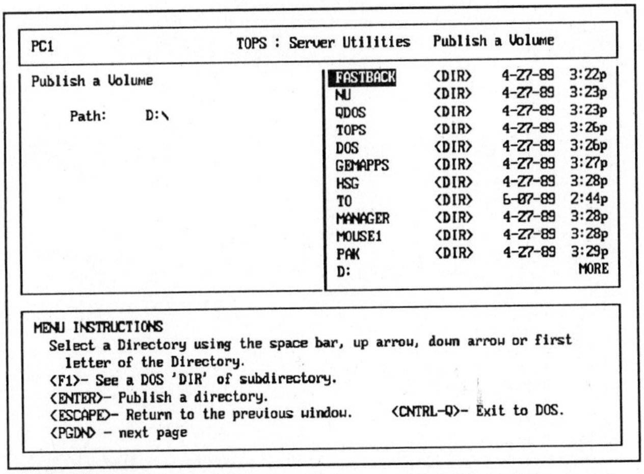

Figure 6-32. Type in the name of the disk drive and press F1 to see a list of the subdirectories on that disk.

To view additional directories:

■ Use the Page Up and Page Down keys to display more subdirectories if the MORE prompt appears at the bottom right corner.

To view subdirectories of subdirectories:

■ Highlight a directory, then press the F1 key again.

To return to the previous display of subdirectories:

■ Press the Esc key.

Selecting the volume

To select a volume for publishing:

■ Move the highlight to the directory you want to publish as explained above and press Enter.

As soon as you press Enter, the name and path of the directory appear in the Path prompt.

■ Verify that this directory is the one you want to publish. If so, press Enter again. If not, press the Esc key to cancel.

Entering an alias

■ Once you have selected the volume to publish, the Alias prompt appears (Figure 6-33).

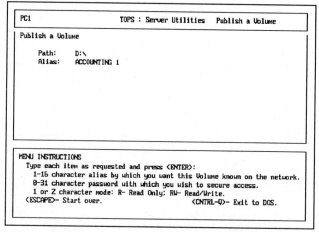

Figure 6-33. You can accept the alias TOPS generates from the directory name, or you can enter a new one of your own.

TOPS automatically provides an alias based on the directory name. You use this default name or create your own alias up to 16 characters long. This alias is the name everybody else sees on the network. If the directory name is not self-explanatory, create an alias that explains the contents.

■ To accept the default name, press Enter.

■ To create a new alias, type in the new name and press Enter. For instance:

```
C:\ 4TH QTR SALES <Enter>
```

Note │ TOPS allows you to use blank spaces in an alias.

Assigning a password

After you create an alias (or accept the default alias), the Password prompt appears (Figure 6-34).

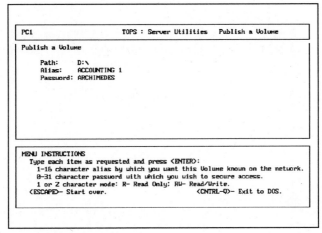

Figure 6-34. The Password prompt.

You should assign a password if you want to restrict access to certain individuals. A password can be up to 16 characters long and it can include spaces. Do not assign a password if you don't need the protection.

To assign a password:

■ Type in the password and press Enter.

To publish the directory without a password:

■ Press Enter.

Tip Choose passwords that prevent lucky guesses. Passwords such as *Password, Computer,* and *Open Sesame* do not provide adequate protection for sensitive files. On the other hand, don't make your passwords so difficult that no one can remember them. Keep them simple. It is self-defeating if passwords are so complicated that network users have to write them down. And remember, they don't have to relate to the subject they protect. (Some managers don't want the passwords to have anything to do with the subject.)

If you forget a password you assigned, you can assign a new one with the Volumes Published option from the Server Utilities menu (described in the next section).

TOPS, however, cannot display what the current password is, so it is a good idea to keep a list of all of your passwords in a safe place, just in case.

Restricting access
■ Whether or not you assign a password, once you press Enter the Mode prompt appears (Figure 6-35).

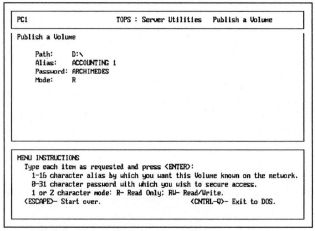

```
┌──────────────────────────────────────────────────────────────────┐
│ PC1                          TOPS : Server Utilities   Publish a Volume │
├──────────────────────────────────────────────────────────────────┤
│ Publish a Volume                                                   │
│                                                                    │
│     Path:      D:\                                                 │
│     Alias:     ACCOUNTING 1                                        │
│     Password:  ARCHIMEDES                                          │
│     Mode:      R                                                   │
│                                                                    │
│                                                                    │
├──────────────────────────────────────────────────────────────────┤
│ MENU INSTRUCTIONS                                                  │
│    Type each item as requested and press <ENTER>:                  │
│      1-16 character alias by which you want this Volume known on the network. │
│      0-31 character password with which you wish to secure access.  │
│      1 or 2 character mode: R- Read Only; RW- Read/Write.           │
│    <ESCAPE>- Start over.                   <CNTRL-Q>- Exit to DOS.  │
└──────────────────────────────────────────────────────────────────┘
```

Figure 6-35. The Mode prompt lets you restrict access to the volumes you publish.

The final step to publishing a volume is defining access privileges for the other network users. The default mode is Read only, represented by the letter *R*. Read only means no one can change the file. To allow other users to change files, you can change the mode to Read/write.

Tip Read only does not prevent other users from copying your files to their computers. It merely prevents them from changing or deleting the original file, and from writing other files onto your disk.

■ To accept the default Read only privileges, press Enter.

■ To change the access to Read/Write, type *W*. You will see both the *R* and the *W* on the screen. Then press Enter.

After completing these steps, the Working... prompt appears while TOPS publishes the volume. When the Path: prompt appears again, you can publish another volume using the same procedures. To end the publishing session and return to the Server Utilities menu, press Esc.

WARNING Do not remove a floppy disk if you currently have a volume published from that disk.

We do not recommend publishing all or part of a floppy disk because it significantly slows network traffic. However, if you must publish a floppy, do *not* remove it while any portion is published. You must unpublish it first.

Viewing a list of published volumes

So far, you've learned to use TOPSMENU's Server Utilities submenu to publish a volume. You can also use it to get a list of the volumes you have published and their attributes. Provided no one is using a volume, you can change its attributes, including the alias, password, and access privileges. Or you can unpublish any volume not currently in use.

To view a list of the published volumes:

■ From the Server Utilities menu, highlight Volumes Published and press Enter.

The Volumes Published display appears (Figure 6-36).

From the list of published volumes, you can select any volume and see who is using it:

■ Highlight the volume and press Enter.

The Clients Using display appears (Figure 6-37).

The Clients Using display indicates all the clients using the volume. If no one has mounted the volume, the No Clients prompt appears.

You can change the attributes of an unmounted volume. (You cannot change attributes if anyone is using it.) To change the alias:

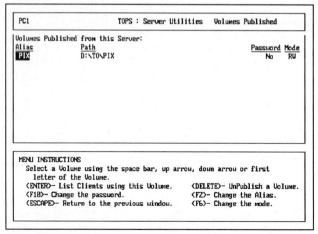

Figure 6-36. Select Volumes Published to see a list of the volumes published from this workstation.

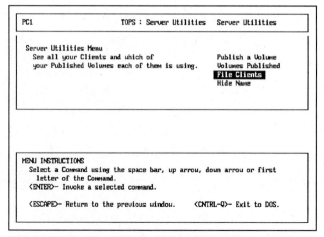

Figure 6-37. The Clients Using display shows you who has mounted your published volumes.

■ From the Volumes Published display, highlight the volume.

■ Select the alias by pressing the F2 key.

The current alias is erased, and the cursor jumps to the Alias column.

■ Type a new alias up to 16 characters long and press Enter

You can also assign, change, or remove a volume's password, provided no one is using it:

■ From the Volumes Published display, highlight the volume name.

■ Select the volume's password by pressing the F10 key.

The Password prompt appears in the middle of the screen.

■ Type in the new password and press Enter.

Press the Esc key to abort and keep the current password (if one has already been assigned). Press Enter without typing anything to remove the password.

You can also redefine a volume's access privileges, if no one has mounted it.

■ From the Volumes Published display, highlight the volume.

■ Select the volume's access mode by pressing the F6 key.

The present access privilege is erased, and the cursor appears in the Mode column of the Volumes Published display. At this point you can define the new access privileges:

■ Type *R* and press Enter to change the access to Read only.

■ Type *RW* and press Enter to change the access to Read/write.

> | Note | TOPS displays an error message if you try to change the alias, password, or access privileges of a volume currently in use. You must wait until the client has unmounted it.

Viewing a list of clients

The Server Utilities submenu also lets you see a list of all the clients who are using your volumes. For example, if you want to unpublish a volume, you might check to see who is using it first. You cannot unpublish a volume until the client unmounts it.

To display the list:

■ From the Server Utilities menu, highlight File Clients and press Enter.

The File Clients display appears (Figure 6-38).

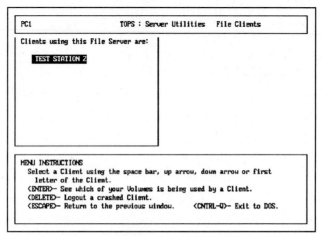

Figure 6-38. The File Clients display shows who is using the volumes you published.

From this list of active clients, you can select any client and check to see which specific volumes it is using:

■ Highlight the client name and press Enter.

The Volumes used by display appears (Figure 6-39).

```
┌────────────────────────────────────────────────────────────────┐
│ PC1                    TOPS : Server Utilities   File Clients    │
│ ┌─────────────────────────────┐                                 │
│ │Clients using this File Server are:│                           │
│ │                             │                                 │
│ │   TEST STATION 2            │                                 │
│ │                             │ ┌─────────────────────────────┐ │
│ │                             │ │ Volumes used by:  TEST STATION 2│
│ │                             │ │    PIX                      │ │
│ │                             │ └─────────────────────────────┘ │
│ └─────────────────────────────┘                                 │
│ ┌────────────────────────────────────────────────────────────┐ │
│ │ MENU INSTRUCTIONS                                           │ │
│ │                                                            │ │
│ │   <ESCAPE>- Return to the previous window.  <CNTRL-Q>- Exit to DOS.│
│ └────────────────────────────────────────────────────────────┘ │
└────────────────────────────────────────────────────────────────┘
```

Figure 6-39. The Volumes used by display shows all the volumes mounted by a particular client.

If no one has mounted any of your volumes, the No Clients using this File Server prompt appears.

Logging out a crashed client

If a client computer crashes, you can log out that client. This prevents your volumes from being tied up should you need to unpublish a volume. To log out a crashed client:

■ From the File Clients display, highlight the client you want to log out and press Del.

Hiding your station

In a few cases, you may want to remain on TOPS, but not have the other network users see your station name. This might occur if you want more security than just passwords. If a client can't see a volume, there will be little temptation to get into it. In essence, this option provides a primitive form of security. It allows you to operate on the network, but doesn't allow new clients to mount your published volumes.

To hide your station name:

■ Go to the Server Utilities submenu.

■ Highlight Hide Name and press Enter.

Your station name is now hidden from the network, and users can no longer mount a volume you have published. You will now see Show Name on the submenu. When you want to show your station name to the network again, select Show Name.

| Note | Anyone who mounted one of your volumes before you hid your name can still use the volume.

A safer and more logical way to keep others off your computer is simply not to publish anything. Or you can publish with a password so you can restrict who gains access.

Unpublishing

You can unpublish a volume and remove it from the network provided no one is currently using it:

■ From the Main menu, highlight Server Utilities and press Enter.

■ From the Server Utilities submenu, highlight Volumes Published and press Enter.

■ From the Volumes Published display, highlight the volume you want to unpublish and press the Del key.

Note │ TOPS displays an error message if you try to unpublish a volume currently being used. You must wait until the client unpublishes it.

Mounting

To retrieve information from another computer on the network, you mount a volume someone has already published. When you mount volumes, you are acting as a client. Your client options are more limited than your server options, but they follow the same pattern. You access these options from the Client Utilities submenu.

Moving to the Client Utilities submenu
To get to the Client Utilities submenu from the Main menu:

■ Highlight Client Utilities and press Enter.

The Client Utilities menu appears (Figure 6-40).

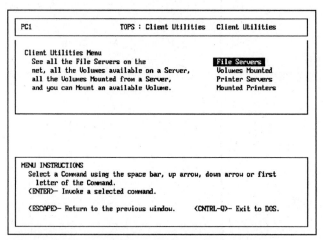

Figure 6-40. The Client Utilities submenu.

Note │ Depending on how your network is set up, you may or may not see a fifth option called *Change Zone*. If your network has more than one zone, you can use this option to move from one to another.

From the Client Utilities submenu, you can select options for mounting and related functions. Mounting a volume requires you to:

1. Select the volume.

2. Assign a drive letter to that volume.

3. Define the access privileges.

4. Furnish the password (if any).

Finding the volume

In order to mount a volume, you must first find and highlight it, using the File Servers option. This option shows you which file servers have published something. By selecting one of those servers, you can then see what volumes it has published. From there, you can mount the volume(s).

To select the server:

■ From the Client Utilities menu, highlight File Servers and press Enter.

The File Servers display appears (Figure 6-41).

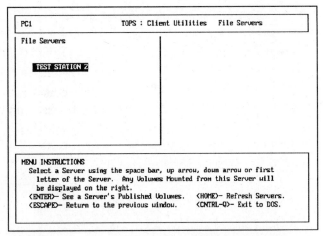

Figure 6-41. The File Servers display lists all the stations that have published at least one volume.

■ Highlight the name of the server you want and press Enter.

The Volumes Available display appears (Figure 6-42).

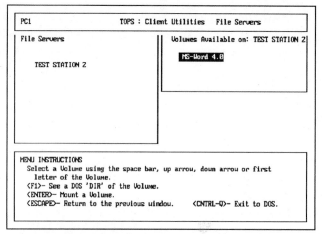

Figure 6-42. Highlight the server name and press Enter to see a list of the published volumes on that server.

If you have already mounted a volume from this server, that volume name appears in the lower right. You may need more information before you know if this is the right volume. To see the contents of a volume:

■ Highlight the volume name and press the F1 key.

The volume's directory listing appears on the left side of the screen. To see the directory listing of a subdirectory, highlight the subdirectory and press F1 again. Although you can look at subdirectories individually, you can only mount the entire volume. To return to previous levels, press the Esc key.

Tip If your network includes Macintosh or UNIX machines, the filenames will be shortened to fit the standard DOS filename format (eight characters, plus a three-character extension). To see the longer, original name, press the F3 function key. Each press of the F3 key switches back and forth between the short and long versions.

Selecting the volume

To select a volume for mounting:

■ Find the volume you want to mount. Highlight its name and press Enter.

After you select a volume, the Choose a Drive Letter prompt appears (Figure 6-43).

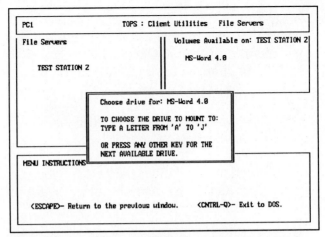

Figure 6-43. After selecting the volume you want to mount, you must give it a drive letter.

You will use the mounted volume just like another disk drive, so you should choose a letter that is different from your existing drives. If you let TOPS assign the letter on its own, it will automatically choose the next available letter. Thus, if you already have A:, B:, C:, and D: drives, TOPS will choose E: for the mounted volume. To accept TOPS's suggestion:

■ Press Enter.

You may prefer to choose a drive letter more closely related to the subject matter. If you mount a volume of letters, for instance, the drive letter L: might help you remember the contents. To choose a different letter:

■ Type in the letter followed by a colon and and press Enter. For example:

```
L: <Enter>
```

WARNING If you assign the drive letter of an existing drive, you can no longer access the local drive. You will not be able to access it until you unmount the volume.

Restricting access

You saw earlier how to restrict access to the volumes you publish. You can also restrict access to the volumes you mount. You might do this if you were worried about accidentally making changes to a file on someone else's computer.

After you assign a drive letter, the Access Mode prompt appears. This prompt asks you to define the access privileges for the mounted volume. Choose Read only if you do not need to make any changes to the files. Choose Read/write if you need to enter new data into a file.

| Note | You cannot override restrictions set by the server when the volume was originally published.

Read only is the default. It allows you to copy files to your own disks, but not to change the original file on the server. To accept the default choice:

■ Press Enter

To select Read/write privileges instead:

■ Highlight Write and Read and press Enter.

Entering the password
At this point, if the volume mount is password protected, the Password prompt appears. You must enter the correct password to mount a protected volume. To do so:

■ Type the password and press Enter.

TOPS passwords can use both upper and lowercase letters. Password entry is case-sensitive — that is, *Shazam* is different than *SHAZAM* or *shaZAM* or *sHaZaM*.

If you enter the wrong password, an error message appears. Retype the password correctly and press Enter.

If you cannot get the right password, press Esc to abort mounting this volume. Check with the TOPS network supervisor or the person who published that volume for the correct password.

If the volume has no password, you will not see the Password display. TOPS now proceeds to mount the volume. At this point, the volume you just mounted appears in the Volumes Mounted display in the lower right.

After completing these steps, you can mount more volumes up to a maximum number of drives allowed by your TOPSKRNL.DAT configuration file (the default is seven with two floppies and one hard drive). When finished, return to the Client Utilities menu by pressing Esc.

Viewing a list of mounted volumes

Use the Volumes Mounted option from the Client Utilities menu to see what volumes you have mounted. With this option, you can also unmount a volume you no longer need.

The Volumes Mounted display shows the volumes you have mounted listed by drive letter. The display also shows the server, the alias, and the access privileges.

To view the list of mounted volumes:

■ From the Client Utilities submenu, highlight Volumes Mounted and press Enter.

The Volumes Mounted display appears (Figure 6-44).

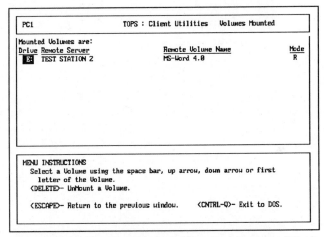

Figure 6-44. Select Volumes Mounted to see a list of the volumes currently mounted on your machine.

Unmounting

It is important to unmount volumes when you aren't using them. This frees up the computer that published the volumes and keeps traffic on the network to a minimum. An uncluttered network is a speedy network. To unmount a volume:

■ From the Main menu, highlight Client Utilities and press Enter.

■ From the Client Utilities submenu, highlight Volumes Mounted and press enter.

■ From the list of mounted volumes, highlight the volume you want to unmount and press Del.

The volume is now unmounted. You can no longer use it until you mount it again.

■ Continuing on

In this chapter, you learned some of the basic differences between Mac files and PC files, and how this affects your use of TOPS. You also learned how to exchange files by publishing and mounting volumes, from both the Macintosh and the PC.

But TOPS can do more than just exchange files. The Mac version also includes a special utility that lets you translate between different file formats as you copy. You'll learn to use this valuable function in the next chapter.

Chapter Seven

■ Translating Files with TOPS

In previous chapters we've reviewed TOPS's facilities for sharing files between workstations. If your network is homogeneous, that is, consisting of a single type of workstation, sharing files is as simple as transferring files from one machine to another. However, if you need to transfer files between dissimilar workstations, such as Macintoshes and PCs, getting the files from one location to another is only half the battle. They must also be translated from one format to another.

In this chapter, we'll examine strategies for converting files between formats. We'll look at TOPS's conversion facilities, as well as several additional options. The topics we'll cover include:

- Not converting at all. Many programs come in both Mac and PC versions, and can read files created in either version.

- Avoiding conversion by using programs that work with *universal* file formats such as ASCII, TIFF, Encapsulated Postscript, DXF, and others.

- Using the file conversion program provided with TOPS.

- Performing file conversions with *pivot* programs that read in files in one format and output in another.

Unlike many chapters in this book, this chapter will not apply to all TOPS users. Therefore, we encourage you to skim this chapter quickly to determine which sections will help you.

■ File formats

Before we go on, let's take a moment to review file format basics and terminology. You need to be familiar not only with the basic file formats on your system, but also with those on other systems in your TOPS network.

Macintosh files

We'll start with the Macintosh file format. Since we usually only encounter Mac files as icons on a desktop and because it is the most complex, the Macintosh file format is probably the least understood.

Each Macintosh file consists of two components, called *forks*. One fork is called the *data fork*, the other the *resource fork* (Figure 7-1). You can best visualize this structure like a combined salt and pepper shaker. Within the single unit one compartment holds the salt and another, separate compartment holds the pepper.

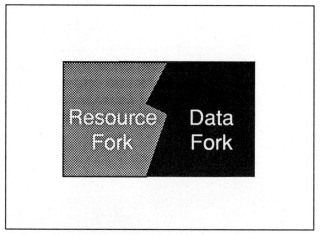

Figure 7-1. The two components of a Macintosh file.

The resource fork contains all of the system resources required by the file. If the file is a program, the resource fork will contain the program's icons, menu, dialog boxes, and other system components. If the file contains data, the resource fork will likely be empty, though not always.

Taken literally, the term data fork can be a bit misleading. In reality, the data fork stores program code as well as data code. If the file is an application program, then the data fork contains code. On the other hand, if the file contains spreadsheet data, a word-processing document, or other program data, the file's data fork might contain only data.

PC files

Life is much simpler on the PC. DOS files do not contain forks or- any of the complex or schizophrenic tendencies of their Macintosh counterparts. They contain either code (.COM and .EXE files) or data, with no other higher structure imposed upon them. And unlike Mac files, which can have lengthy filenames, DOS filenames are limited to eleven characters (eight in the filename and three in the file's extension).

Mac to PC file transfers

When a Mac file is transferred to a PC, the resource fork is sent to a hidden file and then ignored by DOS, since it has no meaning in the PC system architecture. Likewise, when a PC file is transferred to the Mac, all transferred data is placed in the data fork and the resource fork is left empty. The relationship between Macintosh and PC files is shown in Figure 7-2.

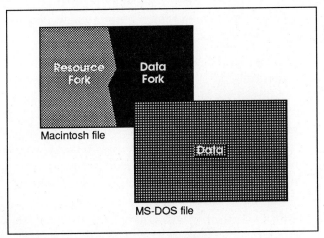

Figure 7-2. PC and Macintosh files.

■ Mac and PC programs

One of the simplest ways to avoid file conversion hassles is to use programs that have both Mac and PC versions, and can read data files from and write data files for the version running in the other environment. On the surface this looks fairly easy, and in many instances it has its merits. However, it is not without pitfalls.

For starters, there is the issue of choice. We'd like to think we choose the programs we use (or they are chosen for us) because they are best suited to the tasks at hand. All other things being equal, this is the way it should be. However, if we make a program's availability in both PC and Mac versions more important than their respective functionality, problems can arise.

Programs available in PC and Mac versions usually come from software publishers who have a best-selling program in one environment and wish to duplicate its success in the other. Good examples of this phenomenon are WordPerfect and Adobe Illustrator. Each was originally a market leader in the PC and Mac markets respectively. Versions were released for the other market with the hopes of realizing the kind of success enjoyed by the original product. As reviews have pointed out, not all of these crossover products have been successful in their new markets. Hence, standardizing on programs with both PC and Mac versions means that someone is likely to get stuck with a second-class program.

Even when a program is a contender in both the Mac and PC marketplaces, data files are not always 100% compatible. Certain features simply cannot be transported between the two environments due to their inherent differences. While this is seldom a major problem (in most cases the discrepancies are minor), it is something you should be aware of. You should also note revision-level differences between a program with offerings in both markets. While most publishers attempt to simultaneously release parallel versions, it doesn't always happen. In that case, it's a good bet that a PC version 2.0 won't read Mac 3.0 files. That guy Murphy again.

■ Common file formats

The next best thing to running the same program in both environments is using programs with the same file format. Although there are very few universal file formats in personal computers (and even fewer that function in both Mac and PC environments), there are enough that they deserve mention.

These universal file formats come in a variety of flavors. Some were designed from the ground up to be equally at home in Mac or PC systems. The TIFF file format is a good example. It can store a wide variety of bit-mapped images in either the Mac or PC environment. At present there appear to be seven dialects of TIFF, but the basic geometric information translates with only a slight accent.

Other universal formats are universal simply because no attributes tie them to one environment or another, or even to a specific program. ASCII text is a good example from this category.

Although the number of such formats is not particularly large, they can be useful. ASCII text is a common file format supported by over a hundred word-processing programs in both the Mac and PC environment. Unfortunately, ASCII text files cannot store all the features and attributes available in today's word-processing products. Nevertheless, most users consider the ability to transfer basic text worth the cost of losing font changes, bold and underline attributes, and other characteristics.

Common file formats can be quite useful as long as the transfer is unidirectional. Most programs can import far more file types than they can output.

The production of this book is an example. The layout was accomplished with Xerox Ventura Publisher. Because the book addresses both IBM PC and Macintosh systems, we needed screen captures from both systems as illustrations. On the PC side of things screen images were saved in IMG image file format. The Macintosh has a handy built-in screen capture facility that outputs MacPaint files. Ventura can read some dialects of this format directly, making it acceptable for Mac screen captures. Since the exchange did not need to be bidirectional, this combination of applications and file formats worked well.

■ TOPS Translators

TOPS for the Macintosh contains a set of translators useful for converting between various pairs of PC and Macintosh file formats. In many cases, the methods for sharing files listed above will not be sufficient. If programs are supported by the TOPS translators, this application can perform the necessary conversions.

Because the TOPS translators are implemented as a Mac application, you must translate files headed for an IBM PC before you actually copy the file from a Mac workstation to a PC. Conversely, if you are transferring a file from a PC to a Mac, you must copy the file first, then translate it once it is on the Mac. We've covered transferring files between TOPS workstations thoroughly in previous chapters, so we'll focus only on using the TOPS Translators application.

Starting the TOPS Translators

The TOPS Translators is an application program. It is not accessible from the Desk Accessories menu like the main TOPS program. It should already be installed on your system, preferably in its own folder. Start TOPS Translators by double-clicking on its application icon. The opening screen will appear (Figure 7-3).

Converting a file is a two-step process. First, tell TOPS Translators the file's current format and the format you want it converted to. The second step is selecting the file for conversion and telling TOPS Translators the name of the output file.

Setting up the translators

The opening screen lists formats in two windows. In the left window are the Macintosh Formats supported by TOPS Translators. On the right are the Foreign Formats. The word *Foreign* is rather misleading. Forgetting for a moment the implication that even dealing with non-Macintosh files is an

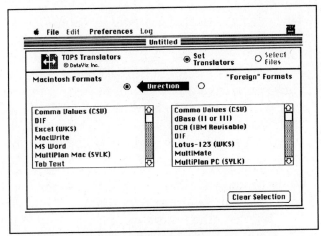

Figure 7-3. TOPS Translators opening screen.

act of treason, a quick review of the supported file formats reveals a list of PC applications. Perhaps the word was chosen to include both PC and Unix files. However, in reality you can think of the word *Foreign* as being synonymous with *IBM PC*.

Find the formats you need in each window, using the scroll bars if necessary. Then select them by clicking on their names. For example, if you wish to convert between Microsoft Word on the Mac side and WordPerfect on the PC side, find each of these formats and select them as shown in Figure 7-4.

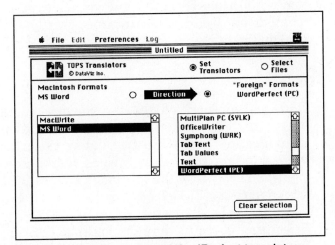

Figure 7-4. MS Word and WordPerfect translators selected.

Once you've selected the two file formats, you must tell TOPS Translators whether to convert from a PC to a Macintosh format or vice versa. A direction arrow pointing to the PC or Foreign file formats indicates that TOPS Translators will be converting from a Macintosh file into a PC file (Figure 7-4). If you wish to reverse the direction of the translation, click on the button at the other end of the arrow. This reverses the direction of the arrow and the translation process.

Although TOPS Translators supports a wide range of file formats, they are limited to three major applications groups: text (word processing), spreadsheets, and databases. Unfortunately, no translators exist for graphics files, for example MacPaint to PC Paintbrush or MacDraw to GEM Draw.

Also keep in mind that the translators only work between similar file types. For example, you can't convert between PC dBase files and Mac Excel.

Surprisingly, TOPS Translators doesn't support ASCII text very well. If you're hoping to convert a word-processing file (such as Microsoft Word on the Mac) into simple ASCII text on the PC, you are out of luck. First, you'll need to convert it into an IBM word-processing format such as WordStar or Word-Perfect. Then use the word processor to convert to ASCII. Most word processors already include an ASCII output function. Unfortunately, this function is not universally implemented (hard paragraph returns when you need soft ones, etc.) and requires an extra step even if it is.

Selecting files

Once you've specified the the conversion parameters, you must select the file to translate and a location for the translated file. First, set TOPS Translators to the Select Files mode by clicking on the button labeled Select Files in the upper right-hand corner of the screen. TOPS Translators' Select File screen appears (Figure 7-5).

Select the source file and the folder for storing the converted file by clicking on the appropriate Drive, Open, and Eject buttons. When you've selected both the file and folder, click on the Convert button.

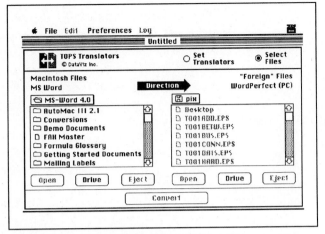

Figure 7-5. TOPS Translators Select File screen.

TOPS Translators will suggest a new name for the file and display it in the dialog box shown in Figure 7-6. Accept the name or enter one of you own. Then click on the OK button to start the translation process.

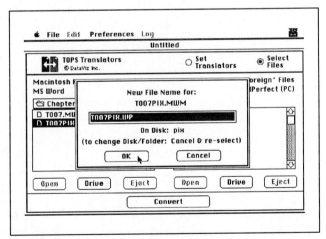

Figure 7-6. Entering the destination file's name.

When converting files from Mac to PC format, you must deal with the differences in the file-naming conventions. TOPS Translators uses the first eight characters of the Macintosh file name as the DOS filename. It then appends the appropriate file extension, based on the file format you specified for the destination file. Thus the file *Company Legal Notes for 1988* on the Mac becomes *COMPANY .DOC* — not a particularly illuminating filename — if you send it to the PC as a Microsoft Word file. Therefore, it's a good idea to enter your own filename rather than accepting the default name proposed by TOPS Translators.

■ Pivot programs

The final method of file conversion has a high Rube Goldberg factor but is useful when no other methods will do. In essence, these programs can import and export multiple file formats. They can take an input file, either from a different system or an intermediate file from the TOPS Translators, and output the final format you are looking for. Figure 7-7 shows the operation of a pivot program schematically.

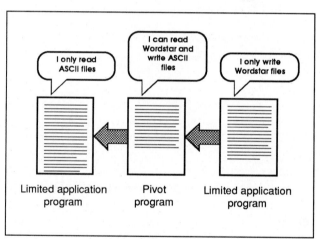

Figure 7-7. Operation of a pivot program.

To help you understand the uses of a pivot program, let's expand our earlier example about making this book. We mentioned that Mac screen snapshots were captured using the Macintosh's system capture function. These files were then copied to a PC where the book was being prepared using Xerox Ventura Publisher. Ventura imported these MacPaint files using the program's native conversion capabilities.

As long as the screen captures were exactly as we wanted them, this method worked fine. But what if they needed to be edited before they were placed in the book? Ventura has no editing capabilities for image files. On the PC side, our screen captures were stored in GEM image format and we could edit them with GEM Paint. But how could we get the Macintosh's screen images (stored in MacPaint format) into GEM image format for editing?

The answer lay in Ventura's ability to convert between several image formats on the input side and the GEM image format on the output side. Loading the Mac screen images into Ventura allowed us to produced output files in GEM image format. These files could be edited, then imported back into Ventura.

As you see, the process of using pivot programs can be somewhat long and tedious. On the other hand, it is often the only way to convert between the desired Mac and PC file formats. Therefore it should not be overlooked.

■ Continuing on

This chapter has shown you three ways to exchange files between Macs and PCs. Now all that's required on your part is some experimentation to find out which method works best for you. The next chapter will show you the ins and outs of printing on and with a TOPS network.

Chapter Eight

■ Printing with TOPS

In previous chapters, we've mentioned the printing capabilities of TOPS. Now we'll take a closer look.

■ Network printing defined

One advantage of local area networks is their ability to access shared data and peripherals. It is often difficult to justify an expensive peripheral, such as a large capacity hard disk, tape backup unit, or laser printer, when it can only be used by one individual. Such equipment becomes much more affordable and attractive if more than one person can use it. In many workgroups, a PostScript laser printer is the most expensive hardware, and hence an excellent candidate for a shared resource. Fortunately, TOPS makes network printing not only more affordable, but easy to use as well. Even Novell and 3Com networks, which in many ways are far more sophisticated than TOPS, lack TOPS's flexibility when it comes to sharing printers.

Before we jump into this subject, we should mention that this chapter, unlike the rest in this book, is designed primarily with IBM PC TOPS users in mind. AppleTalk is already a resource-sharing mechanism. Allowing more than one user to share a LaserWriter or ImageWriter was one of AppleTalk's primary objectives. Consequently, it leaves little for TOPS to improve on. The IBM PC, on the other hand, presents a real opportunity. The designers of the IBM PC seemed intent on making sure you attach more than one printer to each computer. So if you are an IBM PC user and your TOPS network has common printers, read this chapter carefully.

In this chapter, we'll show you how to get the most out of your printers, whether you're using:

- a shared printer

- a local printer

- a network printer

In addition, you'll learn to speed up your printing with print spooling. But first, let's discuss what we mean by shared, local, and network printers.

First things first

As you've probably guessed by now, learning the lingo is half the battle of mastering a network. Printers are no exception, but we'll restrict ourselves to a few new terms in this chapter, namely *local printer*, *shared printer*, and *network printer*. We'll also clue you in on the difference between TPRINT and NETPRINT.

Local printers

Local printers are connected locally to a specific computer. A local printer can only be accessed from the system connected to it. Although we often think of a local printer being attached to a standalone computer, local printers can also be linked to systems in a network. What separates a local printer from shared printers is that *local printers can only be accessed by the computer to which they are attached.*

A local printer can be any type: PostScript, HP LaserJet or compatible, Epson MX/FX-80 or compatible, and so on. Since most Apple printers were designed to be shared, local printers are more likely to be attached to IBM PCs in a TOPS network.

Shared printers

A shared printer is attached to one workstation in network, just like a local printer (Figure 8-1). But a shared printer is accessible to everyone on the network. As a matter of fact, even the computer to which it is attached must access a shared printer through TOPS.

A printer is designated as a shared printer once it has been *published*. For now, think of publishing a printer like publishing a disk drive or directory. Once a printer has been publish-ed, any user on the network can mount it. The process is the same as mounting a disk drive or directory, which we've al-ready covered. We'll discuss publishing and mounting printers in more detail in the next section.

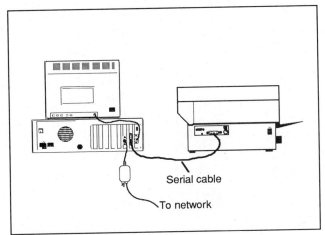

Serial cable

To network

Figure 8-1. A shared laser printer connected to an IBM PC.

Network printers

A network printer is attached directly to the network, rather than to one of the computers. A section of a typical TOPS network with an IBM PC and a LaserWriter is illustrated in Figure 8-2. Compare it with the illustration of a shared printer in Figure 8-1. Although any printer that can attach to an AppleTalk network can be configured as a network printer, in today's marketplace, network printers are generally limited to PostScript laser printers. Of course, if Hewlett-Packard ever decided to put an AppleTalk port on the HP LaserJet, it could be a TOPS network printer.

One final point should be made about the term *network printer*. Up to now we have used the term somewhat fast and loose, applying it to any printer connected to a network, regardless of how that connection is made. Now that we have defined the terms *local printer*, *shared printer*, and *network printer*, we will use them precisely from here on. We will only use the term *network printer* when referring to a printer connected directly to a TOPS network, as described above.

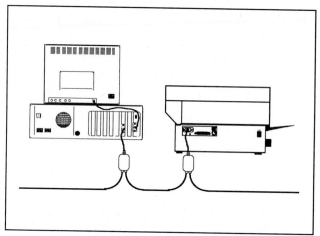

Figure 8-2. A network laser printer connected to a TOPS network.

■ Printing to a shared printer

Now that we've defined the different types of printers in a TOPS network, let's see how to use them. In this section, we'll focus on shared printers.

Like its cousin the shared drive, a shared printer must be published and mounted. And like the disk drive, there's more than meets the eye to successfully configuring a shared printer to meet the needs of a TOPS workgroup.

Publishing a shared printer on your IBM PC

Before a printer can be shared, it must be *published*. Publishing converts a local printer into a shared printer. It stands to reason, then, that a printer must be connected directly to the system that is going to publish it. Also, a printer can only be published on a system that has server software loaded. In other words, a workstation set up for client-only operation *cannot* publish a printer.

Tip The best things in life aren't free, and neither is print server capability. In fact it costs 45K (of RAM that is) more than file server capability for a grand total of 200K. Add to this figure DOS, the PC FlashTalk, or Ethernet drivers and you've eaten up half of the memory in a 640K system. This barely leaves enough room for most PC application programs, and you can only dream about running Windows, Lotus 1-2-3, Ventura Publisher, or any other large memory program on a system with print server capabilities. Clearly not every workstation is destined to be a print server.

If your network has multiple printers, be judicious in your selection of shared printers. Publishing an 80-column Epson MX-80 while leaving an HP LaserJet attached locally to a workstation doesn't make much sense. Typically, you should publish the fastest, most capable, and most widely supported printer.

Before you publish a printer, you must load the TOPS printer server software. The TOPSPRTR module provides printer server capabilities. You must load the TOPSTALK and TOPSKRNL modules first, so you will probably want to add it to the AUTOEXEC.BAT file or other batch file used to load the TOPS file server modules. If you use the LOADTOPS command to load the TOPS file server modules, you'll still need to load TOPSPRTR, since the print server software is not automatically loaded by that program. See Chapter Five, "Loading and Starting TOPS," for complete instructions.

Tip Make sure that all users can boot the system acting as a printer server. Otherwise, you won't be able to use the printer if the system's owner calls in sick or routinely decides that 10:00 A.M. is a far more civilized time to start the workday.

Once the TOPSPRTR software is loaded, you can publish a printer. Keep in mind that *loading the TOPSPRTR software does not publish the printer*. That task is accomplished by the TOPS PUBLISH or the TOPSMENU commands. We'll look at the TOPS PUBLISH command first, since it yields the greatest understanding of how a shared printer is published. In addition, you will probably find TOPS PUBLISH more useful, since it can be included in a batch file, and executed automatically when the system is booted or TOPS is loaded.

TOPS PUBLISH command
The TOPS PUBLISH command is entered at the DOS prompt to designate a printer as shared. The syntax of the command is as follows:

```
TOPS PUBLISH device AS printer USING path [/E]
[/P [password]] <Enter>
```

Look imposing? Let's divide and conquer. We'll take the command line one part at a time.

TOPS PUBLISH — This tells TOPS you wish to publish a resource. Note that this is the same way the command to publish a disk drive or directory from the command line starts.

device — The next parameter in the command line is the DOS name of the local printer. Round up the usual suspects for this one: LPT1:, LPT2:, PRN:, COM1:, and so forth. The colons are necessary to distinguish between a printer device and a file name. Otherwise, TOPS PUBLISH will attempt to find a directory called LPT1 and publish it instead of the printer device LPT1:. It's a small distinction, but an important one.

printer — This parameter is the name the published printer will be known as on the network. This name can contain up to 16 characters and range from the sublime to the ridiculous. Descriptive names such as HP LaserJet, NEC SilentWriter, etc. are always appropriate.

path — The path parameter tells the printer server software where to store the spool files. We'll cover spooling in more detail later in this chapter.

/E — This parameter is optional. If you include it in the command line, the print spooler directory will be cleared (nuked, zapped, obliterated), so be careful if you use this switch.

/P [password] — The /P parameter is also optional. If you wish to limit access to a printer, you can require that users enter a password when they mount that printer. You can enter the password in the command line, or wait for TOPS to prompt you for one by entering only the /P parameter.

Let's look at a simple, but fairly common example to put all of this together. We'll use the system shown in Figure 8-3, consisting of three IBM PCs with an HP LaserJet hooked up to one of the systems.

Let's further assume that the printer is connected to Jedd's system on the LPT1: printer port, that Jedd wants the spool

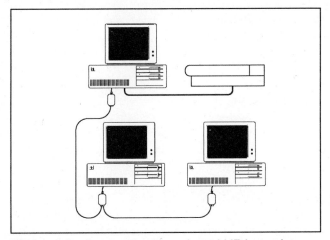

Figure 8-3. A network with a shared HP LaserJet.

directory to be C:\SPOOL, and that the printer is to be christened *Jedd's Jet*. Assuming all of this, the TOPS PUBLISH command that Jedd would enter to publish the printer is:

```
TOPS PUBLISH LPT1: AS JEDD'S JET USING C:\SPOOL
<Enter>
```

Note that each of the parameters shown in the example above is required. You'll also note that we haven't used any of the optional parameters. For most installations, they aren't necessary. Now that we've examined the TOPS PUBLISH command with it various parameters, let's look at publishing a printer using TOPSMENU.

Publishing a printer with TOPSMENU

As we've discussed in previous chapters, TOPSMENU is a menu-driven program that accomplishes many of the same tasks carried out by the TOPS commands. Its purpose is to let you carry out file and printer publishing and mounting operations from one program, as opposed to typing in commands.

The TOPSMENU program is started from the DOS prompt by entering:

```
TOPSMENU <Enter>
```

The TOPSMENU main menu screen will be displayed. Select the Server Utilities. One of the Server Utilities menu items is Publish a Printer. Select the Publish a Printer menu item and press return. You should see the Printer Server submenu shown in Figure 8-4.

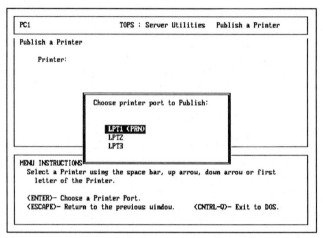

Figure 8-4. TOPSMENU Publish a Printer submenu.

You need to give TOPS specific information to publish a printer. The TOPSMENU Publish a Printer screen contains four fields for this information. Let's look at each one.

1. The first field indicates the local printer you wish to publish. Select the port the printer is connected to. In most cases this will be LPT1:, although any port may be selected. Keep in mind that you can only publish one printer per workstation.

2. The next field is the printer's network name, sometimes referred to as an alias. Enter a name up to 16 characters in length, preferably a descriptive one.

3. Like the TOPS PUBLISH command, you can also enter a password, forcing each user to invoke the password in order to mount the printer. If you don't want to restrict access, simply press return. Unlike restricting files or directories, restricting access to a printer doesn't make much sense unless one of your co-workers is prone to printing pornographic material or queueing 1,000 page print jobs. But if you do want a printer to be private, you can use the password option — or just keep the printer local.

4. The Spool Directory is a required field. TOPS stores the printer stream from your applications in spool files (speed-

ing up the printing time in an application significantly). TOPS then sends the contents of these files to the printer in the background, while you continue working in the foreground. When the print job is complete, the spool file is deleted, freeing up the disk space it occupied. You must enter the path of the directory you wish TOPS to use for its spool files. Keep in mind that you must enter a directory that already exists; TOPSMENU will not create the directory if it isn't already present on the disk. If you aren't sure which directories currently exist on the disk, press the F1 function key. A list of directories will be displayed on the screen, as shown in Figure 8-5.

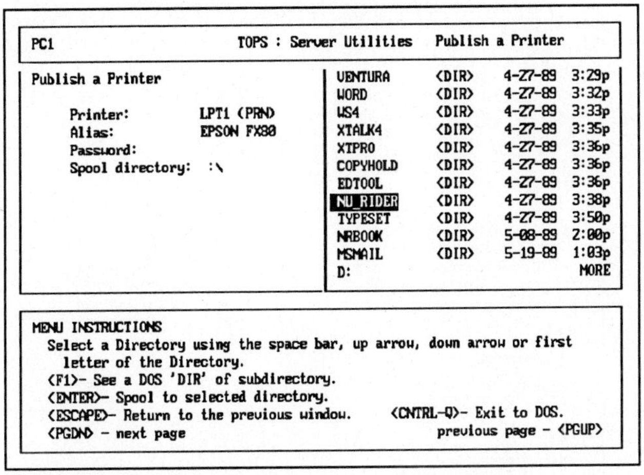

Figure 8-5. Selecting a Spool Directory.

Highlight the directory you want for the Spool Directory. Then press Enter to select it.

Once you've entered this information, check it for accuracy. If you wish to change any of the data, use the up and down arrow keys to highlight the field you wish to change, then enter the correct information. If you decide you don't really want to publish the printer, press the Escape key.

That's all there is to it. Your printer is published and may now be mounted and used by others on the TOPS network.

Mounting a shared printer

Once a printer has been published, any member of a TOPS network can mount it and use it. In this section, we'll show you how to mount a published printer, completing the connection between your application program and the shared printer.

To mount a shared printer, you'll need to call on TOPSMENU again. Start the TOPSMENU program by going to the DOS prompt and entering:

```
C:\TOPS\TOPSMENU <Enter>
```

(We're assuming you put TOPS in the C:\TOPS subdirectory. If not, substitute your actual location.) Select Client Utilities from the TOPSMENU main screen. Once you've selected Client Utilities, your screen looks like Figure 8-6.

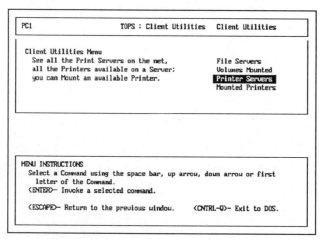

Figure 8-6. TOPSMENU Client Utilities screen.

Two menu selections in the Client Utilities screen relate to shared printers. The first, *Printer Servers*, allows you to find out which printers have been published and provides the mechanism for mounting these printers. The second menu item, *Mounted Printers*, lets you query the status, names, and other information about the shared printers you have mounted. Since you must mount a printer before it will show up in the Mounted Printers display screen, let's start with the Printer Servers menu item. Highlight it using the cursor keys, then press Enter. Your screen will look like Figure 8-7.

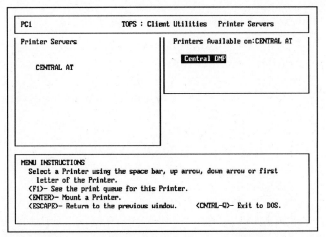

Figure 8-7. TOPSMENU Client Printer Servers screen.

The upper left-hand box contains a list of all print servers in your zone. A print server is the workstation that published the printer. If you want a list of print servers in other zones, press the F1 key. Additional zones on your network will be displayed, and you can select the zone you wish to review.

Once you have selected the print server, the list of attached printers appears in the upper right-hand box. To select the printer, highlight the printer name and press Enter. The final step in mounting the printer is to tell TOPS which local printer port you wish to assign to the shared printer. The printer is now mounted and can be used by your application programs.

Tip Keep in mind when you are assigning one of your system ports to the shared printer that the port does not actually need to exist on your system. For example, let's say you have a system with an IBM ProPrinter connected to LPT1: that you wish to keep as a local printer. You also want to mount the shared printer Jedd's Jet. You can assign Jedd's Jet to LPT2: which doesn't actually exist on your system, keeping your ProPrinter available on LPT1:.

The hardest part of using a shared printer is publishing and mounting. Now that you've cleared that hurdle, you only have a few more steps to go. In the next section, we'll explain how to use a shared printer from an application program.

Printing from an IBM PC application

In many respects, printing to a shared printer from within an IBM PC application is no different than printing to a local printer. That's one of the beauties of TOPS: its ability to provide network functionality without getting in the way.

Selecting the printer port

The first factor to consider when using a shared printer is the port your application is printing to. With a local printer using a parallel interface, you simply hook it up to LPT1: and off you go; everything just works. Life gets a little more complicated if your local printer hooks up via a serial interface rather than a parallel one, or if you have two or more local printers. The same is true with a TOPS shared printer.

Tip If you don't have any local printers connected to your system, it is a good idea always to mount a shared printer as LPT1:. This is the default output port for most IBM PC applications, and therefore the output port selection that will give you the greatest compatibility.

Still more complications arise if you have a local printer to be used along with a shared printer on the TOPS network. You'll need to review which applications you'll be using with the local printer and which ones with the shared printer. Let's look at an example of a system with a local printer with 132-column capability, and an HP LaserJet as a shared printer. We'll further assume that Lotus 1-2-3, WordPerfect, and Xerox Ventura Publisher are the major applications. The local printer will be used for the output from Lotus because of its 132-column capabilities. WordPerfect and Xerox Ventura Publisher need the print quality of the HP LaserJet, so the shared printer will be used as the output for these programs. Now, which printer will be configured as LPT1: and which as LPT2:?

Most IBM PC printer interface cards can be configured as either LPT1: or LPT2:, although LPT1: is almost always the default. So our local printer is a good candidate for LPT1:, since the printer card is probably already configured that way. The next question is whether WordPerfect and Ventura can address a printer at LPT2:. Since the answer is yes, the shared printer should be mounted as LPT2:. That means WordPerfect and Ventura (and any other applications programs wishing to use the shared printer) will need to be configured to output to an HP LaserJet on output port LPT2:.

Application printer configuration

Configuring an application program for a specific printer has always been an issue in the IBM PC, so this topic isn't new for most readers. In most standalone systems, though, your application programs only have to be configured for a single, locally attached printer. In a TOPS environment with shared printers, you may have two or more dissimilar printers available. You want to be able to access them all from within your applications.

Most newer IBM PC programs support multiple printer configurations and allow you to switch between various printers. Examples of these programs are WordPerfect, any Microsoft Windows program, and any GEM program (including Xerox Ventura Publisher). To work with these programs, simply install the necessary printer drivers to match the local and shared printers you have available.

Tip Wherever possible, designate a printer that prints plain ASCII text as LPT1:. This allows you to use DOS to redirect DOS output to a printer and run older application programs without problems. Most dot matrix printers and laser printers designed for IBM PCs fit this bill. You should avoid using a PostScript printer as LPT1:.

Printing from DOS using TPRINT

Once you have mounted a shared printer, it functions just like a local printer with a single exception; you cannot use the DOS PRINT command to print files to that printer. You must use the TOPS TPRINT command instead. The TOPS print queue conflicts with the DOS print queue established by the DOS PRINT command. Keep in mind as you review this section that TPRINT is only necessary when printing files from the DOS prompt. If you only print from within applications, you don't need to use TPRINT.

Tip To avoid confusion we recommend that you rename the DOS PRINT.COM program to PRINT.$$$ or some other filename that won't execute, or better yet delete it from your system. This way you won't accidentally run PRINT when you really should be using TPRINT.

The command syntax for TPRINT is very similar to the DOS PRINT command:

```
TPRINT /R LPT# [/Q] [/T] [filename1,
filename2..] <Enter>
```

Let's take a look the components of the command line to see how they are used.

TPRINT /R — This tells TOPS to add a file to a remote printer's queue, or interrogate the status of the queue. The TPRINT command is used to manage other printing tasks, so it is important to remember the /R parameter.

LPT# — This tells TOPS which printer port you'd like to print to. Although it's a bit indirect, this parameter tells TOPS which mounted printer you'd like to print to. When you mount a shared printer, you must assign it a printer port alias. The TPRINT command uses this port alias to identify which printer you want.

/Q — The /Q parameter instructs TPRINT to display the contents of the specified printer's queue.

/C — This parameter must precede the filename(s) of a file you wish to delete from the shared printer's queue.

/T — The /T command deletes all of *your* print jobs from the remote printer's queue. Note that you are the only one who can control your files in a remote printers queue. By the same token, you cannot control the files placed in a remote printer's queue by other users on the network.

filename1, filename2... — If you enter one or more filenames without the /T parameter, these files will be added to the queue of the remote printer. When you enter the filenames, be sure to include the full path specification if they aren't in the current directory. If the /T parameter is encountered in the command line, TPRINT will delete the file(s) you name from the remote printer's queue.

If you are familiar with the DOS PRINT command, you'll notice the similarity between PRINT's and TPRINT's command syntax.

■ Printing to a local printer

Before we jump into our discussion of network printing, we'll spend a moment reviewing local printing. If your first reaction is "Why should I have to do anything special for local printing?", your instincts are right on. Since printing from your workstation is a local transaction, why should TOPS get in the middle of it? The answer depends on whether you are printing from an application or from the DOS prompt.

If you are doing local printing from within any IBM PC application, TOPS is not involved in any way. You don't have to do anything that you wouldn't have to do anyway.

On the other hand, if you are printing from the DOS prompt, you must use TPRINT, as demonstrated in the previous section, with a single exception. Instead of entering the /R parameter to indicate you are printing to a shared printer, you must enter /P in its place to communicate to TOPS that you wish to print to a local printer. TPRINT interprets all the other parameters (/Q, /C, /T, filename1...) the same as for a shared printer.

However, before you rush out and attempt to print a file to a local printer, there's one more step you must address. You need to install a background print queue. If you've published a local printer, this is already taken care of. The TOPSPRTR command installs a background print queue that can be used by other users when they print to your local printer, as well as by TPRINT to queue print files from your workstation. If you haven't published a local printer, you'll need to load the TOPS background print scheduler INITPRIN.

INITPRIN is loaded from the DOS prompt with the command line shown below.

```
INITPRIN LPT#:
```

Simply enter the command INITPRIN followed by the printer port your local printer is connected to. TOPS will make sure a printer is connected. Then install a background print scheduler for that port. Once you've run the INITPRIN command, you can use TPRINT to add files to the local printer's queue, as well as interrogate the printer queue's status. Of course, you can still print directly to the local printer from your application program, just as you can with the DOS PRINT command. If you attempt to print from an application while the background print scheduler is busy printing a file, the application will be getting a busy message, so it must wait until the background queue is empty. Other than this, it's business as usual.

Network printing

In its simplest form, network printing involves printing from a TOPS workstation to a printer connected directly to the network, rather than to one of the workstations. As such it has the potential of being a rather complicated topic, considering the number of permutations of workstations and printer types. While the possibilities are almost endless, the reality of network printing under TOPS is closer to generic vanilla ice cream than to Baskin-Robbins 31 flavors.

Let's start by examining the printer. In order for a printer to be networked directly, as opposed to shared over the network, it must be physically attached to the network. In the case of TOPS, that means it must have an AppleTalk or Ethernet port. Currently, the Apple ImageWriter and PostScript printers, such as the Apple LaserWriter, QMS PS Jet+, and Varityper VT 600, are the only printers that come equipped with an AppleTalk port. To find a printer with an Ethernet port we have to enter the rarefied atmosphere of $100,000 high-speed page printers, effectively nullifying this category. By default, we've narrowed the printer field to PostScript laser printers equipped with an AppleTalk port.

On the workstation end we have a similar situation. While any workstation should be able to access a networked Post-Script printer over AppleTalk under TOPS, this is not the case. As we stated earlier in this chapter, while AppleTalk arguably has its faults as the basis of a local area network, it is unexcelled as a printer sharing scheme. Hence, the folks at TOPS realized that they could not improve upon Apple's system, and wisely choose to omit this capability from TOPS. Mac users, therefore, don't use TOPS to print to network printers.

So then, what do we have to talk about? Well, in most TOPS

networks we're left with IBM PCs sharing network PostScript printers over AppleTalk. Fairly specific stuff.

NETPRINT vs. TPRINT

Two TOPS programs support network printing. Depending on what type of printing you are doing, you'll need to use one or both of them.

NETPRINT will probably be the program you'll use the most. It allows you to print to a network printer from within your application. The next section in this chapter describes NETPRINT's use in detail.

Occasionally, you will want to print to a network printer from the DOS prompt, in much the same manner as you use the DOS PRINT command on a local printer. In order to accomplish this, you must use the TPRINT command. If you remember from the previous section, TPRINT is also used to print to a shared printer from the DOS prompt. Using TPRINT with a network printer is discussed in a later section.

Printing from an application

If this section were written two years ago, it would be long and complex. Macs and PCs were the Hatfields and McCoys of computers, and saying you supported PostScript from your PC application was likely to leave you wishing for the days of the Spanish Inquisition when life was easy. Running applications wasn't any easier either. By the time you got done using the TOPS conversion routines to go from your Epson MX-80 output to PostScript, and sent your reincarnated output over the network, you'd usually end up saying "What's so great about PostScript anyway? I think I'll stick with dot matrix printer output." Fortunately, things have changed. TOPS still has all of its conversion routines to and from the major IBM PC printer outputs (ASCII, Epson MX-80, Diablo 630, etc.) to PostScript. However, most major PC applications today directly support PostScript output, particularly word processing, Microsoft Windows, GEM, desktop publishing, and graphics applications.

Tip If your application doesn't directly support PostScript output, don't use it with a network printer. Period. Yes, TOPS can convert from a number of common printer formats to PostScript. However, it is not an easy task to get everything set up to do so, and the end result isn't always satisfactory. If you're the type that enjoys a challenge and are tempted to ignore this counsel, here's one more piece of advice: Go run five miles — it's just as grueling and much better for you.

NETPRINT does only one thing — it allows PC users to print to a network printer. You don't need it to print to a shared printer. But if you want to print to a network printer *from inside an application program*, you must load the separate NETPRINT module.

Configuring NETPRINT

In order to run NETPRINT, you'll need to install it on your system, usually in the same \TOPS directory used for the rest of the TOPS programs. Next you'll need to configure NETPRINT with the CONFIGUR program. If you review the NETPRINT documentation, you'll see that NETPRINT supports a numbing collection of options. It also supports a menu-driven mode as well as a command line parameter mode. However, you can ignore most of this if you stick with our earlier advice, and only use network printers with application programs that directly support PostScript output. Enter the following command line at the DOS prompt to configure NETPRINT properly.

```
CONFIGUR /L /W- /T45 LPT# "L=Printername" <Enter>
```

Let's take each parameter individually so you have some idea of how we're setting up NETPRINT. Keep in mind that the CONFIGUR program writes a configuration file that NETPRINT reads each time it's loaded, so you'll only need to run CONFIGUR once, unless you wish to change one of the parameters.

CONFIGUR — This starts the CONFIGUR.EXE program from the DOS prompt.

/L — This parameter tells NETPRINT you wish to print to a network laser printer (as opposed to a network ImageWriter, or other class device).

/W- — The /W- parameter turns off the PostScript translation feature of NETPRINT. PostScript translation refers to

NETPRINT's ability to take output in Epson MX-80 form (or one of several other formats) and convert it into PostScript before sending it to the network printer. Since your application will already be producing PostScript output, there is no need for translation.

/T45 — This parameter controls the NETPRINT *timeout*. Simply stated, timeout is the amount of time NETPRINT waits after receiving the last character in a print job before deciding that the job is really complete, closing the print spool file, and starting to output the job to the network printer. Setting the delay to 45 seconds will allow your application plenty of time to assemble its print job and will avoid NETPRINT prematurely closing the spool file and missing part of the print job.

LPT# — The LPT parameter should be quite familiar to you by now. This is the local printer port that you want NETPRINT to use. As with a shared printer, you should specify a printer port that physically doesn't exist in your system, or that doesn't have a printer connected to it.

"L=Printername" — Each device on an AppleTalk network must have its own unique name. If you have only one laser printer attached to the network, you can omit this parameter. On the other hand, if multiple printers are connected to the network, you will need to specify the one you wish to print to. For example, if you have an Apple LaserWriter and NEC LC890 connected to the network, the Apple will be named LaserWriter and the NEC will be named SilentWriter. Keep in mind that these are names assigned by their manufacturers, not by you. If you have two or more of the same printer (for example, three Apple LaserWriters), they will be named LaserWriter, LaserWriter1 and LaserWriter2. Check the printer manual if you aren't sure of the network name selected by the manufacturer. Also check to see if the printer can be renamed to allow a better description of where and what it is.

Tip It is possible to run NETPRINT without the TOPS server or client modules. All that is necessary is NETPRINT, the AppleTalk driver (ALAP), and a protocol stack program called PSTACK. In certain memory-hungry applications such as Xerox Ventura Publisher, most Microsoft Windows applications and others, you can obtain the benefits of network printing without sacrificing as much memory as you'd need if either the server or client modules were loaded. You will need to load these programs from the DOS prompt in the following order to accomplish this:

```
ALAP <Enter>

PSTACK <Enter>

NETPRINT <Enter>
```

Printing from your application

Once you've loaded NETPRINT, printing to a network printer is as simple as printing to a local printer. Configure your application for a PostScript output device, and direct the program's output to the printer port you specified for the network printer when you ran the CONFIGUR program. Then print as you normally would.

If you are printing a large print job from your application, you'll notice that the printing proceeds much more quickly than when you are printing to a local PostScript printer. This is because NETPRINT is spooling the printer output to a disk file first. Once the application has stopped printing, or timed out, NETPRINT will start printing to the network printer in the background. When your application is done printing and the timeout period has expired, your system's speaker will beep. This is just NETPRINT's way of letting you know that the print job has been completely captured to disk, and that it is busy sending it to the network printer.

WARNING Be careful when you turn off your system. Make sure that any spooled print jobs have been completely printed, and that the network printer is idle.

Just because you've finished printing from your application and are ready to turn your machine off doesn't mean that NETPRINT has sent the print job to the network printer completely. If not, turning your system off will not only halt any print job in progress but may also destroy data currently in a spooled file that hasn't been printed.

Printing from the DOS prompt

The final topic we'll cover in this chapter is printing from the DOS prompt to a network printer. Beyond the normal uses of printing from the DOS prompt, you'll probably end up using this method of accessing a network PostScript printer quite often. The reason is that most applications that really take advantage of a PostScript printer (such as desktop publishing, presentation graphics, etc.) need all of the system RAM they can get. In many cases this means that there isn't enough room to load TOPS, or even NETPRINT, when these applications are running.

The solution is to use the print-to-disk features of these programs to capture the PostScript output into a file that can then be sent to the network printer. The print files can then be sent to the printer at a later date, using the TOPS TPRINT command. The format for the TPRINT command is shown below.

```
TPRINT /X [devicename/N] [zone/Z] filename
<Enter>
```

Now let's dissect it:

/X — This parameter indicates that TPRINT is printing to a network printer.

devicename/N — If your network has more than one network laser printer on it, you must specify the network name, or if you have a PostScript laser printer from a manufacturer other than Apple. For example, if you have an NEC LC890 laser printer on the network you would enter *SilentWriter / N* in the command line.

zone/Z — If your network has multiple zones, you'll need to add this parameter to your command line. If not, you can consider it optional. Enter the zone where the target laser printer resides, followed by a /Z. For example, if the laser printer is in zone @Marketing, this parameter would be entered as @Marketing/Z.

filename — Enter the filename of the file you wish to print.

Unlike the NETPRINT command, which incorporates a print spooler, TPRINT will not return you to the DOS print until the print job is complete.

■ Spooling

One of the important features of the TOPS network program is its ability to save the printer output to a disk before sending it on to the printer. This process is called *spooling*. It is not unique to TOPS. However, it is an important part of the TOPS printer support.

The TOPS spooler works by intercepting printer output from your program, and storing it in a *spooler file* on a local or network disk. The output is accumulated in this file until the application has finished printing. At this point the spooler file is closed, and your application thinks it is done printing, and will return you from the print function. In almost all cases, TOPS can accumulate printer output in a spooler file faster than the printer could accept it directly. Thus, one of the benefits of the TOPS spooler is that you spend less time printing from your application.

Once the printer output has been captured, the TOPS spooler will attempt to establish communications with the selected printer. If another printer job is in process, it will wait until it is complete. This is another benefit of the TOPS print spooler; you don't have to worry about waiting around for a network printer to become available. When it establishes communications with the printer, it sends the printer output it captured from your application to the printer. When this process is complete, the spooler file is deleted from the disk, reclaiming the space it occupied.

Spooling on a PC

There isn't much to print spooling on a PC running under TOPS. When you run the TOPSMENU to mount a shared printer, or NETPRINT to access a network printer, a spool file is automatically set up. You can specify which directory you want the spooler files to be temporarily created in (remember, each spooler file is deleted once its contents have been sent to the printer).

TOPS Spool for the Macintosh

As we've mentioned earlier in this chapter, TOPS does not get involved in printing from the Macintosh. Instead, the standard LaserWriter drivers are used to print to network printers. TOPS leaves these tasks to the Macintosh system software, rather than redirecting output to network printers under TOPS as it does on the IBM PC.

However, TOPS does provide spooling capabilities through TOPS Spool. TOPS Spool operates in the way described above. When you print from a Macintosh application, the output is directed to a capture file on your system boot disk. Once the application is done printing, the capture file is closed, a connection made to the selected network printer, and the output is sent to the printer.

The TOPS Spool program is controlled through a desk accessory. To open the TOPS Spool control panel, select the TOPS Spool menu item from the Apple menu. The control panel appears, as shown in Figure 8-8.

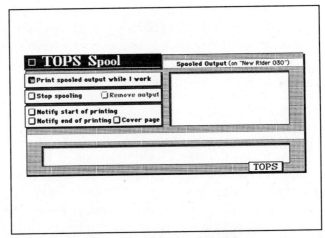

Figure 8-8. TOPS Spool Control Panel.

You can selectively enable and disable TOPS Spool by clicking on the Stop Spooling button. When this button is active, spooling is disabled. Printer output is sent directly to the network printer when TOPS Spool is inactive. You can also control whether you want TOPS Spool to send output to the printer while you are working in the foreground. This is helpful if you are working on an application which is slowed down significantly by TOPS Spool sending output to the printer in the background. If you disable the Print Spooled Output While I Work button to disable background spooling, you can still direct your applications printer output to a capture file. The only difference is that TOPS Spool won't send it to the printer until you click on the Print Spooled Output button.

One of the useful features of TOPS Spool is its ability to notify you when the print job starts and when it stops. To select these features, simply enable them by clicking on their respective buttons.

Tip Notify at End of Job is particularly useful on busy Appletalk networks, or if you are printing large jobs. In either of these cases, it can be many minutes before you print job is done. Without notification, you must constantly open the TOPS Spool desk accessory to determine whether your job has finished. If you enable notification, you can go back to your work without worrying about the printer (the original concept behind the spooler in the first place).

TOPS Spool maintains a print queue, which is a list of all of the print jobs waiting to be printed. You can remove any of the files in the print queue, or change the order in which they will be printed. If you wish to delete a file from the print queue, first select it, then click on the Remove Output button. The file will be removed from the print queue. If there are other files below it in the queue, they will be moved up.

You can also rearrange the order in which print jobs will be sent to the printer. To change a print job's order, drag it with the mouse to the end of the list to make it the last print job, or on top of the job you wish it to be in front of. The print queue will be displayed in its new order. Keep in mind that if you attempt to move a print job currently being output, it will abort the job (after prompting you of course), and it will start over from the beginning. Obviously, you won't want the change the order of a 70-page print job after 55 pages have been printed.

■ Continuing on

Shared and Network printer support are two of the more important features of TOPS. We've shown you how to print from your applications and from DOS using the TPRINT and NETPRINT commands. We also discussed publishing a shared printer using the TOPSMENU and TOPS PUBLISH commands. Finally, we examined TOPS's spooling features.

In the next chapter, you'll learn how to select, install, and operate an electronic mail system on the TOPS network.

Chapter Nine

Sending Electronic Mail on a TOPS Network

People have fantasized about the paperless office for years. You get tired of the little notes, phone messages, and endless forms that clutter up your desk. You get frustrated when your memos don't get answered, because you have no way of knowing if they were even read.

Most people agree that the paperless office is about as likely as the paperless bathroom. But a network with electronic mail goes a long way toward solving the paper mess. Although electronic mail doesn't eliminate paperwork, it does streamline office communication, turning your network into an automated message center. Not only can you send messages on the computer, but you are also alerted when someone reads your message. In addition, you can attach a computer file to a message so you don't have to run down the hall with floppy disks or wait for the recipient to pull the file off the network.

In this chapter we'll start with the concept of electronic mail (E-mail) — what it is and how it can make your office more efficient. Next, we'll outline the minimum system requirements and give a brief overview of several E-mail applications for the Mac and PC, chosen because of their proven compatibility with TOPS:

- freE-Mail (an invention of the authors)

- Microsoft Mail

- QuickMail by CE Software

- TOPS InBox

Once you've decided which application to use, we'll tell you how to install it painlessly. Finally, we'll close the chapter with tips on running each program, so you'll have no trouble fitting E-mail into your TOPS network. We don't promise to make you an E-mail expert, but by the end of the chapter you should be able to log onto E-mail and send and receive a message.

What is E-mail?

Simply put, E-mail applications use a post-office approach to turn your computer network into an electronic messenger service. To do this, one Macintosh acts as the switchboard for a collection of E-mail users. (To simplify things, we'll adopt Microsoft's terminology and call the post-office Mac the mail server, although the other E-mail applications have different names for the central server: QuickMail calls it a MailCenter, and InBox a Message Center.) The mail server stores the E-mail data in a central file, keeps track of E-mail users, notifies a user when he or she has a message, and alerts the sender when a message is read. One person is the E-mail manager, probably your TOPS network manager. He or she keeps the E-mail user list current, handles problems, and maintains the E-mail network.

As you can see, the concept behind E-mail is pretty simple. But don't let that fool you — E-mail is a powerful ally on any network system.

■ Product overview

Now that you understand what E-mail does, let's look at the programs that work best with the TOPS network.

Hardware requirements

Essentially, if you can run TOPS, you can run these applications. Nevertheless, we also recommend a hard disk to run the mail servers. It takes a lot of storage space to hold E-mail for even a medium-sized network. QuickMail also requires a minimum of a Macintosh Plus at every node. Each Mac should be running System 5.0 or higher and needs System 6.0 to take advantage of all the sound effects.

freE-Mail

Though we've listed it as software, freE-Mail does not exist as a standalone program. In fact, it doesn't officially exist at all. You create a freE-Mail system by publishing and mounting designated folders or subdirectories on each computer on the network for message text files. If you spent all your money on a TOPS Network, then a freE-Mail system can provide you with a limited electronic mail capability at no extra cost. Keep in mind, though, that the only thing you will be able to do with it is send each other messages.

Microsoft Mail

Without question, Microsoft Mail has the fewest features of the products listed here, but its features were well chosen. Its design is simple enough for the average person to use without the manual.

To start with, Microsoft Mail has a clean user interface. Because the standard message window is simple and to the point, users don't need to spend a lot of time navigating through commands. They just type their messages, select a recipient from the scrollable user list, and hit the SEND button. The phone message window resembles a phone message pad and works the same way as the standard message window. It also has a graphic message option that works by pasting graphic images to and from the clipboard. These messages can only be read on Macs. Your PC just gives you a polite reminder that you need a Macintosh to see what was sent.

If you use Microsoft Word 4.0 on the Macintosh, you can send your open text file across the E-mail network directly from Microsoft Word using the SEND MAIL command from Word's FILE menu.

Getting started is no trouble. Microsoft Mail takes only a few minutes to set up on both PCs and Macs. Installation involves just one disk, and installing the server requires only one extra step over installing a user. The manual gives a one-page quick installation section for experienced users, a more detailed installation for everybody else, and even a tutorial to walk you through the features. The program also has an on-line help file if you prefer getting screen-fed. Microsoft Mail was designed as a modular application, so that you only have to buy the features you need.

QuickMail

Designed very much like a mainframe E-mail network, Quick-Mail offers the most power of the three applications. Unfortunately, the current version of QuickMail only works on Macintosh computers, a problem for networks with PCs as well as Macintoshes. As of this writing, a PC version of Quick-Mail is still in development.

QuickMail has an impressive list of features:

- On-line help is available any time.

- Each MailCenter has a Bulletin Board for public messages.

- QuickMail can create up to 16 MailCenters per Macintosh.

- You can design your own forms to fit specialized needs.

- The conferencing feature allows you to talk to several different stations at once.

- The privacy option locks out all but the most urgent messages.

- The message sorting capability allows you to rank messages by history, urgency, subject, sender, or date sent.

- You can attach up to 16 different files to one memo.

Three different types of MailCenters are possible: *On-line MailCenters* control communications within the network, allowing subgroups to have their own MailCenter with their own Bulletin Board. *Printer MailCenters* output to a printer so users with no computer can still receive E-mail in hard-copy form. And *Telecom MailCenters* can bridge to other companies' QuickMail E-mail networks and information services such as MCI Mail, GEnie, and others.

Scripting allows many QuickMail features to be automated. For example, you can configure a Telecom MailCenter to connect with MCI Mail automatically at a specific time of day. It will then send its store of E-mail through the Telecom Bridge and afterwards pick up any mail waiting to be delivered. If a given E-mail message arrives with the first line "Attn: Muffy

Smith," The Telecom MailCenter will deliver it to Muffy Smith's station. If it can't find Muffy Smith, it will deliver the message to the custodian for proper routing.

As you can see, QuickMail offers a great chance to allow your E-mail network to grow with your company's needs.

InBox

The biggest advantage InBox has over other packages is its elaborate security features. Not only does it have password protection for its each user and the administrator, it can also scramble transmissions to prevent unwanted listeners from tapping into a network's E-mail.

InBox also gives you the best features for the PC side of your network. Like Sidekick, it has a "Hot Key" that lets you access InBox from any application. (With Microsoft Mail, you have to leave your application and start up your mail server from DOS before you can access your mail.)

Like QuickMail, InBox features a bulletin board for public messages

Finally, InBox gives you a choice of running the Message Center as a dedicated server or a background server. For a larger network, having a dedicated Message Center can bring a greater percentage of its CPU to bear in managing the network.

■ Installation procedures

Now that you've picked out your E-mail program, it's time to install it. To make this a smooth process, we've split each installation into four sections:

1. Installing the mail server

2. Configuring the mail server

3. Connecting a new E-mail user

4. Installing a PC E-mail user (where applicable)

For each application, we've provided step-by-step directions and filled in a few gaps in the manual. Let's get cracking.

Choosing the mail server

When installing a mail server, you will have to choose a Macintosh (PCs are not supported as E-Mail servers) that gets used least during the day. If you install the mail server on a busy machine, the E-mail network slows down. This recommendation has one drawback, however; people who use their computers infrequently tend to be less experienced. Consequently, they may have more problems with their computer and may even bring down the whole network. With this in mind, consider the stability of the Macintosh you choose before you commit it to handling your company's E-mail.

Installing freE-Mail

To create a freE-Mail system, just make a folder or subdirectory on every computer labeled:

```
(station name or user's name)
```

Publish the folder or subdirectory on the network and you're ready to receive freE-Mail. Anytime you need to give someone a message, send a text file across the network to the proper folder.

Of course, everyone will have to check their freE-Mail folders regularly, since there won't be any way to signal new messages. You get what you pay for.

Installing Microsoft Mail

Choosing the mail server is the most difficult part of installing Microsoft Mail (MS-Mail). The manual gives excellent installation instructions, but we have reviewed the process below for your convenience.

Setting up your mail server
■ Insert the MS-Mail disk into the disk drive and double-click on the disk icon to open its window (Figure 9-1).

| Note | If you do not have zone support you will have an icon labeled Microsoft Mail User instead of Microsoft Mail.

Use the Font/DA mover to install the Microsoft Mail desk

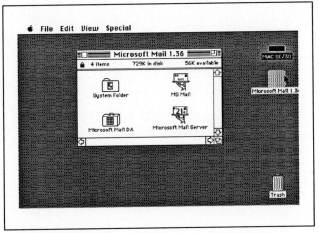

Figure 9-1. Double-click on the MS-Mail disk icon to open its window.

accessory into the computer System Folder. This will allow you to open Microsoft Mail from any application.

⎡**Note**⎤ You must have Font/DA Mover version 3.2 or later to install Microsoft Mail.

■ Double-click on the Microsoft Mail DA icon.

■ Open the System file in your startup disk's System Folder.

■ Select Microsoft Mail from the left column and click on the copy button (Figure 9-2).

Your Microsoft Mail desk accessory is now installed.

■ Drag the Microsoft Mail User icon into the System Folder.

■ Drag the Microsoft Mail Server icon into the System Folder as well, if you are configuring a server..

■ Select Restart from the Special Menu on the menu bar.

After the "Welcome to Macintosh" screen is displayed, the "The Microsoft Mail Server is loading..." screen appears. The next screen will ask for the name of the mail system. This name will be used by all interconnected networks, so choose the name carefully.

■ Type in the name and click on the Set button.

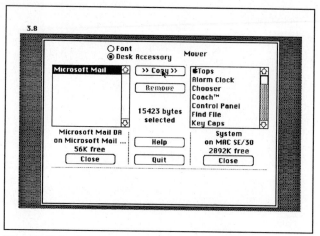

Figure 9-2. Select Microsoft Mail from the left
column of the Font/DA Mover window and click on the
Copy button.

The mail system will then welcome you using the name found
in the Chooser desk accessory.

Configuring the mail system

■ On the network server, choose Microsoft Mail from the
Apple menu.

The Sign In window will appear with the Your Name field
highlighted (Figure 9-3).

Microsoft Mail version 1.36
Please enter your name & password...
Your Name	Network Manager
Password	••••	OK

Figure 9-3. Use the Sign In window to configure your
Microsoft Mail system.

■ Type:

```
Network Manager [Tab]
```

This will advance you to the Password field.

■ Type:

```
mail [Return] (or click OK)
```

Note For security reasons, bullets will hide the characters on screen.

The Network Manager's Message Center screen appears.

■ Double-click on the Management icon.

The User Management window appears (Figure 9-4).

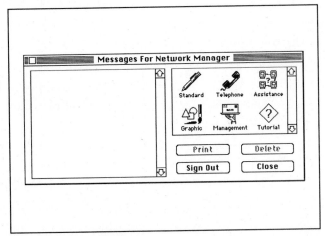

Figure 9-4. With the User Management window, you can add new users to your mail system.

■ Click on the Management icon.

■ Click on the Add New User button.

■ Type the name you want to appear on the mail system.

■ Press Tab, to enter a password if desired.

Note If you do not enter a password for a user, Microsoft Mail automatically signs the user onto the system when the computer is turned on.

Tip If your office does not require security, you may find that the convenience of automatically logging on the system at startup outweighs your desire for a password.

■ Click on the Add button to add your name to the user list.

■ Repeat the last three steps to add other users to the mail system.

■ Click on Quit to Return to the Message Center.

■ Click on Sign Out to finish.

Connecting a new user to the mail system

Once the mail server is set up, you need to install Microsoft Mail on the other computers in your office. This is even easier than setting up the mail server.

■ Insert the Microsoft Mail Master disk into the floppy drive.

■ Use Font/DA version 3.2 or greater to move the Microsoft Mail desk accessory to the System file.

TO09MMCU.EPS

■ Open the Chooser desk accessory and type the name of the user exactly as it was entered into the mail system (Figure 9-5).

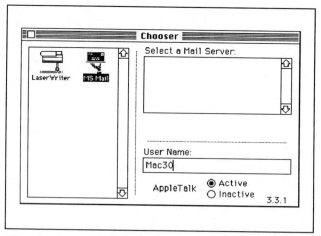

Figure 9-5. In the Chooser, type the user's name just as you entered it in the mail system.

■ Drag the Microsoft Mail User icon (or the Microsoft Mail

icon for multiple zone support, if purchased) into the System Folder.

■ Select Restart from the Special Menu on the menu bar.

During startup, the screen displays the message, "Welcome to Microsoft Mail, (whatever name you chose above)."

Installing a PC Microsoft Mail user

As with most programs, installing Microsoft Mail on a PC is more difficult than on a Macintosh. That doesn't mean it's hard to do. Just make sure you have your user name handy exactly as registered on the mail system and your password if any. Here we go.

■ Turn on the PC.

■ Insert the Microsoft Mail disk for PCs.

■ At the DOS prompt, type:

    A:SETUP

The first screen introduces you to the Setup program (Figure 9-6). If you want, you can quit at this point or continue with the Setup commands.

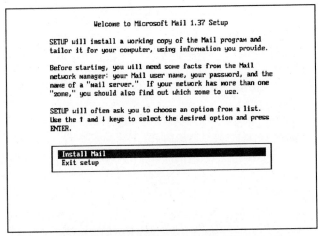

Figure 9-6. The opening Setup screen begins the process of installing a mail user on a PC.

■ Press Enter to continue.

The next screen identifies the available drives on your PC.

■ Use the arrow keys to select a drive for Microsoft Mail and press Enter.

The next screen allows you to choose the subdirectory where you will install the Microsoft Mail programs.

■ Type in the name of the subdirectory you wish to create and press Enter (or just press Enter to accept the default subdirectory).

The screen lists the names of the files being copied to the disk drive and subdirectory you chose. Afterward, a screen message appears to explain screen flicker.

■ Press Enter to continue.

Setup will test for screen flicker for a few seconds. If your screen goes crazy, don't panic. Just answer the on-screen questions about your PC's monitor, and Setup will customize Microsoft Mail to your monitor.

After Setup has modified the program accordingly, it will ask which zone your computer is in.

■ Press Enter to continue.

The next screen asks for the name of your mail server.

■ Press Enter to continue.

Setup then asks if you want to update your AUTOEXEC.BAT file to include your Microsoft Mail subdirectory in the Path= line. This will allow you to access Microsoft Mail from anywhere in DOS.

| Note | If you include Microsoft Mail in your AUTOEXEC.BAT file, you must load your TOPS network drivers (LOADTOPS or LOADCLNT) for the PC before loading Microsoft Mail.

■ Press Enter to continue.

Next, Setup asks if you want to be notified every time new mail has arrived for you (Figure 9-7).

| Note | Choose Yes, only if your AUTOEXEC.BAT program automatically loads TOPS.

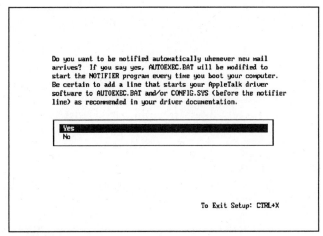

Figure 9-7. A screen message asks whether to alert you each time you receive mail.

Unless TOPS will be active on your system at all times, there's no point having the Notifier active. There won't be anything to notify you about unless TOPS is running to connect you with the rest of the network.

The Notifier program is a TSR (Terminate Stay Resident) program, which means it loads itself into regular memory and stays there no matter what other application is running. If you are using any other TSRs (especially public domain software), the Notifier may fail to function. If the program does not work, get rid of other TSR programs on your system.

■ Answer Yes if you plan to keep TOPS loaded in memory all the time. Otherwise, answer No. Press Enter to continue.

The next screen gives you the option of using a mouse with Microsoft Mail.

■ Select Yes if you have a mouse, No if no mouse is available, and press Enter.

Setup informs you that the installation was successful.

■ Restart your PC by pressing Ctrl-Alt-Del.

■ To start the mail program, type `Mail` at the DOS prompt if you have automatically loaded Microsoft Mail. Otherwise, type Notifier, enter your name and password, and then type Mail.

Installing QuickMail

Although QuickMail is the most powerful E-Mail package discussed in this book, it's almost as easy to install as Microsoft Mail. As we stated earlier, we'll install the mail server first, then configure the Mail Center, and finally take care of each user installation. (No PC version was available when this book went to press.)

- Make a backup copy of the QuickMail Administrator Disk.

- Copy the QuickMail Administrator backup to your mail server's hard disk.

- Open the newly created folder on the hard drive.

- Drag the QuickServer icon into your System Folder.

- Double-click on the QuickMail Administrator icon.

A dialog box appears, reporting the initialization status. When initialization is complete, the configuration dialog box appears (Figure 9-8).

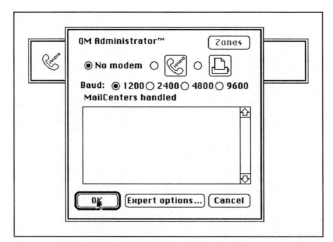

Figure 9-8. Following initialization, the configuration dialog box appears.

- Click on OK to continue.

- Pull down the File menu and select New MailCenter.

The New MailCenter dialog box appears (Figure 9-9).

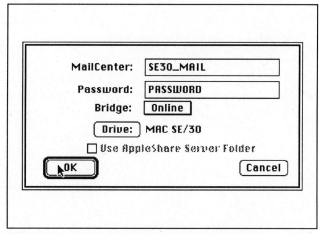

Figure 9-9. Use the New MailCenter dialog box from the File menu to create your electronic post office.

■ Enter a name for your MailCenter (mail server). Only alphabetic characters can be used. Spaces will be replaced by the underscore (_) character.

■ Press Tab to move to the password field and enter a password.

This password will allow access to the MailCenter later, so do not lose it.

■ Click on OK.

■ Click on More... to continue.

The first configuration screen appears (Figure 9-10).

Click on OK to accept the default configuration shown in each of the configuration screens.

Configuring the MailCenter
Configuring the MailCenter is just as easy as installing Quick-Mail.

■ Select Create from the User menu.

The User dialog box appears (Figure 9-11).

■ Type the user's first name and press Tab.

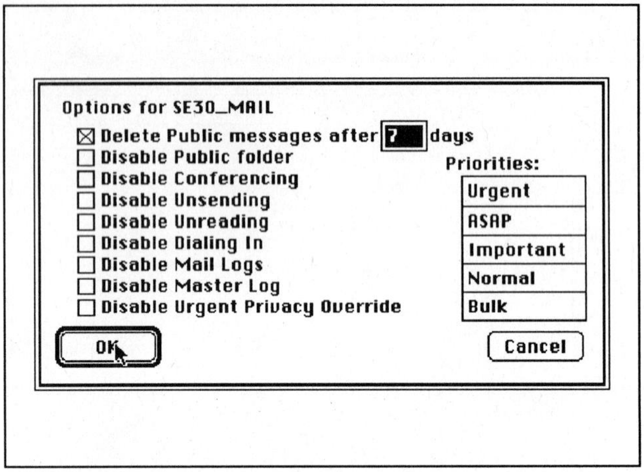

Figure 9-10. The configuration screens allow you to change the defaults of your QuickMail mail system.

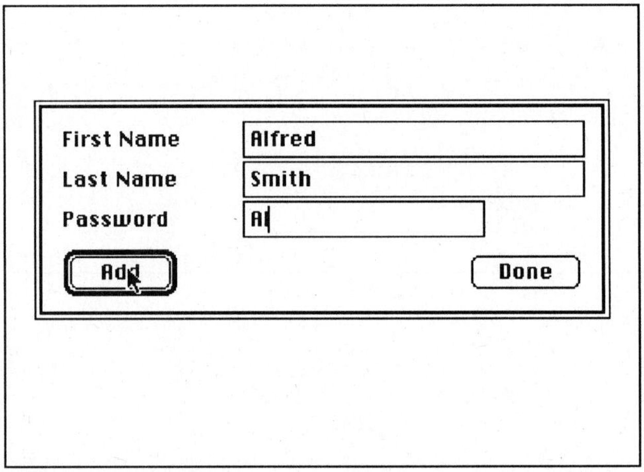

Figure 9-11. Identify users with the User dialog box.

This will advance you to the last name field.

■ Type the user's last name and press Tab.

This will advance you to the password.

■ Type the password for the user.

Note Don't forget to give each user his or her password or he or she will be unable to use the mail system. If passwords aren't necessary, you can skip them at this point.

■ Click on the Add button.

QuickMail adds the name to the user list. Repeat the above steps for each user you wish to add.

■ Click on the Done button.

If you haven't already done so, select a custodian for the MailCenter. *Custodian* is just another name for your E-mail administrator, the person in charge of updating user lists and other maintenance of your E-mail network.

■ Select Configure (your MailCenter name) from the File Menu.

The MailCenter dialog box appears (Figure 9-12).

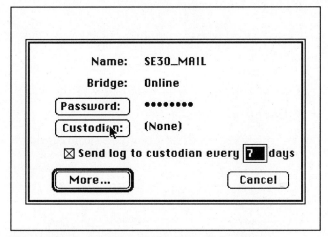

Figure 9-12. Use the MailCenter dialog box to designate one user as custodian.

■ Click on Custodian button.

The user list will now appear (Figure 9-13).

■ Click on the name of the person who will be your E-mail administrator.

QuickMail now enters the user list into the MailCenter.

Installing a QuickMail user
Now it's time to install the users. You're almost done.

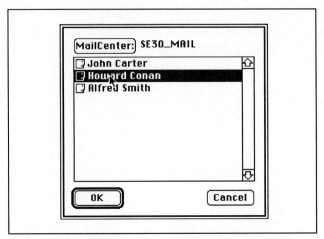

Figure 9-13. Clicking on the Custodian button displays a list of users.

Note Don't forget to install a QuickMail User on the mail server Macintosh.

■ Insert the QuickMail User disk into the Macintosh.

■ Double-click on the QuickInstall icon.

The Installation dialog box appears (Figure 9-14).

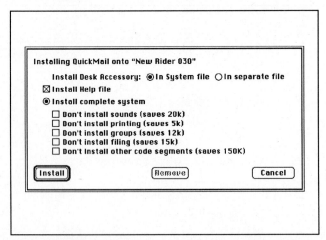

Figure 9-14. The installation dialog box allows you to install individual users.

The options on the installation screen are designed to save disk space. Refer to your user manual for more information.

■ Click on Install to install the QuickMail desk accessory.

■ Click on Restart in the Restart dialog box.

All you have to do is Log In to QuickMail, and you're done.

■ Click on the MailCenter button.

The screen displays a list of zones and the MailCenter for each one(Figure 9-15).

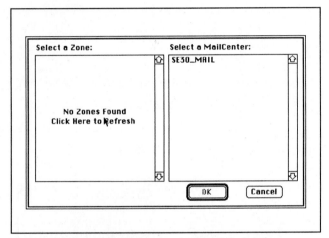

Figure 9-15. Clicking on the MailCenter button displays a list of zones.

■ Select your MailCenter name from the list provided. If your MailCenter name is not on the list, select different zones until it appears on the list.

■ Click on the OK button.

The Log-In screen appears (Figure 9-15).

■ Click on the Name button.

A list of user names will appear (Figure 9-16).

■ Select your name from the list.

■ Click on the OK button.

■ Enter your password.

■ Click on the Log-In button.

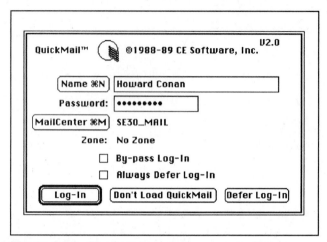

Figure 9-16. The Log-In screen appears after you select the MailCenter name.

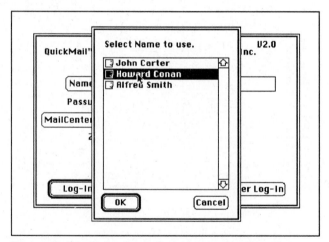

Figure 9-17. To log in, select your name from the user list.

Installing the InBox mail server

We have to admit that of the three programs, InBox is hardest to install. It still won't take more than a couple minutes for each Macintosh, but the PCs on the network will take a little longer. Don't let InBox/PC discourage you. With a some patience and practice, you'll do just fine.

Let's start with the mail server.

- Insert the InBox Administrator disk into your mail server's disk drive.

- Copy the Administrator and Message Center programs onto your startup disk for the Macintosh.

Tip Make sure that you have at least 100K of memory available on your server's disk for each E-mail user on the network. For a large network, a hard disk is mandatory.

- Create a folder on your hard disk for message center data files and name it MESSAGE CENTER FILES.

Configuring the mail system
- Click on the Administrator icon on the startup disk.

- Enter a password for the Administrator program. You will be asked to enter the password a second time for confirmation (Figure 9-18).

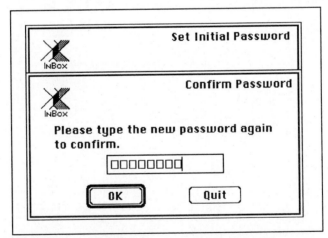

Figure 9-18. InBox asks you to enter your password twice, just to be sure.

From now on, you will need to enter this password to run the Administrator program. If you forget the password, copy the Administrator files onto your hard disk (or startup disk) again. You may then assign a new password.

- If you wish to use the chosen Macintosh for applications besides the mail server, click on the Background button.

If you choose to have the mail server run as the background

task, you must have at least 512K of spare RAM on the chosen Macintosh. To send mail from the Macintosh, you need at least 1MB of RAM. If you don't run the mail server run as a background task, the Macintosh cannot be used for any other work. But the advantage is that the mail server will run faster.

WARNING Running the InBox Administrator in the background gives unpredictable results. We recommend running the Administrator as a dedicated server.

■ Click on the New button.

■ Select the folder MESSAGE CENTER FILES and click on Open twice. If you can't find the folder, click on the DRIVE button until it appears in the file list.

■ Type a name for your message center data files. For example, "TOPS Post Office Data."

The address (user) list request window appears (Figure 9-19).

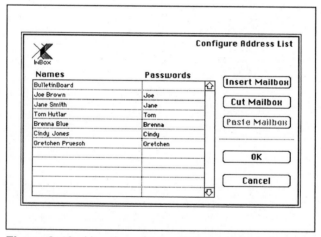

Figure 9-19. Use the address list request window to add users to the Message Center's files.

■ For each user that will be connected to the message center, type in a name and a password.

■ Use the Tab key or press Return to move from box to box.

When you've added all the names you want, click on OK.

The next dialog box (Figure 9-20) allows you to:

- check the date and time
- enter a name for the message center
- enter a news flash.

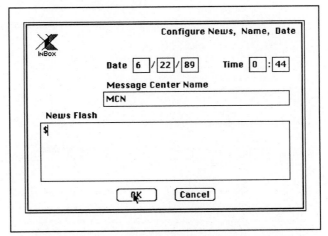

Figure 9-20. This dialog box allows you to name the message center, check the date and time, and enter a news flash.

A news flash will be displayed on the user's computer each time he or she logs into the message center.

■ If the date or time is wrong, use your mouse to select the incorrect field(s) and type in the correct number.

■ Enter the name for the mail center. For example, *TOPS Post Office.*

■ Enter a news flash, if desired. For example, announce who the administrator is and where he or she can be reached.

⎡ **Note** ⎤ To test that everything runs smoothly, type something here, even if it's only one character.

■ Click on OK.

Connecting a user to the mail system
It's time to install the users to InBox — another easy task.

■ Insert the InBox Connection Installer disk into the User's Macintosh.

■ Double-click on the Installer icon on the InBox Connection Installer.

A menu appears (Figure 9-21).

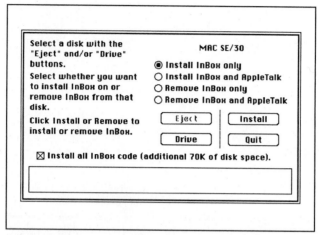

Figure 9-21. The user installation program begins with this menu.

■ Select the correct message center for the user and click on the Select button.

■ Choose the startup disk under your drive option and click on the Install button.

■ Click on the Quit button.

■ Double-click on the InBox Startup icon on your installation disk.

■ Enter your name.

■ Enter your password.

■ Click on the OK button twice.

Installing the InBox/PC Network Driver

Installing the InBox/PC Network Driver takes fewer steps than on the Macintosh, if everything works smoothly. However, because InBox/PC is a TSR program, your TOPS network software may cause loading problems. Don't worry, though; this section offers you a solution to the problem.

Although the user's manual gives you an optional way to install InBox/PC, for most users, the Setup program is the best way to install the software. If you don't want to use Setup, you can copy the software to the Inbox subdirectory using the DOS COPY command. You will have to modify your batch files yourself, but then you may have to anyway.

Before beginning, make a backup of your InBox/PC software. Replacing corrupted original program disks can be costly. After you've made a backup of your installation disk, put the original disk in a place safe from fire, flood, and magnets.

For simplicity's sake we'll assume you have a hard disk called C:. Without a valid subdirectory for its files, the setup program will quit so we'll start by creating a new subdirectory:

■ At the C:\ prompt type:

```
MD INBOX
```

■ Insert your backup copy of the Installer disk into the B: drive and type:

```
B: SETUP C:\INBOX C:\
```

The setup program copies two files to your InBox/PC subdirectory, INST.EXE and IB.EXE. INST.EXE configures InBox/PC. IB.EXE runs it.

Setup also makes two changes to your AUTOEXEC.BAT file. First, it adds the INBOX subdirectory to your PATH. Then it adds another line: SET INBOXDA=C:.

After the Network device driver line (in this case LOADTOPS) Setup adds: IB -R -S. This line starts InBox/PC on your machine. IB loads the program into memory, -R keeps it running but out of the way and -S dedicates 12 K of RAM to InBox while it's installed.

To change the amount of memory allocated to InBox, you can change the -S parameter to any of the following:

-M gives you 16K of RAM

-L gives you 40K of RAM

-N# gives you #K of RAM (You must replace # with a number from 12 to 40.)

To test your installation, reboot your machine. Did InBox Load? If not, don't worry. Your AUTOEXEC.BAT probably sent DOS to run the LOADTOPS.BAT in your \TOPS subdirectory and bypassed the remainder of the AUTOEXEC.BAT program, where the InBox loading command resides. All you have to do is add the InBox loading commands to the LOAD-TOPS.BAT. The next few steps will take care of the problem.

■ Go to the /TOPS sub directory by typing:

```
C cd..
C\cd TOPS
```

■ At the prompt type:

```
C\TOPS edlin LOADTOPS.BAT
```

This will allow you to change your batch file.

■ At the * type:

```
8i
```

■ At the 8* type:

```
IB -R -S
```

> **Note** You can take this opportunity to use one of the other memory configurations in place of -S. Remember: -M = 16K, -L = 40K, and -N# = (An amount of RAM between 12K and 40K, your choice).

At the 9* type:

```
[Ctrl]Z   (or press F6)
```

At the * type:

```
EXIT
```

At this point, you only have to remove the IB -R -S from your AUTOEXEC.BAT file, and you're done with the installation./

■ Return to the root directory by typing:

```
cd\
```

■ Type:

```
edlin AUTOEXEC.BAT
```

■ At the * prompt type:

```
L
```

This shows you the contents of your AUTOEXEC.BAT file.

■ Find the IB -R -S line and delete it. It will appear some-where after your network device driver For example, if it is line 7, type:

```
7D
```

If it is line 8 type:

```
8D
```

And so on.

■ At the * type:

```
E
```

When you reboot your machine this time, everything should work fine.

Configuring InBox/PC

Once the InBox/PC driver is installed, configuring your sta-tion is easy.

■ At the DOS prompt type:

```
INST
```

The installer menu appears.

To move around the menu, use the arrow keys or the Tab key. After exploring the menu a bit, return the cursor to the Name prompt.

■ Type your name:

```
Muffy Smith
```

■ Type your password.

Notice that you cannot see what you type in this field. This may throw you a bit, but it's a standard safety feature. It protects you from co-workers who lean over your shoulder to see what you're doing.

If you find it monotonous to enter your name and password every time you log in, then Tab the cursor to the next section.

This is the Remember option. If you hit the space bar at the Name prompt here, a check mark appears. InBox now assumes you will always be the person logging in on this machine. Press Tab again and you can make InBox remember your password. Just hit the space bar one more time.

Next, you have to decide what sort of alert you want to signal an incoming message. Alert Audibly beeps at you whenever a new message comes in. Alert Visually prompts you with a banner display. You can also choose to be alerted every five minutes until the new message is opened. We don't recommend this option unless you are extremely forgetful.

The Journal option allows you to print hard copies of all the messages you send out. This section gives you the choice of printing either phone messages, memos, or both.

The Network Tuning Functions allow you to set how many times InBox/PC tries to gain access to the Message Center and how long the program waits before each retry.

For the Network Tuning Retries Ctrl-E deletes the current entry so you can enter the new value. The manual recommends you enter 7 here if your network uses bridges and/or modems.

For the Network Tuning Retry Interval, Ctrl-E deletes the current entry. For most purposes, one tick should be sufficient, although you should probably increase this value by one for every zone you have on the network. For example, a three-zone network should have a three-tick pause between retries.

If you have a printer connected to the network and plan to print hard copies of your messages, you need to set the printer option. If your printer already uses carriage returns at the end of each line, leave this option unchecked. If it requires a carriage return prompt, check this option.

You're almost done. In fact, you can stop at this point, because the next two commands are optional. If you like the default Hot Key and if you only have one Message Center on your network, just hit the F1 key to install your parameters. Otherwise, read on.

The Hot Key is the most important of the last two options because F1 may already be used by another application. You may want to pick a combination of keys for your Hot Key to minimize conflict with other applications. A good combination is Alt-~ since the ~ (tilde) key is seldom used for anything.

To change the Hot Key, simply press F7. InBox asks you to press your new Hot Key selection. Check the Hot Key section of the menu to see if your new key is now registered. If it isn't press F7 and try again.

If you have several Message Centers on the network and you want to change from one to another, press F5. This takes you to the Message Center window. Using the arrow keys, scroll through the list of available Message Centers until you find the one you want. Press Enter and InBox will assign you to that Message Center.

When you are satisfied with your configuration, press F1 to log your changes. If you've had second thoughts about the configuration, just select Cancel and InBox will forgive all your transgressions.

Tip Sometimes you may want to change your configuration even though there is no Message Center operating. If this is the case, typing INST at the DOS prompt will not meet with success. You will get a message telling you that InBox could not find any Message Centers. If this happens, press your Esc key, then Enter, and InBox returns you to the DOS prompt. This time type:

```
INST L
```

The Configuration menu will appear without connecting you to a Message Center. In fact, you won't be able to select a Message Center. However, all the other menu options will be available.

■ Some hints on running E-mail

Now that you have your E-mail application installed and running, it's time to show you some tips on using it in your day-to-day operations. We'll break this section into four parts. First we'll give you some general tips that will be useful for all the applications discussed. Then we'll focus on each application separately with more specifics.

General tips

Make sure your E-mail administrator has a thorough knowledge of your software. If people know there is an expert available, their feelings of frustration will be minimized.

Keep messages brief. If you can't get your point across in 50 to 100 words, it'll probably save time to call the person directly. If you want a record of the message, then send a memo, but be sure to make and save a copy as a text file for yourself.

Use the journalistic approach in message writing. Stick to the facts and put your most important points first. If you need to express an opinion make sure the reader knows it's an opinion.

Don't chat on an E-mail network. Too much casual conversation can eat up valuable memory space, especially if your mail server is on a floppy disk. Delete old messages as soon as possible. You don't want to tie up memory with outdated news.

Use the QuickMail and InBox bulletin boards to keep one another informed when you discover new tricks and tips to improve your E-mail and TOPS networks use.

Microsoft Mail tips

You may need to send an urgent message to someone with a application file attached. Unfortunately general message, the only ones you can attach files to, cannot have an urgent status in Microsoft Mail. To get around this, simply create two messages. First, generate an urgent telephone message announcing you are sending a general message with an attached application file. This message will automatically appear on the person's computer screen. You can then send the general message with the file with confidence that it will be noticed.

If you want to send a graphic message from a Macintosh station to a PC station, remember that the PC cannot read it. Send a text file to the PC station telling the person to go to the nearest Macintosh station. Then send the graphic to that Macintosh.

QuickMail tip

Set your PC users up on a Printer MailCenter that accesses the printer they normally use. They'll be able to reply across the TOPS network by sending text files created in a word processor.

InBox tips

InBox requires you to scroll down the list of addresses to select the name of a message recipient. If you have a frequently used name at the bottom of the address list, constant scrolling to find the name can get very tedious. As a solution, InBox allows you to set up routing lists. These lists always appear at the top of the address list in italics. That way you can select the frequently contacted name easily.

You cannot run InBox from the DA menu when in MultiFinder on the Macintosh. To run InBox in MultiFinder, use the Multi-InBox application. Because of limited space, we did not include the instructions for installing MultiInBox. Nevertheless, you can find some straightforward installation instructions in a short pamphlet included with InBox 2.2.

■ Continuing on

Congratulations — you have mastered the basics of E-mail on your TOPS network. You should now be able to do all of the following:

- Explain to someone else what E-mail is and how it works.

- Set up any of the four E-mail systems described in this chapter.

- Use our tips to help run your E-mail network.

With E-mail, you will never lose a message again, we promise. Well, okay, we don't promise. This isn't a perfect world, and things still have a habit of getting lost in the mail. But remember, you're one step closer to a paperless office.

Part Three

▪ Managing TOPS

Once you've mastered the basics, you can supercharge TOPS with advanced techniques. The next two chapters show you how.

Chapter Ten

Building Bigger and Better TOPS Networks

Now that your TOPS network is up and running, you need to consider two things: how to keep it running, and where to go from here. Just like the installation of your TOPS network, the management and expansion of your TOPS network requires careful planning. It's often easier to fix a problem before it happens.

This chapter gives you an overview of network management and expansion. It's not intended as an in-depth analysis of the subject, but as a good starting point. Explaining all aspects of network management and expansion in full detail would require a whole book.

In this chapter, we will also discuss some widely used hardware and software that can simplify your job. Keep in mind that new products are introduced into the microcomputer industry at a staggering rate; the products mentioned in this chapter are by no means the only ones available.

Before we start, let's introduce a new concept: the *internet*. An internet (also known as the internetwork) is a system of two or more networks tied together by gateways or bridges. For the rest of this chapter, we will use internet to refer to a collection of connected networks.

You may be wondering why we are talking about connecting networks. Why not just extend the one we have? As networks get larger and users become more power hungry, the network that has served so well in the past begins to slow down and become unreliable.

One solution to an overtaxed network is to isolate the power users. This works well until the power users figure out that their network resources are gone. The other disadvantage to isolating power users is that power users soon teach their colleagues how to use the network to its full extent. Obviously, you can't isolate everyone.

The best solution to an overtaxed network is the internet. Power users can be isolated on their own small network but still have the resources of a large network via a gateway or bridge. *Gateways* are nodes that separate and manage dissimilar networks, such as DECnet and TOPS. *Bridges* are links between similar networks, such as two TOPS networks. For the purposes of this chapter, we will be talking about bridges when we use the term internet.

A key part of the internet is the zone. A zone is a subnetwork of the internet, literally a small network by itself.

Expanding your TOPS network

As your company expands, the demand on your network also increases. You may need to expand your TOPS network and possibly connect it to other networks in the company. Expansion requires:

- analysis and planning

- hardware and software selection

- more analysis and planning

Before you can expand your network, you must have a solid grasp of it. It's hard to build on something you don't understand fully. You also need to consider your budget. Faster and bigger may be better, but most budgets impose limits. Always consider existing resources you can use or tie into first. What you already have available may surprise you.

Plan any considered changes on paper first. While analyzing your network, some needs to consider are:

- speed

- greater subdivision

- longer distance

- easier access

- more entry points

- more shared resources

- ability to tie in to other networks

Network expansions that are not planned carefully can cause problems when it's time to manage or troubleshoot.

Selecting hardware and software

Numerous products exist to help you to expand your network. What you choose depends on your needs and your budget. In general you can expand your internet in four ways:

- Install dedicated servers.

- Improve or upgrade hardware.

- Improve or change the cabling.

- Install repeaters, bridges, gateways, or star controllers.

Dedicated servers

Although TOPS is designed to be a distributed file network system, there may be situations when you want to set up TOPS to run on a dedicated server. As your network expands, it will handle more file transfers and the files will also get larger. The increased demand on your distributed-server-based system will cause the network to drag its heels on other tasks, such as word processing, database searches, and so on.

To combat this problem, consider a single dedicated file server. One benefit of a dedicated file server is ease of management. When all users save their files onto one hard disk, security is easier to maintain, and you only have to back up a single hard disk.

If you have a dedicated server, you can use it for several serving tasks. For example, a single machine can be a TOPS server, an E-Mail server, and a printer server at the same time, freeing up the other computers on the network.

Tip One way to increase the performance of a Macintosh-based dedicated server is by turning on the RAM cache in the Macintosh Control Panel. This technique also improves the performance of non-dedicated TOPS file servers. Another trick is to leave the TOPS DA open on the server (visible when using Multi-Finder). Apple's Finder is generally a poor program to run TOPS under if you want maximum performance.

To use an inexpensive PC clone as a centralized storage area only, consider the DayStar FS100 LocalTalk File server board. The FS100 allows an inexpensive hard disk PC to become an AppleTalk file server.

Improve or upgrade hardware

Three things that determine how fast a computer works — CPU speed, RAM capacity, and hard disk capacity — also affect how fast you can transfer information from one machine to another on the network. If your system has a fast CPU, it can execute instructions faster and perform user-requested tasks in less time. Higher RAM capacity means more of each program can be stored in RAM. Disk access is reduced. If you run Multi-Finder on a Macintosh, more RAM means you can load more programs at the same time. The speed of the hard disk is also important.

Tip Develop these three areas in tandem. If you simply improve the speed of the hard disk but not the system, you won't see much improvement. Likewise, if you team a fast computer with a slow hard disk, your computer will always have to wait for the hard disk. If you put all your money in RAM, you'll find some of the RAM might not be used.

Improve or change cabling

Cabling is the highway that information travels on. As traffic increases, you'll need to improve it. The bigger, longer, and faster you want the highway, the more expensive it will be. AppleTalk is the standard protocol. However, if you want to transmit at a higher speed with the same cabling, you'll need to go to FlashTalk from TOPS or DaynaTalk from Dayna Communications. If you want to make the cabling longer as well as faster, you might consider the Ethernet or the fiber-optic solution from DuPont. In the following section, we will briefly discuss these alternatives.

FlashTalk

FlashTalk is a protocol developed by TOPS to be used over AppleTalk networks. It allows PCs and Macs to communicate at up to 770 Kbps. FlashTalk is fully compatible with the AppleTalk protocols. On PCs, FlashTalk is built into every FlashCard you buy from TOPS and the card is set to use it automatically. However, if you choose to, you can turn off FlashTalk when you set up your FlashCard. On the Macs, you'll need to install both the FlashTalk software into the system folder and the FlashBox hardware between the CPU and the interface boxes. Keep in mind that each FlashBox requires an AC plug nearby. FlashBoxes use power to amplify the network signal.

DaynaTalk

The DaynaTalk box is a FlashBox-like device that helps increase the performance of an AppleTalk network. DaynaTalk clocks in at 850 Kbps, which makes it slightly faster than FlashBox. However, the speed increase won't be that noticeable. The biggest advantage DaynaTalk has over FlashBox is that DaynaTalk Boxes do not need to draw electric current from an AC plug-in. DaynaTalk draws its power through the serial port on the Macintosh.

Ethernet

Ethernet allows data transmission with EtherTalk at speeds up to 10 Mbps. It can support up to 254 active AppleTalk users with up to 1023 total devices. In order to use EtherTalk, you need to install Ethernet cabling. There are two ways to interface your computer systems with Ethernet cabling: through a gateway and through direct connection. A gateway requires installing an interface box between the two different networks. Direct connection requires you to put each machine onto the Ethernet network. The disadvantage of a direct connection is that you can't use a LaserWriter on an Ethernet network without a gateway.

On Mac IIs and Mac SEs, two products from Kinetics (called EtherPort II and EtherPort SE) make the connection simple. On the Mac Plus, since there is no expansion slot, you can use Kinetics' EtherSC, which connects to Mac Plus's SCSI port. Many other companies offer similar solutions. On the PC side, TOPS 2.1 now supports the 3COM Ethernet cards.

Fiber optics

Everyone predicts that fiber optics will be the cabling solution of the future. This cabling can transmit information at speeds of up to 180,000 miles per second. Signals can travel between stations more than 30 miles apart without repeaters, and carry more than 1,300 two-way conversations. It is also relatively immune to wiretapping, radio frequency interference (RFI), electromagnetic flux (EMF), and crosstalk. Unfortunately, at this time the only advantages offered by DuPont's fiber-optic products are longer networks and relative immunity from wiretapping. Information still travels at 230 Kbps.

Repeaters, bridges, gateways, and star controllers

Building bigger networks often means combining several small networks and sending signals longer distances. Repeaters, bridges, gateways, and star controllers address these problems and allow for better network management and easier troubleshooting.

Repeaters

Repeaters allow you to increase the length of your network, and also increase the number of nodes allowed on each network. With the TOPS repeater, you can extend the network to 3,000 feet and the number of nodes from 32 to 254. You can also use the TOPS Repeater with a bridge to connect different zones or networks that are separated by a moderate distance. Another repeater that works the same as the TOPS Repeater is Farallon's PhoneNet Repeater. The basic repeater configuration is shown in Figure 10-1.

| Note | No computer should have to travel over two repeaters to retrieve files or to print. Doing so significantly cuts down the efficiency of the network.

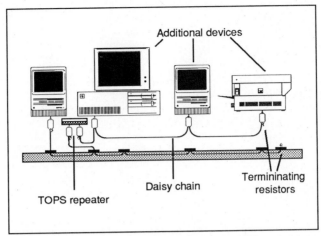

Figure 10-1. Use a repeater when the cable run of your network exceeds 1000 feet.

Bridges

Bridges provide a link between two similar networks. They allow the networks to function independently, but also provide a path between the different networks. Through bridges, resources such as file servers and printers can be shared. The primary use for bridges are:

- to increase network efficiency

- to connect networks that are far away

- to provide dial-in access

- to increase the number of nodes

Bridges allow you to increase the efficiency of your network by allowing you to separate a huge network into smaller logical groups called zones. This is usually called a *full bridge* or *local bridge*. In this configuration, only one bridge is needed per link. You can separate each department into smaller networks and connect them through bridges. By keeping the layout of your networks close to the layout of the office, it becomes easier to locate people and services (such as printers) on the network. In this arrangement, each smaller zone is free from unnecessary traffic. You can also use bridges to isolate high-demand users, freeing other users from having to work with a bogged-down network. Figure 10-2 shows an example of a simple bridge connection.

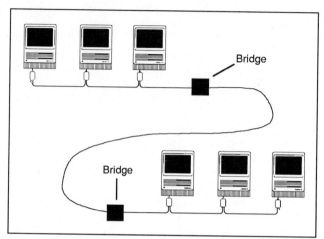

Figure 10-2. A simple bridge connection.

Bridges also allow you to connect networks over a modem. This type of connection is referred to as a *half bridge* or *remote bridge*. To establish a remote bridge, two bridges and two modems or a full duplex connection are needed, as shown in Figure 10-3. The modem setup connects distant networks over normal phone lines while the full duplex connection is used to connect distant networks over a leased phone line or dedicated cable.

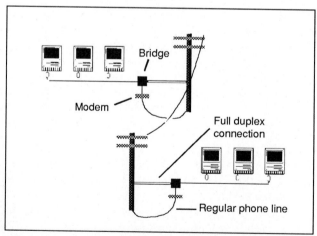

Figure 10-3. A remote bridge uses two bridges and two modems or a full duplex connection.

Because of slow modem speeds (usually ranging from 1,200 to 19,200 bps compared to AppleTalk's 230 Kbps), networks connected by remote bridges operate significantly slower. Only electronic mail, file transfer, and small-document printing is recommend for this arrangement.

Bridges that are connected to modems also allow remote users to dial in and function as if they were on the network. The speed limitations of remote bridges also apply to dial-in access.

Just like repeaters, bridges allow you to separate your network into different small networks or zones. This way you can significantly increase the number of nodes possible on your network.

Available bridges
Currently, there are several good bridges to choose from. The more popular bridges are:

- Hayes' Interbridge
- Shiva's TeleBridge
- Shiva's NetBridge
- Infosphere's Liaison

Hayes Interbridge
Hayes Interbridge is the grandaddy of AppleTalk bridges. It offers all the features mentioned above except for dial-in access. It gives you the basics for setting up a local or remote bridge.

> **Note**   On a remote bridge, Interbridge will only interface directly with a Hayes-compatible modem.

Shiva NetBridge
This product has most of the features offered by Interbridge, but can only function in a local or full bridge capacity. If you want remote bridge capability from Shiva, you need to go to their TeleBridge.

Shiva TeleBridge
TeleBridge specializes in remote bridging; you cannot set up local bridges with this product. It does allow Macs on the network to share a modem for outgoing calls, and also allows advanced users to configure TeleBridge to work with nonstandard

modems. With this feature, you can use a specialized high-speed modem for the remote connection.

Infosphere Liaison

Liaison is unusual because it is a software-only bridge The program runs in the background on a Macintosh and doesn't need dedicated hardware. It has all the features mentioned above, plus extensive dial-in security control. You can limit access to the answering bridge, the zone, or the entire network. Because this bridge relies heavily on the computing resources of a Mac, you might want to make sure the Mac that runs Liaison is a dedicated server or used lightly.

Gateways

A gateway is a relay station that not only bridges two networks but also acts as a translator between incompatible networks, allowing files and other services to move between them. Three gateway programs that connect other PC networks to AppleTalk are:

- FastPath

- GatorBox

- Netware 2.15

FastPath

Kinetic's FastPath allows you to connect AppleTalk nets to Ethernet wiring. With FastPath, you can hook several AppleTalk networks to TCP/IP and DECnet Ethernets. Mac users have access to systems and services on the Ethernet, and users of VAXes, UNIX machines, PCs, and terminals on the Ethernet can access services on the AppleTalk network.

GatorBox

GatorBox from Cayman systems allows users to integrate Macs on AppleTalk networks into Ethernet network environments. Using GatorBox, Macs can share files with systems such as Suns, VAXs, Apollos, and Macs running UNIX that support Network File System (NFS). NFS is developed by Sun Microsystems, and is the equivalent of the Apple Filing Protocol (AFP) offered by Apple. GatorBox's software translates AFP requests into NFS requests and NFS responses into AFP responses. The translation is so complete that Mac users access the NFS server as if it were an AppleShare server. GatorBox also offers terminal services, mail services, print services, and presentation services.

Netware 2.15

If you are running Novell on your PC network and AppleTalk on your Mac network and you want to connect them, you could upgrade your Netware LAN to the Netware Mac version. With all the necessary protocol conversion built in, this version can act as a gateway between your PCs and Macs. Mac users treat the Novell server as if it were an Appleshare server.

Star Controller

With a Star Controller, you can set up an active star network, which allows you to connect up to 12 daisy chains or trunks. In many ways it behaves as a multiple repeater that can handle up to 12 networks. Figure 10-4 shows you how you can use the Star Controller from Farallon Computing.

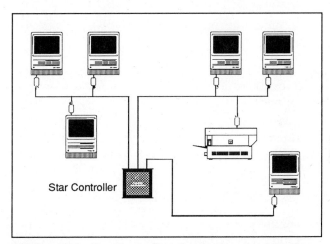

Figure 10-4. Farallon's Star Controller allows longer cable runs as well as acting as a network hub.

User education

You should constantly inform the users of all the changes you've made that could possibly affect them. People usually don't like it when their favorite printer is gone and they don't know where to print. Let the users know how these changes might affect the way they work; help them take advantage of the improvements you made.

Network management

No system runs perfectly forever; your TOPS network or internet is no exception. Without careful planning, standardizing software and hardware, monitoring and fine tuning the network, maintaining data integrity, and educating users, your TOPS internet could give you more pain than convenience.

Planning

To plan and design your internet effectively, you must understand your present and anticipate your future. Take the time for extensive analysis and careful design. You need to find out what kind of budget you are working within, what your users' needs are, and how your network is working now. Your solution must satisfy your users given these parameters.

Don't buy or implement anything you can't use now, but at the same time don't purchase anything that will be obsolete in a year. If you buy into technologies that are relatively old, chances are your equipment will be outdated quickly. New technologies, however, are usually expensive and sometimes unproven. Whenever possible, thoroughly research any new technology before you purchase it or add it to the network.

Standardizing software and hardware

Keep your network simple. The simpler the design, the easier it will be to maintain. Although you can buy a variety of programs to enhance your network and internet, they won't always work together. If you use a lot of network maintenance and troubleshooting programs, you may find that their incompatibilities are causing more troubles than they cure.

Application standardization
Application programs deserve some cautions also. Avoid having more than one or two software packages within any one software category. For example, over 50 different word processors exist just on the PC and Macintosh platforms.

Some of these can create files that are usable in other word processors, some of them cannot. For example WordPerfect on the Macintosh can read and write Microsoft Word documents, but Wordstar on the PC can only read and write Wordstar and ASCII files.

Generic ASCII files are readable by just about all word processors, but the hard returns and lack of formatting make them impractical for day-to-day. Therefore, the most practical word-processing package for a network is one supported by all of the computer platforms on the network.

Tip Cross-platform programs like Microsoft Word and Word-Perfect are usually good choices to put on the standards list, because their files are easily interchangeable between the Macintosh and PC platforms.

Ask your network users what software they prefer (from the network-compatible choices you give them) and make the process as democratic as possible. The needs of your various departments may preclude the use of only one or two word processors. If a small minority of users need a specific product that is incompatible with the majority's choice, the rules will need to be bent. Just remember that their software product must not interfere with the rest of the network. If their choice affects the network, it is your job to make them aware of it and remove them from the network if they insist on using the offending software.

In addition to using compatible software, it helps to standardize your software release levels. You can run into frustrating problems if some of your users are behind the rest of the network and have outdated software. Like a stubborn parent dealing with a teenager, older versions of a given software will not be able to understand files from an updated version. As the network manager, you must be sure to upgrade everybody to avoid these problems.

PCs and Macs promote individuality, and individuality spawns creativity, but too much variety on the network chews up valuable time for both you and your users. Users get confused because they have to keep track of each person's software choice and version number in order to exchange files.

The trick in establishing network standards is to balance user individuality with network compatibility and manageability.

Tip Your absolute minimum for standardization should be to make sure that, for any given program, all users are working with the same version.

Operating system standardization

Standardization is even more important for operating systems. Keep all of the operating systems on their respective platforms at the same level across the network. This is especially true with Macintoshes. Because the Macintosh operating system contains printer information, users can end up playing leapfrog with the laser printer initialization.

For example, a Macintosh user with System 5.0 prints a file out to a LaserWriter. The Mac operating system, recognizing that the printer has not been initialized, does so. Another user with System 6.0 prints something a few minutes later. Since the LaserWriter was not initialized with System 6.0, the operating system assumes the printer is not initialized and does so with 6.0. The first user comes back to print again with System 5.0. That system, not recognizing the 6.0 initialization, reinitializes the laser printer again. Each initialization adds thirty seconds to a minute to each print job. With enough print jobs, that could add up to an hour of lost productivity each day.

While it is important to have the same release level for computer operating systems on your network, you need only worry about the major release levels. For example, System 5.0.2 and System 6.0.2 are vastly different on the Macintosh and could cause network clashes. On the other hand System 6.0.2 and 6.0.3 look virtually identical to the network, the only difference being 6.0.3 is for use by the Macintosh SE/30 while 6.0.2 is for use by all other Macs.

Tip As completely new operating systems become available, wait before installing them on network computers. Quite often operating systems have teething pains and the only pacifier is the older operating system.

Monitoring and fine-tuning the network

The world is continually changing, and so is your company. Needs change; people and resources move around. You should have a map or list that shows the configuration of your system. Update it regularly to track developing problems. You must also have a way to monitor the network or internet so that you can correct a problem as soon as it occurs. For example, you might want to isolate power users from the rest of the users or you might want to balance your internet by grouping each heavy user with several light users in interconnected smaller networks called zones. If there is heavy use of a laser printer, you might increase the capacity of that device or put another one in the same area. If a user is using a distant printer and there is another printer closer, you might inform him/her to start using the closer printer to curb heavy traffic over the length of the network. Remember — depending on the way the network is laid out, the closest printer physically may not be the closest printer on the network.

When you make changes, make them one at a time. If you make too many modifications at once, you won't know where to look if something goes wrong. It's like a chemistry experiment: if you throw everything into the beaker at once, you have no way of knowing which chemical made it explode.

To make productive changes, you must have a way to monitor activity on your internet. Three programs, NetCheck, Inter-Poll, and Traffic Watch, allow you to keep track of your network's daily activity.

NetCheck

Farallon's NetCheck allows you to find out what's connected on the network. You can customize the search criteria so you only have to look at what you're interested in. Once you've found what you want, you can generate reports, which you can save for reference. By comparing new reports with old reports, you can easily see any differences that might contribute to a problem. Because it is a Desk Accessory for the Macintosh, you can invoke NetCheck any time you want. Included with the package is a program called LWStatus. LWStatus lets you view the printing status of LaserWriters on the network. It can save countless hours tracking breakdowns on the network. We recommend it for small to medium networks.

InterPoll

InterPoll from Apple is a grown-up version of NetCheck. Not only can you find out what's on the network and where everything is, you can even test individual devices across the network and find out what version of Macintosh system software is running on each system. We recommend this program for maintaining and troubleshooting medium to large networks.

TrafficWatch

For fine-tuning a network, Farallon's TrafficWatch is a must. TrafficWatch allows you to monitor the amount of activity each user generates and the amount of requests each devices receives. Not only does it allow you to watch this as it occurs, but it can also record activities at specified intervals like time-lapse photography. Along with TrafficWatch, Farallon also includes TrafficChart, NodeHint, and LWStatus. Traffic-Chart is a Microsoft Excel Macro which allows you to transform the data generated by TrafficWatch into easy-to-read charts. NodeHint allows you to assign node numbers to Macs on the network. While a Mac selects a unique node number at random when it starts up, sometimes you might want to have control over what number gets assigned to each node. Once assigned, the number stays with that node until there is a conflict, at which point a new random number will be assigned.

Although these programs help you keep track of what's happening on your network, you might sometimes want access to a given user's machine. Timbuktu and MacChuck are designed to allow a remote Mac to take control of another machine on the network. Timbuktu allows remote access to a Macintosh; MacChuck to a PC.

Timbuktu

Timbuktu from Farallon is almost like being in two places at the same time. If another Macintosh user on the network calls you for help with an application program, you simply call up Timbuktu from your Mac's desk accessory menu and immediately obtain full control of the user's computer (also equipped with Timbuktu) without leaving your office. On your computer, you can see everything on the user's screen. The other machine accepts input from your keyboard and your mouse. You can show the user what to do from your own desk. Of course, the user must first allow you access, and can terminate the connection at any time. Users can also choose to have no guests and allow only observer access to their computers. Each system can be protected by a password, to prevent unauthorized access.

Timbuktu also has a feature called SoftScreen which allows you to operate a Mac II family computer which has no keyboard, monitor, or video card. This feature is crucial if you want to dedicate a Mac II for file and mail service, but don't want a monitor and keyboard sitting wasted. Timbuktu is serialized just like TOPS; every machine must have a different copy of Timbuktu.

Tip You can also use Timbuktu to mount folders and volumes as well as start TOPS on other network users' machines.

MacChuck

While Timbuktu allows you to operate another Mac over the network, MacChuck allows you to operate PCs from a Mac. In order to run MacChuck, you need to install the driver and program on the target PC. On the Mac side, you just launch the application. The PC application will then appear as a window on the Mac.

■ Maintaining data integrity

Data integrity is the foundation of successful information management on a network. You measure this integrity by your data's security and reliability. A network manager faces three major obstacles in maintaining data integrity:

- data security — unauthorized tampering or access

- data corruption — viruses

- data reliability — hardware failure

Data security

It's important to safeguard your network without bogging down the flow of information. You need to protect your information from prying eyes and from intentional or unintentional sabotage. The two methods currently used for safeguarding data are *data encryption* and *data restriction*.

Data encryption means encoding a file so that it can't be read until it's decoded. The biggest drawback is the time it takes to encode and decode the file. In addition, this method does not prevent other people from obtaining the file and trying to decode it themselves. Two recent entries in this field are Camouflage from usrEZ Software and Sentinel from Super-Mac. Both programs offer the federal government's Data Encryption Standard (DES), as well as their own faster proprietary schemes.

Data restriction uses passwords to limit access to data on the network. If you don't have the password, you can't open the file. Entries in this field include Alsoft's MultiDisk, Symantec's HD Partition utility, Kent Marsh Ltd's MacSafe and NightWatch, and Magna's Empower. All of these programs, except NightWatch, allow you to partition your hard disk and assign a password to restrict access. Night-Watch, on the other hand, works to protect your system at night. With it, you can secure your system so that only people with a key disk (created using NightWatch) and the right password can boot up the hard disk.

WARNING **If your hard disk crashes, a hard disk partition can cause problems. Recovery software sometimes views the partition as one big file, making file recovery difficult if not impossible.**

Data corruption

For the past few years, users and computer support personnel have been battling a problem called computer viruses. Viruses are self-replicating programs often designed to corrupt data files or applications. Once they sneak into your system, they attach themselves to files or applications and multiply. Like a flu virus, they spread everywhere, infecting whatever they are designed to attack. You have no way of knowing where, when, or how they may strike. They could garble all the data on all the computers on your network before you even suspect they are there.

Most viruses attack only Macintoshes, because of the Mac file structure. The viruses use the resource forks on Macintosh files to pass themselves from one system to another. Since the operating system uses file resource forks like a handle on a skillet, it's easy to concentrate the infection on a certain part of the file for maximum spread. PCs, on the other hand, lack the sophistication of resource forks, so PC viruses are limited to certain application programs and their files. Therefore, we will only discuss virus protection for Macintoshes, since they stand to lose the most data.

The only sure-fire way to protect your network from these malicious creatures is abstinence. If you or your users don't put any new software or files onto your network, you'll be safe. However, this solution is not realistic or helpful. What good is a system that doesn't allow you to add anything to it? Also, it is next to impossible to prevent network users from putting anything new onto their computers. Fortunately, several software packages can help you fight this epidemic. We'll briefly discuss examples: Vaccine, Virex, and SAM.

Vaccine

Vaccine was the first non-commercial software to come to the rescue of virus-plagued Macintosh users. Thanks go to Mr. Donald Brown of CE Software (the makers of QuickMail), who released this program as a public domain software so that all users can have some protection. Vaccine is a preventative program; it attempts to stop the infection before it happens. Installation is simple; all you do is copy the program into the system folder. It does a fairly good job against most viruses. CE Software has not updated it frequently enough to battle some of the newer viruses.

Virex

Virex is a commercial virus-fighting program for the Macintosh. It is not a preventative program like Vaccine; rather, it is a fixer program. If you suspect a volume is infected, you can use Virex to seek and destroy all viruses it recognizes. Since new viruses emerge all the time, anti-virus programs become outdated rather quickly. HJC Software offers a yearly subscription for users to get upgrades every time a new virus is discovered and remedied.

SAM

SAM is the most comprehensive virus fighter. Not only does it attempt to prevent viruses from spreading in the first place, it also eliminates the viruses that exist on a hard disk. It even has an option allowing you to scan every floppy you put into your disk drive.

The cost of a commercial product seems less prohibitive when you consider that, without these programs, your only cure for an infected disk is complete reformatting. Even with these programs it takes about 15 minutes or more per machine to clear an infected disk, not to mention all the floppies that might be infected by contact with the infected disk. You need to balance the value of your time against the cost of the solution you choose. Finally, user education is still the most important element in virus prevention. You must have a procedure for everyone to follow, one that allows you to inspect every new piece of software you plan to put on the network.

WARNING Don't install any new software anywhere on the network without testing it for viruses. Even commercial programs from major vendors can carry a virus, thereby infecting the entire network.

Avoiding hardware failure

In the early days of microcomputers, hard disks were not very reliable and we were reminded constantly to back up our data — often by the hard disk crashing. Hard disks are getting more reliable and crashes are now rare. But they do happen, and backups are still a necessity. A crash without backup could mean a loss of weeks, months, or even years of work. A high price to pay, especially when so much hardware and software is available to make backup relatively painless. The basic steps to a successful backup program are:

- analysis and planning

- hardware and software selection

- testing

- user education

Analysis and planning

Your system must be tailored to the needs of both your users and the network administration staff. It must also fall within the department's budget. Your backup program needs to be as transparent as possible. A complicated or arbitrary system cuts down productivity, and can create resentment and frustration. At the same time, the system must have enough checks to ensure the smooth running of the system.

TOPS is a distributed file server system; it would be taxing to fully back up every system on the network. One strategy is to restrict what applications people put on their systems, so that all systems are identical except for data. This way, you only need to back up the data on each system; you can even access each machine's data over TOPS and back up the files across the network. Keep in mind that AppleTalk can only communicate at 230K; sending huge files across the network will bog it down for other users. A network backup would need to be done in off-hours and should utilize some of the faster network hardware like FlashCards and FlashBoxes with FlashTalk

If you've set up TOPS with a dedicated server, backup is even easier; you only need to back up the server. If each system has different application programs and files, you'll have to back up each system individually. By using speedy backup software and speedy hardware, you can at least cut down some of the time. You can also request that users put all data that needs backing up into a special partition or folder on their system. At the end of the day, they need to copy the data partition or folder into a centralized server for backup. This can eliminate the need to back up every system on the network. These are only a few suggestions; you'll need to spend time to find the best solution for you.

Selecting backup hardware and software

The hardware and software needed to backup your network depends on your specific network setup. A network with only four Macs on it could get by with a tape backup and a user responsible for backing up all of the machines across the network every Friday. A large network with Macs and PCs could use a dedicated server with a timed backup software system and large-capacity removable hard disk that polls all of the machines on the network and performs system backups in the middle of the night without user intervention.

Hardware

What kind of hardware you use depends on the amount of information to be backed up and your budget. You have four alternatives:

1. floppy disks

2. tape drives

3. removable hard disk cartridges

4. Bernoulli cartridges

Floppy disks

Floppy-based backups can be executed on 3.5-in. and/or 5.25-in. disks and utilize your existing equipment. For 3.5-in. backup, you can choose from the Macintosh's 400K, 800K, or 1.44MB drives or the PC's 720K or 1.44MB 3.5-in. drives. In 5.25-in. disks — the PC standard — you can use 360K or 1.2MB disk drives. High-capacity floppy systems such as Peripheral Land's Infinity 10 systems, Dolphin's Flipper 20, Mirror Technologies' RM20, and Jasmine's MegaDrive 20 are also available, but their high price and nonstandard formats make them unsuitable for backup.

The Apple 3.5-in. or PC 5.25-in. floppy-based backup is by far the most economical. The drives are already in your existing equipment, so you don't have to spend any more money buying a drive. However, floppy systems are slow. Backing up one 40MB hard drive could take half an hour or more.

Floppy disks also have limited storage. To back up a 20MB hard drive using 800K diskettes, you need at least 25 diskettes. If you lose any one of these diskettes, your whole backup set could be useless (depending on the backup software). Of course, as you step up to high-capacity floppies, the number of diskettes you need will decrease.

Tip If you use high-capacity floppies as a backup, make sure you have at least two machines capable of using high-capacity floppies. If one machine suffers catastrophic failure, the other can still retrieve data.

Tape drives

Tape drives have been around for a long time and are probably the most popular dedicated backup mechanism. The major advantage of tape drives is their high capacity. You can usually back up a whole 80MB hard disk on one tape. Another advantage of some tape drives is that they share the same format for both Macs and PCs.

The Irwin 5080 tape backup system for the Mac and 2080 system for the PC utilize the same 80MB tape format. If a Mac system backed up with the 5080 went down, the PC 2080 drive could retrieve the data from the Mac backup.

Tape drives are slow compared to hard media, but you can usually execute the backup command and leave the system unattended. The major drawback of a tape system is that you cannot boot off a tape. If your hard drive is down, a tape backup won't help you until the hard drive is fixed or replaced.

Removable hard drives

The technology for removable high-capacity drives has been around for a while, but reliability plagued this technology. Syquest conquered the reliability problem and now has a popular removable hard disk. This system is designed to be a primary hard disk system. For our purposes, we are looking at it as a network backup system. If your network has a dedicated server, this drive could be used as the primary drive for the server and the backup drive for the network.

The Syquest drive has a formatted capacity of 42MB and an average access time of 26 milliseconds (ms), as fast as the average hard drive. The cartridges are 5.25-in. square and approximately 1/4-in. thick. Inside the case is a metal platter, just like the ones found in conventional hard drives.

One or two cartridges can easily back up any large-capacity hard drive. In speed, this system can rival even fast conventional hard drives. Imagine backing up a 20MB hard disk in less than five minutes. The most important benefit of this system is that it can easily replace a crashed hard disk. Just pull out the bad hard drive, plug in the backup cartridge, and your computer is up and functional again after a down time of less than 15 minutes. The main disadvantages of these systems are price (over $800 at publication time), and the fact that to back up a cartridge, you need at least two cartridge drives or a dual cartridge drive. If your budget allows, this is by far the best backup solution.

Iomega Bernoulli systems

Iomega has been in the removable business for a long time with its Bernoulli systems. Its latest offering of a 5.25-in. 44MB removable system can easily rival the Syquest system. This system has the same advantages and disadvantages as the Syquest unit. While the Syquest unit has hard-disk cartridges with an access time of 26 ms, the Bernoulli has floppy-based cartridges with an access time of 32 ms. The media is also less expensive than the removable hard disk.

Software selection

Most backup software is aimed at people who back up onto floppies or tapes. In these cases, the program manages the files and distributes the contents of the hard disk onto the floppies. If you are using a removable hard disk system or Bernoulli drive, you will not need a backup program at all.

In this section, we will look at some of the more common backup programs: Redux 1.01 and 1.5, DiskFit 1.5, HFS Backup 2.0, for the Macintosh, and Fastback for the Mac and PC.

Speed

Speed is probably one of the most important features in a backup program. Currently, the fastest program is Fastback, followed by HFS backup, DiskFit, and Redux.

Tip To help speed backups, you can create a partition on your hard disk and put all data into the partition. This allows you to back up the most rapidly changing part of your disk without waiting for a backup of the rest.

Unattended backup

Unattended backup is an important feature, especially for the busy or absent-minded user. In this batch of programs, only DiskFit 1.5, FastBack 2.0, and HFS Backup 2.0 can do scheduled unattended backups.

Hard cartridge support

Teamed with a fast removable system, backup can be painless. The only program that does not support hard cartridge is the current version of HFS Backup.

Selective backup

In some cases, you might not always need to back up everything on your hard disk. The ability to choose exactly what you want to back up can be very convenient. All the programs here offer this feature except DiskFit. With DiskFit, if you don't want to backup a folder, you need to rename the folder by putting the name of the folder in brackets [xxx]. If you did not want to backup the folder, Accounting, you would have to rename it to [Accounting]. A similar feature is the ability to tell the backup program to back up only documents on the hard disk. Again, all the programs here have that feature.

File compression

Fastback has several compression options that can cut file size 20 to 80%.

These are only a handful of the features you'll find useful in these programs. With this representative list of programs we hope you can better decide which program will suit your needs.

Testing

Before you add a new element to your network, you need to test it. You must find out first-hand how it performs and whether it is fully compatible. You can not always trust what you read; everyone's situation is different and there's no way for anybody to anticipate every situation and every combination of software and hardware.

User education

To manage a computer network effectively, you must first understand how people interact with computers. It's important that users understand the procedures and why it is important to follow them. About 50% of your job as network manager is getting your users to cooperate.

■ Conclusion

The tailoring business has a saying that can apply here with a little modification. "Measure twice, cut once." Go over any improvements to your network carefully, and when you think you've solved all the bugs, show your plans to someone else. If you sit down and think about what you want to do ahead of time, you'll have the best chance of utilizing your resources efficiently.

One final bit of advice: If you find yourself managing a larger network than you can handle, try to seek out individuals in each department who are both technically competent and interested in the job. Then give them adequate resources and you'll find them powerful allies. Most important of all, encourage them to reach out and help those around them. The network is a team effort. If your assistants can solve problems before you have to deal with them, you can devote your time to other projects. Maybe, if you're lucky, you'll get an afternoon of golf in once in a while.

Chapter Eleven

◼ Customizing TOPS on the PC

By now you should understand something about networks and TOPS. Most TOPS users don't need to go any further. However, a small percentage may want to modify TOPS on the PC to enhance its performance.

This chapter gives you an in-depth look at customizing TOPS on the PC. To get the most out of it, you should be familiar with the basics of batch programming. Although the methods in this chapter require some extra work, they can help you unleash the full power of TOPS on the PC.

Customizing TOPS on the PC involves three topics:

- understanding TOPS commands for DOS
- using TOPS commands in batch files
- modifying TOPS system files

◼ Understanding TOPS commands for DOS

A quick review before we start: When you load TOPS , you put the TOPS software modules into memory. From that point, TOPS waits for you to tell it what to do. You can issue commands in two different ways: (1) from the TOPS menuing system or (2) directly from the DOS prompt (also called a *command line*).

To use the menuing system, you load the separate TOPSMENU program. This brings up a point-and-shoot menu shell. To work with TOPS, you select from the lists on the screen. You highlight your choice and press Enter. Once you press Enter, the menuing system takes care of issuing commands to TOPS itself.

If you prefer, you can deal directly with TOPS. In that case, you do not load the optional TOPSMENU program. Instead, you type in commands at the DOS prompt.

The individual TOPS DOS commands provide all of the functions of the menu program and more. They also allow you to make custom batch files or custom menuing systems.

This section describes the following:

- the proper format for commands

- commands for server functions

- commands for client functions

- commands for miscellaneous functions

Formatting commands correctly

With few exceptions (such as passwords), TOPS DOS commands begin with the word TOPS or the letters *T*, *X*, or *P*. They are not case sensitive — that is, the computer doesn't care whether you type a command in upper or lower case letters. We have several symbols to explain the TOPS commands, as summarized them in Table 11-1.

Table 11-1. Shorthand for TOPS commands

Item	Definition
[ ]	Parts of the command found in brackets are optional; the command runs with or without it. Do not type the brackets themselves.
lowercase	Indicates a name.
		Represents the word *or*. It separates parameters (optional or not) when only one or the other is needed.
/	Indicates a "switch" — a special extra instruction that modifies the main command.

Figure 11-1 shows a typical command in two forms: (1) as it would be shown in this book and (2) as you might actually type it into the computer.

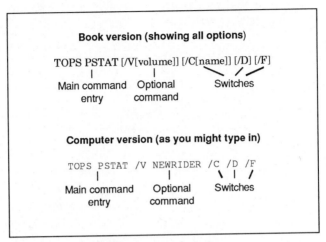

Figure 11-1. TOPS command syntax.

As you can see, the book version is simply a way to format commands so you can tell what is what.

Rather than spend more time explaining the format, we'd like to plunge into some examples. The system will become clear once you've tried it a time or two.

Using server commands

Since servers deal mainly with publishing, you only have to remember three easy commands: PUBLISH, UNPUBLISH, and PSTAT (for publish status). All three commands apply both to directories (which become volumes once published) and to printers.

Publishing a volume

Whenever you want to make a directory available on the network, use the PUBLISH command. Here is the formula:

```
TOPS PUBLISH c:\path AS volume [/X] [/R | /RW]
[/P [password]] <Enter>
```

That may look a little tangled, so let's unravel it:

TOPS Publish is the main command.

c:\path indicates the source drive and pathname for directory to be published. For example, you would type `C:\` to publish your entire C: drive or `C:\BUSINESS` to publish a directory called C:\BUSINESS.

> **Note** If you do not enter a pathname, TOPS uses the current directory.

AS is the part of the command that separates the actual name of the directory from its alias. Notice that you put a space before and after.

volume represents the alias for the volume when published on the network. The alias is the name the rest of the network will see. It can be up to 16 characters long and may contain blank spaces.

/X is an optional addition telling TOPS to skip the XSYNC utility (described later in this chapter). Use /X for directories you publish often or when publishing your entire hard drive.

/R or */RW*, defines access privileges. Read-only (/R) access prevents clients from changing files on your disk. Read/write (/RW) access allows a client to save changes to published files on your disk.

/P [password] assigns a password to a published volume. Passwords can be up to 16 characters long and may contain blank spaces. Unlike most TOPS DOS commands, passwords are case sensitive (*H* does not match *h*). If you just type /P, TOPS asks you to enter a password.

Now a complete example. Let's say you want to publish a directory called *lastqtr* from drive C: as *4th Qtr Sales*, and you decide to give clients read/write access. In addition, you decide to protect the volume with a password (*happy days*). The command for all this would be:

```
TOPS PUBLISH c:\lastqtr AS 4th Qtr Sales /RW /P
happy days <Enter>
```

Unpublishing a volume

The UNPUBLISH command removes a volume from the network. It looks like this:

```
TOPS UNPUBLISH volume | /A <Enter>
```

volume represents the alias for the volume already published.

/A tells the computer to unpublish all volumes you have already published.

For example, if you need to unpublish a directory with the alias "Receive" enter the following:

```
TOPS UNPUBLISH Receive <Enter>
```

Note You must unpublish a volume or printer before shutting down your machine. Otherwise, other users who attempt to access the volume or printer will get an error message.

You cannot unpublish a volume currently being used by a client. To see which of your volumes are are being used, use the PSTAT command.

Displaying the status of published volumes

The PSTAT command allows you to check the status of volumes you've published. Let's look at it in our usual shorthand:

```
TOPS PSTAT [/V [volume]] [/C [name]] [/D] [/F]
<Enter>
```

Time to dissect it:

/V [volume] displays all volumes you have published. If you enter a specific volume name, you can see which clients are currently using that volume.

/C [name] displays all clients using volumes you have published. If you enter a specific client name, you can see which volumes are currently being used by that client.

/D displays all of your directories currently in use.

/F displays all of your files currently in use.

Let's take an example. If you need to see who's using the file of customer listings in your *Customer* directory, type the following:

```
TOPS PSTAT /V Customer <Enter>
```

Using client commands

Since clients deal mainly with mounting, you only have to remember four easy commands: DIR (for directory), MOUNT, UNMOUNT, and CSTAT (for client status). The DIR command deals with servers on the network; the other three commands apply to published volumes and printers.

Getting a network directory

Should you need to see all the servers available on the network or the volumes an individual server has published, use the DIR command:

```
TOPS DIR [server] <Enter>
```

The *server* part of the command displays all volumes published by that server. If no server name is entered, all servers on the network are displayed.

For instance, if you want to see which servers have volumes published, enter the following:

```
TOPS DIR <Enter>
```

Mounting a volume

When you want to mount a published volume from the network, use the MOUNT command, as follows:

```
TOPS MOUNT c: TO server volume [/R | /RW] [/P
[password]] <Enter>
```

Now let's define it:

c: stands for the drive letter assigned to the mounted volume.

Tip DOS considers drives A: through E: to be local drives. It's a good idea, therefore, to assign mounted drives labels F: to Z:.

server is the name of the server that published the volume.

volume is the name of the volume you want to mount.

/R | /RW defines the access privileges you want while using the mounted volume. Use /R if you don't need to make any changes. Use /RW if you need to enter new data or modify a file in some way. Note, however, that you cannot give yourself read/write privileges if the person who published the volume already defined it as read only.

Tip Even though you don't think you've made changes to data, many application programs will attempt to write data or configuration files to disk. Use read-only access when you want to make absolutely sure your application doesn't write to the volume.

/P [password] indicates password protection for a volume. Remember, passwords are case sensitive (*H* does not match *h*). If you just type /P, TOPS asks you to enter a password. If you do not use /P when trying to mount a volume with password-protection, TOPS asks you to enter a password before mounting.

Now let's put it all together in an example: Let's say you want to mount the volume *Contact Letters* (located on the Publications server) as drive L. We'll assume you only need read only access and that the volume has no password. In these circumstances, you would type:

```
TOPS MOUNT L: TO Publications Contact Letters /R
<Enter>
```

Unmounting a volume

When you need to unmount a volume, use the UNMOUNT command, as follows:

```
TOPS UNMOUNT c: | /A <Enter>
```

Here, *c:* is the drive letter of volume you want to unmount.

/A unmounts all volumes. For instance, if you've finished working with all of the volumes you have mounted, type the following:

```
TOPS UNMOUNT /A <Enter>
```

Note You should always unmount before turning off your machine. Otherwise, you could cause problems for the server station, which would still show the volume mounted. (See the TOPS LOGOUT command in the "Miscellaneous commands" section.)

Checking the status

To check your client status on the network, use the CSTAT command, as follows:

```
TOPS CSTAT [c:] <Enter>
```

c: is the drive letter for a mounted volume. Specifying the drive displays the volume and reveals which server it was mounted from. If no specific drive letter is entered, all currently mounted drives are shown.

Miscellaneous commands

The following TOPS DOS commands perform various functions, most of them self-explanatory. We've listed the commands in alphabetical order.

Understanding error messages

If you receive messages reporting errors with the TOPS network driver software, use the ERR command, as follows:

```
TOPS ERR /A <Enter>
```

The computer will then provide information about the error, its causes and solutions.

| Note | This command will not work unless you have TOPS FlashCard.

Getting help

When you need information about a particular TOPS command, or just help with the TOPS DOS commands in general, use the HELP command, as follows:

```
TOPS HELP [command | /A] <Enter>
```

command represents the name of the command you need information about.

/A displays help screens for all commands.

For example, if you want to find out more on how to publish a volume, enter the following:

```
TOPS HELP Publish <Enter>
```

Logging out a client

If a client shuts off the computer without unmounting a volume published from your PC, use the LOGOUT command. Here's how it looks:

```
TOPS LOGOUT name | /A <Enter>
```

name is the name of the client station you wish to logout.

/A logs out all clients using any of your published volumes.

Suppose someone in the accounting department (with the station name of *Accounting*) had mounted a volume you published but turned off the computer without first unmounting the volume. This can causes problems for you, since your server station shows the volume still mounted. Fortunately, you can log out that station by typing the following:

```
TOPS LOGOUT Accounting <Enter>
```

Automating publishing and mounting
Use the REMEMBER command when you have a series of published and/or mounted volumes you use often. With the remember command, you can tell TOPS to publish and/or mount these volumes automatically each time you start TOPS. To use the command, first publish and/or mount the volumes. Then issue the Remember command:

```
TOPS REMEMBER [filename] <Enter>
```

If you don't enter a filename, TOPS stores the publish and/or mount commands in a batch file called TOPSTART.BAT.

Shutting down TOPS
The SHUTDOWN command provides an alternative to using PSTAT followed by UNPUBLISH. It allows you to unpublish and unmount all volumes in one step. Here's how it goes:

```
TOPS SHUTDOWN <Enter>
```

Any clients currently using your published volumes will be notified before the shutdown is completed — kind of like saying, "Everybody out of the pool."

Unloading TOPS modules

If you need to unload any of the TOPS software modules stored in your PC's memory, use the UNLOAD command, as follows:

```
TOPS UNLOAD KRNL (CLNT) | TALK (TALC) | ATALK |
TNETBIOS | /A <Enter>
```

KRNL (CLNT) unloads the TOPS configuration data module — KRNL for servers, CLNT for clients.

TALK (TALC) unloads TOPS network communications module — TALK for servers, TALC for clients.

ATALK unloads both ALAP and PSTACK modules (LocalTalk software drivers for TOPS FlashCard).

TNETBIOS unloads TOPS version of NETBIOS instructions (cannot be unloaded with /A option).

/A unloads all TOPS modules stored in memory, with the exception of TOPS' version of NETBIOS.

WARNING Using the /A option to unload the TNETBIOS module may cause your computer to crash. To avoid this possibility, unload TNETBIOS before unloading any other TOPS modules.

Tip To prevent conflicting system errors, unload modules in reverse of the order you loaded them.

As an example, let's say you want to unload the TOPS server/client configuration data module (KRNL) so you can load the client only configuration. To do so, type:

```
TOPS UNLOAD KRNL <Enter>
```

TOPS version number

The following command will display the version number and serial number of your TOPS software:

```
TOPS VER <Enter>
```

■ Batch files

Even if you don't use the DOS command line very often, you can save yourself a lot of effort by combining TOPS DOS commands in batch files. A *batch file* contains a series or *batch* of commands that run in sequence. You can customize batch files to perform any series of functions you want.

Batch files can make using TOPS easier and more automatic. Batch files can result in significant time savings and cost benefits. This section presents a practical, how-to approach for using batch files and includes sample batch files you can use with your TOPS network. We'll do this in three parts:

- uses for batch files
- creation of batch files
- sample batch files

Uses for batch files

Batch files have unlimited uses for both the novice and the experienced power user. These functions can be grouped into three main categories:

- simplifying tasks
- repeating tasks
- combining tasks

Simplifying tasks

TOPS has already simplified the task of loading the TOPS network software — just enter LOADTOPS (for server use) or LOADCLNT (for client use). These batch files load all the necessary software modules needed into your PC's memory. That's much easier than typing four or five different commands, some (or all) of which you might not even recognize.

Other tasks that TOPS can simplify include publishing and/or mounting the same volumes week after week. Let's say you work in the accounting department. You balance the drafts and receipts in numerous spreadsheets on your PC, all stored according to category. When you want to publish the spreadsheet data for others to use, you can use the TOPS

REMEMBER command to create a batch file that publishes each directory containing the necessary information.

Repeating tasks

Batch files make tasks infinitely more bearable by eliminating the boredom of repetition — even the thankless task of entering TOPS before using every TOPS command.

Let's say you're in charge of a simple TOPS network with two or three PCs and a Macintosh. One of the people using a PC is still a little apprehensive just being around a computer, let alone trying to use a network. You can set up a series of custom batch files for this person that simplify the three or four TOPS commands needed.

For example, a batch file called *Monday* can help someone who needs to do a series of tasks every Monday morning. This file might contain TOPS commands that publish a specific directory containing work assignments for the week, mount the PAYROLL directory from Accounting's PC to enter timesheets, and mount a database for updating client contact records. (The sample batch files at the end of this section illustrate these and other repetitive tasks.)

Combining tasks

Batch files also permit different tasks to be combined into one easy command. You can change directories, open programs, copy or print files, even go somewhere or copy something else when you're done. Anything you can do from the DOS command line can be put in a batch file and made to perform at your bidding.

You can create a batch file named *GoThere* that leaves your current directory (regardless of where it is), goes to your database directory, and starts the database program. Once you exit the program, the batch file can still be waiting and, like a faithful mountain guide, take you back from whence you came (or at least back to the trailhead).

Your TOPS batch files can include a number of combined tasks. LOADTOPS already combines the loading of four different modules. Add TOPSTART and a TOPS command or two (like PSTAT and TOPS DIR) to the same batch file, and you'll be given a complete inventory of your active files, plus a list of available servers every time you get started.

Creation of batch files

Every experienced user has a favorite system for creating batch files. Rather than trying to tell you which is the best way, this section gives you three simple methods for creating batch files you can use with TOPS. They include:

- TOPS REMEMBER command

- simple line editors

- advanced editors and chaining commands

Remember command

The REMEMBER command provides the easiest way to create a batch file for TOPS. Whether from the TOPS menu program or with TOPS DOS commands, REMEMBER gives you flexibility and simplicity.

A common use of REMEMBER involves starting up the TOPS menu program and publishing and mounting volumes the way you'll usually need them. When you're done setting things up, select the REMEMBER command from the menu and press Enter. TOPS does the rest. It stores all your currently published and mounted volumes in a batch file called TOPSTART, then adds TOPSTART to the LOADTOPS batch file. From then on, every time you load the TOPS network software, this set of volumes is published and mounted for you.

When you get a little more adept at using TOPS, the REMEMBER command from the DOS command line opens up new possibilities, allowing you to set up different batch files for different volumes you need to publish or mount. (If you skipped the discussion of this command earlier in this chapter, turn back to the section on "Miscellaneous commands" and read it now.)

For example, suppose you spend half your day working for the director of marketing, answering questions about products, compiling data on customer contacts, and preparing promotional materials. You have to mount volumes containing product spec documents, customer databases, and some basic graphics layout tools, as well as publish your contact data and promotional ideas. Once you've finished publishing and mounting for one day, just enter TOPS REMEMBER Markets, and your new *Markets* batch file will do the job for you every morning.

Other tasks that require a particular grouping of volumes can be stored (remembered) under a different file name. That way you can switch back and forth between your two jobs and never forget which directory you're in or what you're supposed to be doing there.

As effective as the REMEMBER command is, it can only execute TOPS commands. You'll need some extra information if you want to execute DOS or other non-TOPS commands in your batch files. That's next.

Editing batch files with COPY

The simplest line editor in the DOS environment happens to be the COPY command. Although it's not really an editor, you can use it to edit ordinary batch files. Basically, you type the batch file from scratch, then copy what you type from the keyboard into a file on the computer. Here's the command:

```
COPY CON [filename] <Enter>
```

CON stands for *console* (another word for your keyboard and monitor). When you enter the filename with the .BAT extension, it works like any other batch file. Here are a couple of examples:

Your boss is always asking you to find some obscure memo he can't locate. You need a simple batch file that lets you publish your Memos directory as a TOPS volume at a moments notice — we'll call it *Quick*. At the DOS prompt, type the following:

```
COPY CON quick.bat <Enter>
TOPS PUBLISH c:\Memos AS Memos <Enter>
^Z <Enter>
```

DOS responds by telling you that one file has been copied. Presto — your batch file is complete.

| Note | As you can see, the second line ends with a funny symbol called a *control character.* You type this by holding down the control key (CTRL) and pressing Z. You can also get a ^Z by pressing F6. Be sure to press Enter after ^Z.

To unpublish Memos as quickly as you published it, make a batch file called *Done.* Use the COPY command just as you did before. From the DOS prompt, type:

```
COPY CON done.bat <Enter>
TOPS UNPUBLISH Memos <Enter>
^Z <Enter>
```

You will get the same response as before (1 File(s) copied).

You decide to change the name of your Memos directory to Oldmemos in order to separate last year's correspondence from new letters. To edit your existing *Quick* batch file, just retype it on the DOS command line using the new directory name. If you need to remember what your batch file contains, use the TYPE command at the DOS prompt:

```
TYPE quick.bat <Enter>
```

The contents of QUICK.BAT appear on the screen. Now type:

```
COPY CON quick.bat <Enter>
TOPS PUBLISH c:\Oldmemos AS Oldmemos <Enter>
^Z <Enter>
```

If you wish to confirm that QUICK.BAT was changed, you can use the TYPE command again to display its contents on the screen.

Editing batch files with EDLIN

While COPY can help out in a pinch, you don't want to retype a batch file that has several hundred characters every time you change one line. That's where real line editors come into play. Line editors are almost as numerous as computers themselves. If you've got a favorite, don't switch just because of us.

The following examples are given using EDLIN because it normally comes with every copy of PC-DOS. If you prefer another editor, experiment a little to find out how to make the same things happen with your own program. If you've never used a line editor, or are scared to death to try, you can follow these two examples and take a step forward in your knowledge of computer operation.

We're going to add two commands at the beginning of the Markets batch file that unpublish and unmount whatever you currently have on your PC. This saves on memory and speeds up the network.

■ At the DOS command line, start EDLIN and load the Markets batch file by typing:

```
edlin markets.bat <Enter>
```

The screen should read:

```
End of input file
*
```

■ Now list the contents of the batch file. At the DOS prompt, type:

```
L <Enter>
```

The following information will appear on your screen:

1. *TOPS MOUNT D: TO Dave's_PC Clients /P gumdrops

2. TOPS MOUNT E: TO Publications Equipment_Desc.

3. TOPS MOUNT F: TO Don's_Artsy_Mac Page_Layout

4. TOPS PUBLISH C:\DB\Customer AS Customer_Contact /R

5. TOPS PUBLISH C:\Promo\Ideas AS Promo_Ideas

■ Insert the two new commands. At the DOS prompt, type:

```
1i <Enter>
```

The screen shows: 1:*

■ Now type:

```
TOPS UNPUBLISH /A <Enter>
```

The screen shows: 2:*

■ Type:

```
TOPS UNMOUNT /A <Enter>
```

The screen shows: 3:*

■ Type:

```
<Ctrl><Break> (Press the Control and Break keys
simultaneously)
```

The screen shows: *

■ List the modified batch file. Type:

```
L <Enter>
```

The screen shows the following:

1. TOPS UNPUBLISH /A

2. TOPS UNMOUNT /A

3. *TOPS MOUNT D: TO Dave's_PC Clients /P gumdrops

4. TOPS MOUNT E: TO Publications Equipment_Desc.

5. TOPS MOUNT F: TO Don's_Artsy_Mac Page_Layout

6. TOPS PUBLISH C:\DB\Customer AS Customer_Contact /R

7. TOPS PUBLISH C:\Promo\Ideas AS Promo_Ideas

■ Save MARKETS.BAT and exit Edlin. Type:

```
e <Enter>
```

The screen shows: C:\ (or whatever directory you started from).

> **Note** When you end Edlin, it saves a backup copy of your original file. The backup has .BAK for the filename extension. Don't confuse this with your .BAT batch file. You can delete the backup file unless you want to save the extra copy.

We already have added the Unpublish and Unmount commands in the *Persons* batch file, but suppose for the next couple of weeks you need to publish a directory that will contain procedures involving the new company benefit program, as well as memos to be distributed in house and letters to be mailed to all employees concerning the changes.

■ At the DOS command line, start Edlin and load the Persons batch file. At the DOS prompt, type:

```
edlin Persons.bat <Enter>
```

The screen responds: End of input file

■ Now list the contents of the batch file. Type:

```
L <Enter>
```

The screen displays the following:

1. *TOPS MOUNT H: TO Sandy's_Place Personal_History /P sensitive

2. TOPS MOUNT I: TO Sandy's_Place Benefits_Info /R

3. TOPS MOUNT J: TO Sandy's_Place Job_Descriptions /P workplace

■ Insert the new publish command at the end of the file. Type:

```
4i <Enter>
```

The screen responds: 4:*

■ Now type:

```
TOPS PUBLISH c:\Benefits AS Benefits_Work <Enter>
```

The screen shows: 5:*

■ Type:

```
<Ctrl><Break> (Press the Control and Break keys
simultaneously)
```

The screen shows: *

■ List the modified batch file. Type:

```
L <Enter>
```

The screen displays the following:

1. *TOPS MOUNT H: TO Sandy's_Place Personal_History /P sensitive

2. TOPS MOUNT I: TO Sandy's_Place Benefits_Info /R

3. TOPS MOUNT J: TO Sandy's_Place Job_Descriptions /P workplace

4. TOPS PUBLISH C:\Benefits AS Benefits_Work

■ Save PERSONS.BAT and end Edlin. Type:

    e <Enter>

The screen shows: C:\ (or whatever directory you started from).

While Edlin and the REMEMBER command are easy to use, you cannot create those special batch files you've always wanted without spending a lot of extra time and effort. Fortunately, many advanced editors, including high-powered word-processing programs, make it easy to create complex batch files that make use of *chaining* commands together.

Using such an editor gives you the advantage of revising a file without retyping entire lines of text (or the whole thing, as with the COPY command). You can also use existing files to cut and paste commands and functions for new and different purposes. Finally, the power and flexibility of chaining simple batch files together provides infinite combinations of commands to meet your TOPS needs. Refer to the next section for an example of chaining batch files.

Sample batch files

Here are some sample batch files you might use for everyday TOPS needs. Many of these are oversimplified, and a few are more complex than the average user needs to tackle. However, we hope each example might introduce new ideas or creative approaches to problems you are facing right now in your own work place.

The sample batch files in this section include:

• automating startup

• simple publishing

• configuring TOPS data file

• creating weekly batch files

• running another program

- modifying LOADTOPS

- chaining batch files

Automating startup

What could be easier than sitting down at the keyboard, typing your name, and having your computer do the rest? Well, this batch file comes pretty close. Enter the following at the DOS command line (type in your name where it says "me"):

```
COPY CON me.bat <Enter>
LOADTOPS <Enter>
TOPS STATION me <Enter>
TOPSMENU <Enter>
^Z <Enter>
```

The screen responds: "1 File(s) copied"

Now every time you want to start TOPS, just type your name, and the rest is automatic.

Simple publishing

Whenever you need to publish or mount the same directories over and over, use the TOPS REMEMBER command to create a batch file that's easy to recognize.

Tip Enter this example at the DOS command line. You can also perform the same publishing steps from within the TOPS menu program, then use the REMEMBER option from the Main menu before quitting.

In the accounting department, you need to publish several volumes. Enter these TOPS commands on the DOS command line:

```
TOPS PUBLISH c:\Supplies AS Office_Supplies
<Enter>
TOPS PUBLISH c:\Utility AS Gen._Utilities <Enter>
TOPS PUBLISH c:\Tran-Rcv AS Transport-Recv
<Enter>
TOPS PUBLISH c:\Tran-Pay AS Transport-Pay <Enter>
```

Response (once for each line entered):

TOPS: updating directories to be published...

Enter:

```
TOPS REMEMBER Accounts <Enter>
```

Response:

Saving TOPS setup to file C:\ACCOUNTS.BAT

Now, whenever you to publish these particular volumes for others on the network to see and use, just type `Accounts` on the DOS command line.

Configuring the TOPS data file

If you need two (or more) different settings for the TOPS data file, you can use this batch file to quickly change between the two, reload the new file, and keep running with TOPS.

■ Make a copy of the TOPS data file (TOPSKRNL.DAT) and name it TOPSKRNL.2. Edit this file to include all of the changes you need (fewer clients and open volumes, etc.) for a different TOPS operating configuration. Keep both copies of TOPSKRNL in the same directory with your other TOPS network software. (This example assumes these files are kept in a directory named TOPS.)

■ Create the following batch file using Edlin or the editor of your choice. Choose a name that's easy to remember for the function the file performs (i.e., SWITCH.BAT or CON-FIG-2.BAT).

```
TOPS UNLOAD KRNL
REN \TOPS\TOPSKRNL.DAT KRNLTEMP
REN \TOPS\TOPSKRNL.2 TOPSKRNL.DAT
REN \TOPS\KRNLTEMP TOPSKRNL.2
TOPSKRNL
```

WARNING Only run this batch file if you have already loaded TOPS. If the TOPS data file has not been loaded, the first line of this batch file results in an error, the next three lines go ahead and rename all the files (changing your configuration data), but the last line fails also. You must then rename each file before you can properly load the previous TOPS configuration.

Tip It's a good idea to use different station names for your different configurations. That way, after loading TOPSKRNL,

TOPS tells you "Initializing network name: name...." so you know which configuration you've loaded.

Tip You can use three or more copies of TOPSKRNL.DAT by renaming files in series — TOPSKRNL.3 becomes TOPSKRNL.2, KRNLTEMP becomes TOPSKRNL.3, etc.

Creating weekly batch files

Our *Monday* batch file is designed for a the inexperienced computer user. As the name indicates, a batch file of this type can be run once a week on Monday mornings, and that's as close to TOPS as they need to come. Create the following batch file (named, naturally, MONDAY.BAT) using Edlin or the editor of your choice and modify the example to include the volume names your inexperienced user needs.

```
TOPS PUBLISH C:\WP\ASSIGN AS ASSIGNMENTS
TOPS MOUNT E: TO ACCOUNTING TIMESHEETS
TOPS MOUNT D: TO MARKETING CONTACT DATABASE
```

Tip You can also start the programs this user needs by entering the filenames after the TOPS commands.

A *Goodbye* batch file can unmount and unpublish a person's TOPS volumes, as well as unload the TOPS networking software and park the disk head, if necessary, before they shut down their computer. Create the following batch file using Edlin or the editor of your choice and modify the example to include the volume names your inexperienced user has loaded.

```
TOPS UNMOUNT /A
TOPS UNPUBLISH /A
TOPS UNLOAD /A
```

Tip You can also use the TOPS SHUTDOWN command instead of UNMOUNT and UNPUBLISH. This automatically sends a message to all clients using a published volume that the directory is about to be unpublished.

Running another program

A *GoThere* batch file comes in handy if you need to run a different program and return when you're finished. Create the following batch file (named *Go-dBASE*) using Edlin or the editor of your choice and modify the example to include the directory where you want to go and the program name to execute.

```
CD \DBASE
DBASE
CD \
```

Tip If you want to return to another directory instead of the *root directory* (C:\), enter the pathname after the program command, and when you exit the program, *GoThere* takes you where you want to go.)

Modifying LOADTOPS

If you've been using TOPS and have set up a series of volumes you publish on a regular basis (using the REMEMBER command, etc.), you might want to modify your LOADTOPS batch file to take care of some mundane administrative-type tasks. This example shows you how to add two TOPS commands — PSTAT and TOPS DIR — to remind you which volumes you've already published and mounted, as well as all of the servers currently on the network which you can mount more volumes from. Edit the LOADTOPS.BAT file using Edlin or the editor of your choice. Then change it to look like this:

```
ALAP
PSTACK
TOPSTALK
TOPSKRNL
ECHO OFF
IF NOT EXIST \TOPSTART.BAT GOTO NOSTART
ECHO ON
\TOPSTART.BAT
:NOSTART
TOPS PSTAT /V    Add these
TOPS DIR    two lines
```

Chaining batch files

The idea behind *chaining* batch files is to create a linked set of batch files, each ending with the name of another batch file to execute, until the chain is complete and all tasks finished. Let's say you need to have access to three different remote volumes during a given day. However, you don't want to mount all of them at once because of the memory it would take up, etc. By simply entering a MOUNT123 batch file, you can mount the volumes in the order you want and automatically start each program.

Use Edlin, or the editor of your choice, for this example, which shows you how to create a short set of batch files that mount the volumes in the order you want.

■ Create the first batch file called MOUNT123.BAT that starts everything off:

```
REM Mount123 mounts dBASE, Excel, then Word.
CLS
ECHO Mounting database...
DBMOUNT
```

■ Create a second batch file called DBMOUNT.BAT that mounts a database volume, starts the program, and after exiting the program, calls for the spreadsheet mounting batch file:

```
ECHO OFF TOPS MOUNT D: TO Dave's_PC Database
ECHO Starting database...
D:DBASE
ECHO OFF TOPS UNMOUNT Database
CLS
ECHO Mounting spreadsheet...
SSMOUNT
```

■ Create a third batch file called SSMOUNT.BAT that mounts a spreadsheet volume, starts the program, and after exiting the program, calls for the word processor mounting batch file:

```
ECHO OFF TOPS MOUNT E: TO Accounting Spreadsheet
ECHO Starting spreadsheet...
E:EXCEL
ECHO OFF TOPS UNMOUNT Spreadsheet
CLS
WPMOUNT
```

■ Create a fourth batch file called WPMOUNT.BAT that mounts a word processing volume, starts the program, and after exiting the program, displays a "finished" message:

```
ECHO OFF TOPS MOUNT F: TO Publications
Word_Processor
```

```
ECHO Starting word processor...
F:WORD
ECHO OFF TOPS UNMOUNT Word_Processor
CLS
ECHO I'm all done — how about you?
```

When you've completed this series of files, all you need to do is enter MOUNT123, and your volumes are loaded and programs executed, all chained together by your batch files.

Modifying TOPS system files

If you want to fully customize TOPS on your PC, you need to understand the TOPS system files — how to use them more efficiently and how to modify them for your personal needs. We'll give you some nitty-gritty details. If you're not a TOPS network supervisor, you should qualify as one after completing this section.

The TOPS system files consist of three types:

- configuration data files
- system utilities
- special purpose modules

Configuration data files

The TOPS configuration data file TOPSKRNL.DAT holds the variable parameters used by TOPS each time you load it. For ordinary operations, you can use the default settings and never have to bother the data file. However, your station may require a change or two, especially if it has one of the following needs:

- *Network configuration* — adjust for different size networks, either smaller (three to four stations) or larger (ten or more stations) than the average TOPS network.

- *Hardware configuration* — modified hardware that includes something other than one or two floppy drives and/or a hard drive.

- *Station name* — automatically start TOPS with your station name.

- *Memory space* — make better use of your PC's available memory.

- *File service/client capacity* — increase your PC's capacity for handling extraordinary transactions from servers and clients.

- *System application capacity* — your PC won't allow enough applications to be run at once.

- *Application requirements* — your applications require some special networking parameters (or none at all).

Parameters for all of these categories can be customized in the TOPS configuration data file. This section explains how to edit the TOPSKRNL.DAT file using your favorite line editor. (If you don't have a line editor to call your favorite, refer to the section on "Creation of batch files" earlier in this chapter.) We'll give you a line-by-line breakdown of the data file contents, then take a look at which parameters can be modified.

When you load the TOPSKRNL.DAT configuration file into your editor, it looks like this:

```
*1:TOPSKRNL Version 2.10
2:Station Name (15 chars):
 *3:Client
4:Printer redirection time-out, in seconds (20 - 60): 40
5:Flush printer redirection buffer on exit (Y/N): Y
6:TOPSEXEC.COM Path (66 chars): C:\TOPS
7:No. Servers (1 - 10): 5
8:No. Remote Volumes (1 - 10): 5
9:No. Remote Files (5 - 40): 20
10:No. FCBs (2 - 20): 8
11:Last Logical Drive (C - Z): J
 *12:Drive Map (F=floppy, H=hard disk (or ram disk), U=unused)::
13:FFHUUUUUUU
 *14:Server
15:No. Clients (0 - 20): 10
16:No. Published Volumes (0 - 10): 5
17:No. Open Volumes (0 - 20): 10
18:No. Files (0 - 100): 30
```

19:No. Locks (0 - 100): 30
20:No. Directories (0 - 30): 20
21:Buffer Size, K Bytes (4 - 16): 12
22:No. Handles reserved for Server (0 - 8): 3

Note Do *not* modify the lines indicated with an * (1,3,12,14). These lines are required for TOPS configuration and will not load properly if changed in any way.

Lets look at each line in turn.

1:TOPSKRNL Version 2.10 — Version number of your TOPS DOS software. Do *not* modify this line.

2:Station Name — If you enter your station name on this line, you don't have to enter it every time before you publish or mount a volume. (Up to 15 characters long.)

3:Client — Signals TOPS to begin loading client configuration parameters. Do *not* modify this line.

4:Printer redirection time-out — Some applications require a printer to wait longer than normal (TOPS default = 40 seconds) when you or a client print on your published printer. This parameter lets you change the time-out (waiting period) in 10-second increments.

5:Flush printer redirection buffer on exit — Default is YES, telling TOPS to end a print job when you exit an application. Change this setting to NO when using a background printing spooler, such as NetPrint, and redirecting a printer port, such as LPT1.

6:TOPSEXEC.COM Path — TOPS checks this path for the executable file, TOPSEXEC.COM. This file lets you run applications from remote servers. If TOPS doesn't find the file where the path parameter says it is, you can't run remote applications.

7:Number of Servers — You can choose from 1 to 10 servers to access at the same time. TOPS requires 148 bytes for each server defined. Do NOT specify more servers than the number of stations on your network.

8:Number of Remote Volumes — You can choose from 1 to 10

volumes to mount at once. Do NOT specify more volumes than the number of drives defined in lines 11 and 13 following.

9:Number of Remote Files — You can choose from 5 to 40 files to open simultaneously from all mounted volumes. TOPS requires 104 bytes for each file defined. (Most applications don't allow opening of many files at once — 10-15 should work well.)

10:Number of FCBs — You can choose from 2 to 20 File Control Blocks (FCBs) to at once. Since newer applications don't use FCBs, set this number lower than the default unless your application sustains an FCB-related error.

11:Last Logical Drive — You can choose any letter from C to Z as the last letter to assign a mounted volume. Requires 92 bytes for each drive defined. This number *must* equal the number of drive settings in line 13.

12:Drive Map — Signals TOPS that the drive map settings follow. Do NOT modify this line.

13:FFHUUUUUUU — TOPS checks this line before assigning a drive letter to a mounted volume. Define the type for each drive physically or logically attached to your PC, starting with A: for the first letter, then B: and so on. All unoccupied drive letters can be used for mounted volumes.

14:Server — Signals TOPS to begin loading server configuration parameters. Do *not* modify this line. (If you load TOPS for client-only operations, lines 15 through 22 are ignored, which also saves you memory space.)

15:Number of Clients — You can choose from 0 to 20 clients to have access to your server at once. Do *not* specify more clients than the number of stations in your network.

16:Number of Published Volumes — You can choose from 0 to 10 volumes to publish simultaneously. However, since all subdirectories are published along with their parent directory, avoid publishing a subdirectory if its parent directory has already been published.

17:Number of Open Volumes — You can choose from 0 to 20 volumes to be opened at the same time by clients.

18:Number of Files — You can choose from 0 to 100 files to be opened at once from all of your published volumes. This number includes files opened by you and your clients.

19:Number of Locks — You can choose from 0 to 100 locks to be set at the same time. Since newer applications don't use locks, you can normally set this number lower than the default.

20:Number of Directories — You can choose from 0 to 30 directories to be open at once. This number includes directories opened by you and your clients, whether listing files or opening them.

21:Buffer Size, K Bytes — You can choose from 4 to 16 K bytes of memory for your server buffer. Network performance depends on the size of this buffer, since your server uses the specified amount of memory to handle traffic to and from all your clients.

22:Number of Handles reserved for Server — You can choose from 0 to 8 handles for server background processes. Do *not* increase the default number unless required by a specific application.

System utilities

When you use TOPS DOS on your PC, some of things happen behind the scenes that you normally can't see. However, if you need to take a look at these low-level operations, TOPS provides you with five system utilities for examining the details: XSYNC, XDIR, XDEL, TDIR, and TDEL. These utilities allow you to see the TOPS extended directory and hidden files created by normal TOPS operations.

TOPS creates an extended directory file called XDIRSTAT.TPS for each volume you publish. The extended directory stores additional file information that DOS does not keep. For volumes containing both Macintosh and UNIX files, the extended directory preserves the original, longer name of Macintosh and UNIX files, as well as the shortened DOS version of these names assigned by TOPS. The extended directory also includes information about Macintosh icon types and manages Macintosh hidden files — called resource forks — that are linked to the visible Macintosh data files.

> **Note** Because the TOPS hidden files are hidden, you'd be surprised just how many of the buggers are out there, taking up your precious disk space. Remember to use the TOPS system utilities on a regular basis, especially to check for hidden files in directories you haven't published recently. Use XDEL to remove extended directories for volumes you no longer publish or won't be publishing in the near future. Every little byte helps.

Displaying the extended directory

Use XDIR to see the TOPS extended directory for one of your PC directories or for a remotely published volume. This display includes all DOS and UNIX files, plus any Macintosh data files. You can see both the long and short versions of Macintosh and UNIX filenames. With the /A parameter, you can also display Macintosh hidden resource files — the DOS version of resource filenames begin with *R*.

Display the TOPS extended directory using XDIR from the DOS command line, as follows:

```
XDIR [?] [/A] [d:[path]] <Enter>
```

Now let's talk about what that means.

? tells the computer to display HELP information for XDIR command.

/A tells the computer to display Macintosh hidden files information. If you don't use /A, only filenames (original and DOS versions) and file types will be displayed.

d:[path] selects the drive and path for displaying XDIR. If you don't enter a pathname, XDIR displays the current drive and directory.

Updating the extended directory

Every time you publish a volume, TOPS automatically updates the extended directory for that volume using XSYNC. If you publish a volume for the first time, TOPS uses XSYNC to create a new extended directory for the published directory and any subdirectories. XSYNC keeps the extended directory for each volume up-to-date as long as it remains published.

However, for very large directories or directories you don't change very often, you may want to disable XSYNC when publishing these volumes because it can take a while to update the extended directory for them. You can disable the XSYNC update either from the TOPS menu program (when publishing a specific volume) or from the DOS command line (for any volume).

If you want to disable XSYNC when publishing a volume using the TOPS menu program, follow these steps:

1. From Server Utilities menu, select the Publish a Volume option.

2. From the Publish a Volume display, disable XSYNC by typing Alt-X (Hold down the Alt key and press *X*).

3. The NO XSYNC prompt appears in the upper right corner of the window.

4. As long as the NO XSYNC prompt is displayed, TOPS does not update the extended directory for any volume you publish.

5. Whenever you want to enable XSYNC, press Alt-X again. The NO XSYNC prompt disappears, and the extended directory is updated for any volume you publish.

If you want to disable XSYNC when publishing a volume from the DOS command line, use the XSYNC command in this format:

```
XSYNC [?] [/S] [/Y] [/D] [d:[path]] <Enter>
```

Now let's dissect it:

? tells the computer to display HELP information for XDIR command.

/S updates all subdirectories contained within the specified directory.

/Y overrides XSYNC confirmation prompt (normally required when updating an extended directory).

/D deletes a Macintosh Desktop file from the specified directory

⎡**Note**⎤ Desktop files are created when a PC volume is mounted on a Macintosh and appears on the desktop display. Use this parameter to delete the Desktop file if it becomes corrupted.

d:[path] update the extended directory for the specified drive and path. If you don't enter a pathname, XSYNC updates the current drive and directory.

Deleting the extended directory
Use XDEL to delete the extended directory (XDIRSTAT.TPS) for a specific volume, including all hidden files (Macintosh resource files and desktop files).

WARNING **If you delete a Macintosh resource file for a Macintosh application, that application becomes unusable. Deleting resource files can also corrupt certain data files.**

Tip Before you can remove a DOS directory that has been published as a TOPS volume, you must use XDEL to remove all hidden files from that directory. If you try to remove a directory that still contains TOPS hidden files, your PC displays the following error prompt: "Invalid path, not directory, or directory not empty."

When you want to delete an extended directory, use the XDEL command, as follows:

```
XDEL [?] [/S] [/Y] [/N] [d:[path]] <Enter>
```

Now the lowdown:

? displays HELP information for XDEL command.

/S deletes all subdirectories contained within the specified directory.

/Y overrides XDEL confirmation prompt (normally required when deleting an extended directory).

d:[path] deletes the extended directory for the specified drive and path. If you don't enter a pathname, XDEL deletes the extended directory of the current drive and directory.

Displaying TOPS hidden files

When you need to see a quick, easy-to-read listing of a specific directory, including any hidden files, use TDIR to display all of the files in the directory you choose, as follows:

```
TDIR [d:[path]] <Enter>
```

Note TDIR displays the files in a similar format to the DOS command DIR.

If you don't enter a pathname, TDIR shows you the files in the current drive and directory.

Deleting TOPS hidden files

When you only want to remove a few hidden files (and not an entire extended directory), use TDEL to delete hidden files one at a time. Although XDEL deletes hidden files as well, TDEL gives you selective control over which files get deleted and which don't, as follows:

```
TDEL [d:[path]] filename
```

If you don't enter a pathname, TDEL deletes hidden files in the current drive and directory.

Note If you enter a Macintosh data filename, TDEL deletes both the data file and its linked resource file. If you just want to delete a resource file (normally leaving the data file intact), enter the resource filename only.

Special-purpose modules

TOPS provides three special-purpose modules that help you customize your TOPS network to support specific applications you already use. The special purpose modules include: TNET-BIOS, TEXTEND, and INITPRIN.

The function of the three modules, and the memory space they require, are shown in Table 11-2.

Table 11-2. TOPS special-purpose modules

Module	Function	Memory
TNETBIOS	Required for applications using NETBIOS standards	47K
TEXTEND	Required for multiuser version of dBASE III Plus	7K
INITPRIN	Print from DOS command line (does not require loading TOPSPRTR)	22K

TNETBIOS

The TNETBIOS module allows certain PC network applications that require NETBIOS standards to run on a TOPS network. NETBIOS is used by such programs as multi-user databases and electronic mail packages — if you don't know whether your program requires NETBIOS, refer to the manufacturer's documentation. (For more information on TOPS and electronic mail, see Chapter Eight.)

You must configure your network software driver to use TNETBIOS.

■ Start the TOPS setup program:

```
SETUP <Enter>
```

Tip If you have not included TOPS as a defined path, you must run SETUP from the TOPS subdirectory.

■ Select the Configure option from the opening menu:

```
C
```

■ From the Driver Configuration menu: Highlight the network card type installed in your PC and then press Enter.

■ Highlight the Software Interrupt option and press Enter.

■ Select 60 as the software interrupt:

```
60 <Enter>
```

■ Press *Y* to save the driver configuration changes and exit the Setup program.

You have finished reconfiguring your network software driver. You must reboot your computer and load TOPS in order for TOPS to use the new driver settings. If you already have TOPS loaded, unload all TOPS modules (type `TOPS UNLOAD /A <Enter>`), then reboot your computer and load TOPS.

Before you run an application requiring NetBios, you must load the TNETBIOS module, as follows:

- If you have not already, load the TOPS networking software:

  `LOADTOPS <Enter>`

- Load the TNETBIOS module:

  `TNETBIOS <Enter>`

Remember to unload TNETBIOS before unloading the rest of the TOPS modules, as follows:

`TOPS UNLOAD TNETBIOS <Enter>`

WARNING Do NOT use the TOP UNLOAD /A option to unload the TNETBIOS module — your computer will crash. Unload TNETBIOS first, before unloading any other TOPS modules.

TEXTEND

TOPS provides a special module for networks running the multi-user version of dBASE III Plus. Load TEXTEND before you run dBASE III Plus, as follows:

`TEXTEND <Enter>`

Remember to unload TEXTEND before unloading the rest of the TOPS modules. The TEXTEND module does not use the TOPS UNLOAD command; unload TEXTEND as follows:

`TEXTEND UNLOAD <Enter>`

Note If you try to unload the TOPS network software modules while TEXTEND is still loaded, TOPS prompts you with an error message telling you to unload the memory-resident module before unloading the TOPS network software.

INITPRIN

The TOPS module INITPRIN allows you to use background printing on your PC because you cannot use the normal DOS background print queue with TOPS loaded. Load INITPRIN when printing from the DOS command line to a local printer connected to your PC, as follows:

```
INITPRIN <Enter>
```

| Note | Do not load INITPRIN to print on a network or remote printer or from an application program you're using. Also, if you have loaded the TOPSPRTR module, do not load INITPRIN. Refer to Chapter Eight for more information on printing with TOPS.

Remember to unload INITPRIN before unloading the rest of the TOPS modules. The INITPRIN module does not use the TOPS UNLOAD command; unload INITPRIN as follows:

```
INITPRIN /U <Enter>
```

| Note | If you try to unload the TOPS network software modules while INITPRIN is still loaded, TOPS prompts you with an error message telling you to unload the memory-resident module before unloading the TOPS network software.

■ Continuing on

Congratulations. If you've read this entire book, you're ready to put on your TOPS hat and show off your newfound node-how. With the knowledge we've shared with you, you should be able to handle any TOPS challenge.

If you have any questions or suggestions for our next edition, write us at 31125 Via Colinas #902, Thousand Oaks, CA 91362.

■ Glossary

The first step in using TOPS is learning the language. We've defined the terminology you'll need to know in this appendix. We recommend that both the beginning user, who finds the language unfamiliar, and the advanced user, who may be familiar with the terms used in different ways, take the time to skim over the words defined here. Then you can refer back to the definitions when you need clarification.

■ Using the glossary

To make the time spent using this glossary more productive, we have cross-referenced the glossary with italics. You'll find words that appear in italics defined under their own headings.

■ TOPS terminology

Active star

A configuration of networked computers in which information goes from workstations to a central *node*, then on to its destination. The central node manages and controls all the traffic on the *network*. You can arrange a *TOPS* network in an active star *topology* through *devices* such as Farallon Computing's Star Controller.

Address

A unique code that identifies a *node* to the *network*. Also a unique code that identifies an expansion board in an IBM-compatible computer.

Alias
A name (16 characters maximum) given to a *volume* or printer when it is published. This is the *volume* or printer name as seen by other stations on the *network*.

AppleTalk
A set of network communication *protocols* for *LocalTalk* cabling systems. The *driver* that controls how the *devices* address, send, receive, and read the information transmitted over the *network*.

Application software
A program or file containing an executable program. The program will perform a particular task, such as word processing, database management, networking, etc.

ALAP
AppleTalk Link Access Protocol. Establishes and maintains a physical *AppleTalk* link and is the foundation for all other AppleTalk overhead.

ASCII
American Standard Code for Information Interchange. ASCII is a standard way to represent text in microcomputer operating systems.

AUTOEXEC.BAT
An MS-DOS *batch file* that executes automatically on system startup or rebooting.

Background tasks
Functions performed by the computer that allow it to accomplish other tasks. Background functions are invisible to the user. For example, while printing a document in the background, the computer can still accept and process data for another document.

Back up
To copy the contents of a disk, directory, or file to another hard disk, floppy disk, removable high-capacity disk, or streaming tape. (A backup file or disk provides security against the loss of the original.)

Batch file
A text file containing MS-DOS commands intended to automatically execute in a batch. Entering the batch file name at the *DOS* prompt executes the commands in the order found in the file.

Bridge
A hardware device that connects two similar *networks* (*zones*). Bridges extend *networks* to expand the resource pool and control *network* traffic by forwarding only transmissions intended for a different *zone*.

Cables
The physical means of connecting *devices* on the *network*. They contain the wires that carry the signals from one machine to another. TOPS-compatible cables come in three varieties: *twisted-pair*, *coaxial*, and *fiber-optic*.

Centralized server
A computer or machine that serves files to all of the other computers on a *network*. The centralized method has its limitations: Failure of the server can bring down the whole network, and only *peripherals* connected to the *server* are available to *network* users — if you want to share three laser printers, all three of them must be attached to the central server. Only the information on the central server is available to the rest of the *network*.

Client
A computer that can use files from *servers* on the *network*.

Coaxial cable
A connecting cord whose superior shielding lets it carry more information for longer distances. Popular for larger *networks*, coaxial cable is used to install an *Ethernet*-compatible version of *TOPS*.

Connector
A jack or plug that attaches a cable to any device. Some vendors use the term connector interchangeably with *interface box*. We use connector only for the plugs and jacks that attach cables.

Daisy chain layout

A configuration of networked computers in which the beginning and end of a cable are limited to two *nodes* without any deviating cables. To achieve a daisy chain layout, string cables between machines.

Data file

A computer file containing information or data that can be read or processed by an *application*. This could be a word-processing document, spreadsheet, database file, or simple text. Most data files have information formatted in a way that can be processed only by the particular *application* that created it. Text files have no formatting.

Data fork

One of the two parts of a Macintosh file, the data fork stores the data or text. See also *resource fork*.

Decentralized server

Also called a *distributed server.*

Dedicated server

A computer or machine used only for storing and retrieving files for the network. (Some *networks* require a dedicated server to operate.)

Desktop

A Macintosh's working environment. The desktop displays the files temporarily placed on it, the Trash icon, and disk icons.

Devices

A computer or *peripheral* physically attached to a *network*; for example, computers, printers, *file servers*, *bridges*, *gateways*, and modems. See also *nodes*.

Directory

A self-contained group of files stored on a disk. Directories can be created within other directories, forming a hierarchy of directory and subdirectory levels (root directory, second-level directory, etc.). Also used to refer to a listing of files within a directory and accessed by the MS-DOS DIR command.

Disk
A *device* used to store information processed by your computer. Hard disks and floppy diskettes are common storage *devices*.

Distributed server
A *workstation* that can act as a *server* while also performing other computing chores. A distributed server can make any of its *peripherals* available to the *network*. Furthermore, the failure of one machine doesn't affect the rest of the network. *TOPS* can use either the distributed or *dedicated server* strategy.

DOS (MS-DOS or PC-DOS)
The operating system (Disk Operating System) used by IBM PCs and compatible computers.

Driver
The portion of a *network* software package responsible for getting communication out onto the *network* and for ensuring that it gets to its destination *station* without error. Different interface cards require different drivers.

Encapsulated PostScript
A PostScript file with a special structure designed for exchanging graphics among programs. EPS files can be downloaded to a PostScript-compatible *device* over a *network* with *TOPS* TPRINT.

Electronic mail (E-Mail)
A way to send and receive messages among workstations attached to the network. You type in a message and specify the recipient. The E-Mail program routes it to the correct *workstation*. Many E-Mail programs allow files to be attached to a message.

Ethernet
A networking system originally developed by Xerox Corp. capable of transmitting data at 10 megabits per second. *TOPS* can work over Ethernet hardware at a higher speed than it can work with *LocalTalk* hardware. Ethernet compatibility requires more expensive hardware, special boards for Macintoshes, and higher-priced *coaxial cable*.

EtherTalk
This *driver* adapts *AppleTalk protocols* so they can run on the *Ethernet* system.

Fiber-optic cabling
The least common *cable* type. Glass or acrylic fibers transmit the data. Fiber-optic cable can carry more information than other types. However, it requires extra equipment to translate electrical signals into optical signals and back again. Its current use is restricted to specialized environments that can justify its higher costs.

File exchanging
The most basic, essential use of *TOPS* is to trade files among computers. Two concepts hold the key to understanding file exchanges: *publishing* and *mounting*.

File locking
A system used by *network (multi-user) applications* to prevent data files from being written to by more than one user at any one time.

Filename conventions
The rules for constructing filenames. These differ from one operating system to another. *DOS* filenames can be up to eight characters in length with an optional three-character extension. Macintosh filenames can be up to 31 characters long.

File server
A station on a *network* that makes files available to other stations.

Finder
The *application* that maintains the Macintosh desktop. It keeps track of documents and applications and transfers information to and from disks.

FlashTalk
A *LocalTalk network driver* developed by *TOPS*. It is similar to *AppleTalk*, but transmits data at up to three times (770 Kbits) the *AppleTalk* rate (230 Kbits).

Forks

The two parts into which Macintosh files are divided. The *data fork* is an unstructured finite sequence of data bytes. The *resource fork* is the part of a file that is accessible through the Macintosh Resource Manager and that contains specialized data used by an *application*, such as menus, fonts, and icons (as well as the *application* code for an *application* file).

Gateways

Nodes that separate and manage communication between two dissimilar types of *networks*. For example, a gateway is used to connect an *AppleTalk protocol*-based *network* to a non-*AppleTalk protocol*-based system. A gateway contains both hardware and software. The hardware lets different *cable* types interconnect. The software translates the signals from one *network* so they can be understood by the other. The gateway serves as a translator between the *protocols* of the two connected *networks*.

Hierarchical file system (HFS)

A filing scheme used by the Macintosh operating system in which files are organized in folders within folders on hard disks and 800K floppies.

Interface Box

The physical link between the *devices* and the *cable*. On an *AppleTalk*-compatible *network*, every device needs an interface box. The interface box is used with either the *LocalTalk* or modular phone wire types of *cabling*. *Ethernet* does not need interface boxes.

Interrupt

The temporary suspension of a program by a computer to perform other tasks. Usually it is in response to a signal from a *peripheral device* or other external source.

Internet

A *network* that spans *local area networks* by linking them together, often over long distances.

Local
Files, software, or hardware stored in or connected to a computer. See also *remote.*

Local area network (LAN)
A network within a single workplace. In contrast, a wide area network spans long distances and usually links local area networks.

Local disk drive
A disk drive that is physically attached to a computer. See also *remote* drive.

LocalTalk
A physical networking system made by Apple that links computers and *peripheral devices* together to permit communication and data transmission. Also refers to *LocalTalk-*compatible *cabling* systems.

LocalTalk cable
Type of *networking cable* introduced by Apple. Many older *TOPS networks* still use LocalTalk cable.

Macintosh Operating System (Mac OS)
The operating system consisting of ROM- and disk-based routines that the Macintosh uses to perform tasks such as starting the computer, moving data to and from disks and peripheral devices, and managing memory space in RAM.

Memory
The data storage area of a computer system, usually composed of disk memory, *RAM* (random-access memory), and *ROM* (read-only memory). Disk memory is the main data storage area in a computer. Application and data files are stored there even with the computer turned off. See also *RAM* and *ROM.*

Memory resident
Software designed so that once it is loaded, it remains in memory even if other programs are loaded.

Modem
A device that allows two or more computers to communicate serially over a phone line.

Modular phone wire cabling
The type of wire that connects your telephone to the wall jack. Also known as unshielded *twisted-pair* and PhoneNet wiring. This is the most popular *TOPS cabling*.

Mounting
The process of making a *volume* available to your own machine. When accessing a *volume* on the *network*, it is mounted on the *local* computer and appears as though it were residing in the computer — although it could be on any computer in the network.

MultiFinder
A multitasking operating system for Macintosh computers that makes it possible to have several applications open at the same time, including background applications that let you perform one task while the computer performs another.

Multi-user application
An *application* that multiple users can run simultaneously.

Multi-user computer
A system in which many terminals are attached to one central machine. These multi-user computers possess only one brain, one central processing unit (CPU).

NETPRINT
A standalone software utility for PC users who just want to print and don't need to do other *network* tasks for the moment. NETPRINT doesn't give users any other *TOPS* functions, but it provides access to printers attached directly to the *network*.

Network

A scheme for connecting computers. Computers linked by *cables* communicate with the help of network software. Each computer in a network has its own CPU. The network is a highway that carries messages back and forth among these standalone *devices*. The three most important reasons to use a network are to share information, to share resources, and to centralize files. Networks also make it possible to share expensive *peripherals*.

Network circuitry

A computer must have the necessary circuitry inside. This hardware provides a *port* — a connection to the cable that runs to the other *devices*. If necessary, it also translates the signal so it can be sent over the wire to the other machines. Macintosh computers and Sun workstations have *networking* circuitry built right in. PC compatibles, on the other hand, need an add-in board. If an alternative *network* like *Ethernet* is used, all computers need adapter boards.

Network driver software

An *application* that does the actual talking over the network.

Network hardware

All the equipment needed to form a *network*: *devices*, *network circuitry*, *cables*, and *connectors*.

Network interface card

A computer board that forms the physical connection between a microcomputer and a *network*-cabling system.

Network name

The name that a computer, printer, or *volume* displays to the *network*.

Network operating software (NOS)

The program that links the *network* to the computer's native operating system.

Network printer

Certain printers, such as the Apple LaserWriter, that can hook up to the *network* without passing through a computer. These printers are PostScript compatible and have AppleTalk circuitry built in.

Node

Any equipment connected to the *network* (for example, a computer or a printer).

Password

A unique character string that the user must enter to *access* certain files, folders, or *volumes*. Passwords provide *network* security.

Partition

A portion of a *memory device*, such as a hard disk, that is *accessed* as if it were a separate *device*.

Path

The route through a *hierarchical file system*, from one directory down through one or more subdirectories to a file.

Peripherals

Devices that attach to computers, including laser printers, scanners, modems, and plotters.

Port

The *device* or *connector* on a computer where *peripheral devices* are attached. For example, a printer port.

PostScript

A page description language created by Adobe Systems. PostScript is a scheme that allows PostScript-compatible software to send specialized instructions to PostScript-compatible output *devices* like laser printers, film recorders, and typesetting machines. All Macintosh applications support PostScript through the Macintosh Operating System. Many PC programs are capable of printing to PostScript-compatible devices. See Encapsulated PostScript.

Printer redirection

A process that intercepts print files and sends them to a remote or *network* printer rather than a *local* printer *port*.

Printer server

A *station* on a *network* that makes its *local* printer available to other *stations* on the *network*.

Print spooling

See *spooler*.

Protocol

A set of procedure rules that govern the transmission of information across a *network* by controlling timing, error correction, and format.

PSTACK

Protocol Stack. The implementation of *protocol* for a *node*.

Publishing

The process that makes a disk into a *server*. Publishing notifies all *network* users with the right *access* to see and use the published *volume*. A published *volume* can allow reading and writing by the *network* users or be made *read only*.

Queue

The line of jobs waiting to be sent to a printer.

RAM

Random-access memory: volatile computer *memory* used to hold *application* programs during their execution. Turning off the computer clears the RAM. DOS machines have a maximum of 640K of conventional RAM.

Read-only access

An *access* mode that allows a user to read, but not change, a file's contents.

Read/write access (R/W)

An *access* mode that allows a user to read, and/or change (write) a file's contents.

Remote
Files, hardware or software stored in or directly connected to a *station* on a *network* other than your own. See also *local*.

Resource fork
The part of a Macintosh file that contains information about the icons, graphical interface, menus, and other information about the file. *DOS* cannot read or display the information in a resource fork. See also *data fork*.

Repeater
A *device* that extends the length of a *network*. When a *cable* gets too long (about 1000 feet) the signal starts to fade. The repeater corrects this by amplifying *network* signals and sending them further.

Ringing
Excessive signal overlap that causes one signal to cancel another and obscure data.

Ring layout
A configuration of network computers in which all the machines are hooked up in a circle (for example, IBM's Token Ring). Do not use this arrangement with TOPS.

ROM
Read-only memory: computer *memory* in which information vital to computer operation is permanently stored or burned in. It is not lost when the computer is turned off or the power is interrupted in any way. You cannot write to ROM.

Root directory
The top-level directory of a *DOS* hierarchical file system.

Server
A computer disk, subdirectory, or folder that stores files and makes them available to the *network*.

Shielding
A method used to protect cables carrying data from stray signals such as Electro Magnetic Flux (EMF) and Radio Frequency Interference (RFI).

Single-user application
Applications designed to be run by one user at a time.

Spooler
An *application* that lets printing take place in the *background* without interfering with your computer tasks. It also allows users to send documents to the printer without waiting for the printer to finish its current job. Print jobs are placed in a *queue* and printed as the printer becomes available. *Local* spoolers put your *local* print jobs in a *local queue. Network* spoolers put print jobs from all *stations* in a central *queue.*

Star layout
A configuration of *networked* computers with a central hub. That hub can be active — when it performs some of the *network* functions — or passive — when it does nothing except provide a physical connection between machines

Station
Each computer on the *network.* Each station receives a name from its user when the user signs onto the *network.* PC station names can be up to 15 characters long. Macintosh station names can be up to 31 characters long.

Text file
A file containing text only (no formatting information). *ASCII* is most common microcomputer convention. See also *data file.*

Topology
The way machines are connected in an arrangement or layout.

TOPS
An inexpensive *networking* scheme that can link Macintoshes, PCs, Sun computers, and others.

TOPS Spool
An *application* for printing documents in the *background.* Users send their documents to TOPS Spool instead of the printer. TOPS Spool makes a temporary disk copy, then passes this file on to the printer. Meanwhile, the user can go back to work. See also *spooler.*

TOPS Translators
A Macintosh *application* from Data-Viz that allows file conversion from one document type to another while transferring a file across the *network*. TOPS Translators comes with *TOPS*.

TPRINT
A TOPS software utility that allows users to *publish* a printer the way a disk is published. TPRINT also allows the user to send or dump files to *network* printers.

Trunk layout
A *TOPS network topology* with a central trunk — in this case a *cable*. From there, other *cables* branch out. At first glance, a trunk layout resembles a *daisy chain*. The difference is that an extra length of wire runs from the *connector* back to the central *cable*.

Twisted-pair cable
A connecting cord containing wires wrapped around one another. (Twisting reduces interference between the signals.) These cables can be shielded or unshielded. See *shielding*.

UNIX
A widely used, *multi-user*, multi-tasking operating system originally developed by Bell Laboratories and used on Sun workstations.

Unmount
To break the connection to a remote *volume* or printer.

Unpublish
To make unavailable any resource a *server* has previously published and made available to the *network*.

Virus
A self-replicating computer program, often designed to corrupt data files or applications. They are transferred from one computer system to another by disk or modem. Once in a system, they attach themselves to files or applications and multiply. Like a flu virus they spread everywhere, infecting whatever they are designed to attack.

Volume
Any disk, directory, or subdirectory *published* on a *network*. It is possible to *publish* more than one volume at a time. (When a directory is published, all subdirectories and files in that directory are also published.)

Workstation
See station.

Write
To transfer information from the computer's *RAM* to a disk. Writing a file to a disk stores the information on the disk.

Zone
A logical grouping of *nodes* to form a *network* within a larger group of interconnected *networks* joined together through *bridges*. Zones subdivide a very large *network* to control traffic and make *networking* easier.

Manufacturers Reference

Hardware

Tops, A Sun Microsystems Co.
950 Marina Village Pkwy.
Alameda, CA 94501
(415) 769-8700 or (800) 445-8677

TOPS Connectors, TOPS Repeater, TOPS FlashCard, and TOPS FlashBox

Apple Computer, Inc.
20525 Mariani Ave.
Cupertino, CA 95014
(408) 996-1010

AppleTalk Cabling, AppleTalk network interface boxes, LaserWriters, and AppleTalk PC boards

Belkin Components
14550 S. Main St.
Gardena, CA 90248
(213) (515) 7585 or (800) 223-5546

BelTalk and QuickNet network interface boxes

Cayman Systems, Inc.
One Kendall Sq., Bldg. 600
Cambridge, MA 02139
(617) 494-1999

GatorBox

Dayna Communications
50 South Main St., 5th Floor
Salt Lake City, UT 84144
(801) 531-0600

DaynaTalk network interface boxes

DayStar Digital, Inc.
5556 Atlanta Hwy.
Flowery Branch, GA 30542
(404) 967-2077 or (800) 962-2077

FS100 File Server Board for the PC, LT200 LocalTalk Inter-face Board for the PC

Du Pont Electronics
515 Fishing Creek Rd.
New Cumberland, PA 17070
(717) 938-6711 or (800) 237-2374

Du Pont Fiber Optic AppleTalk LAN

Farallon Computing, Inc.
2150 Kittredge St.
Berkeley, CA 94704
(415) 849-2331

PhoneNET Components, Star Controller, and PhoneNet Repeater

Hayes Microcomputer Products, Inc.
PO Box 105203
Atlanta, GA 30348
(404) 449-8791

Interbridge

Iomega
1821 W. 4000 South
Roy, UT 84067
(800) 422-8828

Bernoulli drives

Irwin Magnetics
2101 Commonwealth Blvd.
Ann Arbor, MI 48105
(313) 930-9000

5080 and 2080 tape drives

Jasmine Technologies
1740 Army Street
San Francisco, CA 94124
(415) 282-1111 or (800) 347-3228

MegaDrive 20

Kinetics, Inc.
2540 Camino Diablo
Walnut Creek, CA 94596
(415) 947-0998

FastPath, EtherPort II, and EtherPort SE

Mass Microsystems
550 Del Rey Ave.
Sunnyvale, CA 94086
(408) 522-1200

DataPak removable hard drive

Mirror Technologies
2644 Patton Road
Roseville, MN 55113
(612) 633-4450 or (800) 654-5294

RM20 removable hard drive

Nuvotech, Inc.
2015 Bridgeway, Ste. 204
Sausalito, CA 94965
(415) 331-7815

TurboNET network interface boxes

Peripheral Land, Inc.
47800 Westinghouse Drive
Fremont, CA 94539
(415) 657-2211 or (800) 288-8754

Infinity 10 and 40 removable hard drives

Shiva Corp.
155 Second St.
Cambridge, MA 02141
(617) 864-8500

NetBridge and TeleBridge

3Com Corp.
3165 Kifer Rd.
Santa Clara, CA 95052
(408) 562-6400 or (800) 638-3266

3Com Ethernet cards

■ Software

Tops, A Sun Microsystems Co.
950 Marina Village Pkwy.
Alameda, CA 94501
(415) 769-8700 or (800) 445-8677

TOPS PC, TOPS Macintosh, InBox, and NetPrint

Apple Computer, Inc.
20525 Mariani Ave.
Cupertino, CA 95014
(408) 996-1010

InterPoll

CE Software
PO Box 65580
W. Des Moines, IA 50265
(515) 224-1995

QuickMail, Vaccine

DayStar Digital, Inc.
5556 Atlanta Hwy.
Flowery Branch, GA 30542
(404) 967-2077 or (800) 962-2077

FS100 File Server System

Farallon Computing, Inc.
2150 Kittredge St.
Berkeley, CA 94704
(415) 849-2331

Timbuktu, PhoneNET Traffic Watch, CheckNET

Fifth Generation Systems, Inc.
11200 Industriplex Blvd.
Baton Rouge, LA 70809
(504) 291-7221 or (800) 873-4384

Fastback for the Mac and PC

HJC Software, Inc.
P.O. Box 51816
Durham, NC 27717
(919) 490-1277

Virex

Infosphere, Inc.
4730 SW Macadam Ave.
Portland, OR 97201
(503) 226-3620

Liaison, ComServe

Microseeds Publishing
7030-B West Hillsborough Ave.
Tampa, FL 33634
(813) 882-8635

Redux

Microsoft Corp.
16011 NE 36th Way; Box 97017
Redmond, WA 98073
(206) 882-8080

Microsoft Mail, Microsoft Word

Novell, Inc.
122 East 1700 South
Provo, UT 84601
(801) 379-5900 or (800) 453-1267

Netware LAN and Netware Mac

Personal Computer Peripherals Corp.
4710 Eisenhower Blvd., Bldg. A4
Tampa, FL 33634
(813) 884-3092 or (800) 622-2888

HFS Backup

QMS, Inc.
One Magnum Pass
Mobile, AL. 36618
(205) 633-4300

AppleTalk-compatible laser printers

Symantec Corporation
10201 Torre Avenue
Cupertino, CA 95014
(408) 253-9600

Symantec Utilities for Macintosh, and SAM

SuperMac Technology
485 Potero Ave.
Sunnyvale, CA 94086
(408) 245-2202

DiskFit

3Com Corp.
3165 Kifer Rd.
Santa Clara, CA 95052
(408) 562-6400 or (800) 638-3266

3Com, 3S/200, 3S/400

Vano Associates, Inc.
PO Box 12730
New Brighton, MN 55418
(612) 788-9547

MacChuck

XTree Company
4330 Santa Fe Road
San Luis Obispo, CA 93401
(800) 634-5545

XTree Pro, XTree Mac

TOPS Planning Checklists

Additional copies of the TOPS planning checklists in Chapter Two are provided here. You can remove them from the book and use them to plan your network. If you prefer, you can photocopy them, at their actual size or enlarged, and maintain a supply of forms for documenting changes in your network and planning large networks.

Sketch: Draw proposed layout, writing in station names and length of cable runs. Use separate sheet if necessary. Circle stations that need terminating resistors.

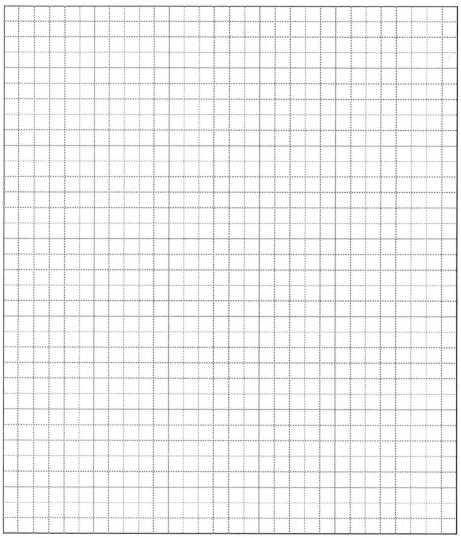

Total cable length: _____   Total DIN-8 interface boxes: _____

Cable type: ☐ Phone wire ☐ LocalTalk ☐ Mixed ☐ Other   Total DB-9 interface boxes: _____

Topology: ☐ Daisy chain ☐ Trunk   ☐ Star

Sketch: Draw proposed layout, writing in station names and length of cable runs. Use separate sheet if necessary. Circle stations that need terminating resistors.

Total cable length: _____   Total DIN-8 interface boxes: _____

Cable type: ☐ Phone wire ☐ LocalTalk ☐ Mixed ☐ Other   Total DB-9 interface boxes: _____

Topology: ☐ Daisy chain ☐ Trunk ☐ Star

Station name: _____   Type of device: _____

Operating System/version #: _____   TOPS serial#: _____

TOPS version #: _____

AppleTalk port

☐ DIN-8   ☐ DB-9

Cable

☐ Phone wire   ☐ LocalTalk   ☐ Other _____

Interface box

Brand _____

Self-terminating: ☐ Yes   ☐ No   Connector: ☐ DIN 8   ☐ DB-9

Computers

RAM: _____   Hard disk volume(s):

                                         Size _____MB   Name _____

Floppy disk(s): (fill in number of matching drives)   Size _____MB   Name _____

_____   360K   _____   1.2MB   Size _____MB   Name _____

_____   1.44MB   _____   400K   Size _____MB   Name _____

_____   720K   _____   800K   Size _____MB   Name _____

Board settings (PCs only)

Network board: IRQ _____   I/O _____   DMA _____   Serial board: IRQ _____   I/O _____

Video board: IRQ _____   I/O _____   DMA _____   Other board(s): IRQ _____   I/O _____   DMA _____

Bus mouse: IRQ _____   I/O _____   IRQ _____   I/O _____   DMA _____

Printers

Standalone network device: ☐ Yes   ☐ No

Page Description Language (PDL) or Emulation: _____

Ports: ☐ AppleTalk   ☐ DIN 8   ☐ AppleTalk DB-9

        ☐ Serial   ☐ Parallel

        ☐ Dedicated laserboard

Printer driver: ☐ TPRINT   ☐ NetPrint

Printer driver version #: _____

Auto-Publish settings

Volumes/printers _____   _____   _____

to auto-publish _____   _____   _____

                 _____   _____   _____

Volumes/printers _____   _____   _____

to auto-mount   _____   _____   _____

                 _____   _____   _____

◼ Index

W

X

Z

New Riders Library

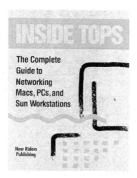

INSIDE TOPS

The Complete Guide to Networking Macs, and PCs
New Riders Publishing
320 pages, 100+ illustrations
ISBN 0-934035-72-5

A how-to book for installing, using, and maintaining TOPs on Macintoshes, and PC compatibles. The reader is instructed on the networking basics, making physical connections, sharing files with dissimilar machines, and how to profit from a local area net work.

INSIDE DESIGNER

Techniques for the Electronic Canvas
Frank Lenk with illustrations by Sû Allison
320 pages, 100 + illustrations
ISBN 0-934035-70-0 **$21.95**

A clear and concise introduction to Micrografx Designer, the powerful IBM-compaticble graphics and design package. Dozens of real-world examples, suitable for users at all levels. *Inside Designer* also includes an introduction to the Windows operating environment.

Optional Designer Disk available.

INSIDE XEROX PRESENTS

A Guide to Professional Presentations
Martha Lubow
384 pages, over 100 illustrations
ISBN 0-934035-66-0 **$21.95**

Inside Xerox Presents teaches you how to turn this exciting new program into an indispensible business tool. Clear-cut, easy-to-follow instructions teach you the inside secrets of Xerox Presents.

Organize and produce top-notch presentations – add impact to your visuals, speaker notes and audience handouts to create a complete presentation. Streamline the design process with tricks, tips and shortcuts not available anywhere else.

Optional disk available for instant point and click productivity.

INSIDE XEROX VENTURA PUBLISHER

A Guide to Professional-Quality Desktop Publishing on the IBM PC
James Cavuoto and Jesse Berst
704 pages, 330 illustrations
ISBN 0-934035-59-8 **$29.95**
2nd Edition

The best reference guide to Xerox Ventura Publisher is now even better! *Inside Xerox Ventura Publisher*, 2nd Edition, has been completely rewritten for Ventura Publisher Version 2 and includes more of what readers have asked for: more hands-on examples, more easy-to-use charts, and more time-saving tips and tricks.

PUBLISHING POWER WITH VENTURA

The Complete Teaching Guide to Xerox Ventura Publisher
Martha Lubow and Jesse Berst
624 pages, 230 illustrations
ISBN 0-934035-61-X **$27.95**
2nd Edition

Unlock the inner secrets of Xerox Ventura Publisher Version 2 with this well-written tutorial. You'll learn how to create your own great-looking business documents by producing the "real world" documents presented in this book. These documents include reports, newsletters, directories, technical manuals, and books. Companion software is available.

DESKTOP MANAGER   *Software*

ISBN: 0-934035-34-2 **$99.95**
Supports Version 1 and 2

Desktop Manager is the desktop accessory software for IBM and compatible personal computers that helps you manage your Ventura Publisher documents, running transparently from within the Ventura Publisher environment. A multifunction software utility, Desktop Manager provides file management, timed backup, document control, style sheet settings, and report generation. This desktop utility program comes complete with an 180-page guide.

MANAGING DESKTOP PUBLISHING

By Jesse Berst
320 Pages over 150 illustrations
ISBN: 0-934035-27-X **$9.95**

The essential handbook for the modern writer and editor. *Managing Desktop Publishing* shows you how to save production time by preformatting documents. Learn to manage your files, styles and style sheets. Also presented are the elements of style you need to succeed in today's desktop publishing arena. Companion software is available.

STYLE SHEETS FOR BUSINESS DOCUMENTS
(Book and Disk Set)

Martha Lubow and Jesse Berst
320 pages, 150 illustrations
ISBN 0-934035-22-9 **$39.95**
Supports Version 1 and 2

Introducing a cure for the common document—*Style Sheets for Business Documents*. This book and disk set contains more than 30 predesigned Xerox Ventura Publisher templates for creating top-quality business documents. Style sheets are presented for proposals, reports, marketing materials, ads, brochures, and correspondence. More than 100 pages of design tips and tricks are also included.

STYLE SHEETS FOR TECHNICAL DOCUMENTS
(Book and Disk Set)

By Byron Canfield and Chad Canty
320 Pages 150 illustrations
ISBN: 0-934035-29-6 **$39.95**
Supports Version 1 and 2

Get the maximum out of Xerox Ventura Publisher with these advanced technical document formats. This book/disk combination presents more than 25 ready-to-use templates for creating technical documents and books. Also includes techniques for creating pictures and tables, plus advanced tips for modifying formats to fit your needs.

STYLE SHEETS FOR NEWSLETTERS
(Book and Disk Set)
By Martha Lubow and Polly Pattison
320 Pages over 150 illustrations
ISBN: 0-934035-31-8 **$39.95**
Supports Version 1 and 2

This book and disk set presents more than 25 predesigned Xerox Ventura Publisher templates for creating one-, two-, three-, and four-column newsletters. Just open the chapter template, load in your own text, and print. A complete description of every style sheet and key tag for all chapter templates is also included.

VALUE PACK!
All three Style Sheet sets for just **$99.95**

INSIDE XEROX FORMBASE
Rod Potter
320 pages, 100+ illustrations
ISBN 0-934035-68±7 **$21.95**

Inside Xerox FormBase provides straightforward, step-by-step intructions on form design. Users progress from basic to advanced techniques, learning to create, store, and manage professional forms with underlying databases. Covers spreadsheets, graphics, and tables.

Order from New Riders Publishing Today!

Yes, please send me the productivity-boosting material I have checked below.

(Make check payable to New Riders Publishing.)

❏ Check enclosed.

Charge to my ❏ VISA ❏ MasterCard

Card #_____

Expiration:_____

Signature:_____

Name:_____

Company:_____

Address:_____

City:_____

State:_____ZIP:_____

Phone:_____

The easiest way to order is to pick up the phone and call 1-800-541-6789 between 9:00 AM and 5:00 PM PST. Please have your credit card available and your order can be placed in a snap!

IT

Quantity	Description of Item	Unit Cost	Total Cost
	Inside TOPS	$21.95	
	Inside TOPS Disk for MAC	$17.95	
	Inside TOPS Disk for IBM	$14.95	
	Inside Designer	$21.95	
	Inside Designer Disk	$14.95	
	Inside Xerox Presents	$21.95	
	Managing Desktop Publishing	$ 9.95	
	Inside Xerox Ventura Publisher, 2nd Edition	$29.95	
	Publishing Power with Ventura, 2nd Edition	$27.95	
	Publishing Power Disk	$14.95	
	Style Sheets for Business Documents–Book/Disk Set	$39.95	
	Style Sheets for Newsletters–Book/Disk Set	$39.95	
	Style Sheets for Technical Documents–Book/Disk Set	$39.95	
	All three Style Sheets (*Value Pack Save $19.90*)	$99.95	
	Desktop Manager (software)	$99.95	
	Shipping and Handling: See information below.		
	Sales Tax: California please add 6.5% sales tax.		
	TOTAL:		

Send to:

✹ **New Riders Publishing**
P.O. Box 4846
Thousand Oaks, CA 91360
(818) 991-5392

Shipping and Handling: $4.00 for the first book and $1.75 for each additional book. Floppy disk: add $1.75 for shipping and handling. If you need to have it NOW, we can ship product to you in 24 to 48 hours for an additional charge and you will receive your item over night or in 2 days. Add $20.00 per book and $8.00 up to 3 disks for overseas shipping.

New Riders Publishing ● P.O. Box 4846 ● Thousand Oaks ● CA 91360

1-800-541-6789	1-818-991-5392	1-818-991-9263
Orders	**Customer Service**	**FAX**

Order from New Riders Publishing Today!

Yes, please send me the productivity-boosting material I have checked below.

(Make check payable to New Riders Publishing.)

❑ Check enclosed.

Charge to my   ❑ VISA   ❑ MasterCard

Card #_____

Expiration:_____

Signature:_____

IT

Name:_____

Company:_____

Address:_____

City:_____

State:_____ ZIP:_____

Phone:_____

The easiest way to order is to pick up the phone and call 1-800-541-6789 between 9:00 AM and 5:00 PM PST. Please have your credit card available and your order can be placed in a snap!

Quantity	Description of Item	Unit Cost	Total Cost
	Inside TOPS	$21.95	
	Inside TOPS Disk for MAC	$17.95	
	Inside TOPS Disk for IBM	$14.95	
	Inside Designer	$21.95	
	Inside Designer Disk	$14.95	
	Inside Xerox Presents	$21.95	
	Managing Desktop Publishing	$ 9.95	
	Inside Xerox FormBase	$21.95	
	Inside Xerox Ventura Publisher, 2nd Edition	$29.95	
	Publishing Power with Ventura, 2nd Edition	$27.95	
	Publishing Power Disk	$14.95	
	Style Sheets for Business Documents–Book/Disk Set	$39.95	
	Style Sheets for Newsletters–Book/Disk Set	$39.95	
	Style Sheets for Technical Documents–Book/Disk Set	$39.95	
	All three Style Sheets (*Value Pack—Save $19.90*)	$99.95	
	Desktop Manager (software)	$99.95	

Send to:

✆ **New Riders Publishing**
P.O. Box 4846
Thousand Oaks, CA 91360
(818)991-5392

Shipping and Handling: See information below.		
Sales Tax: California please add 6.75% sales tax.		
TOTAL:		

Shipping and Handling: $4.00 for the first book and $1.75 for each additional book. Floppy disk: add $1.75 for shipping and handling. If you need to have it NOW, we can ship product to you in 24 to 48 hours for an additional charge and you will receive your item over night or in 2 days. Add $20.00 per book and $8.00 up to 3 disks for overseas shipping.

New Riders Publishing ● P.O. Box 4846 ● Thousand Oaks ● CA 91360

1-800-541-6789	**1-818-991-5392**	**1-818-991-9263**
Orders	**Customer Service**	**FAX**

To order: Fill in the reverse side, fold, and mail

|||||

BUSINESS REPLY MAIL
FIRST CLASS PERMIT NO. 53   THOUSAND OAKS, CA

POSTAGE WILL BE PAID BY ADDRESSEE

NEW RIDERS PUBLISHING

P.O. Box 4846-P

Thousand Oaks, CA 91360